The Expressive Instinct

The Expressive Instinct

How Imagination and Creative Works Help Us Survive and Thrive

Girija Kaimal

OXFORD
UNIVERSITY PRESS

OXFORD
UNIVERSITY PRESS

Oxford University Press is a department of the University of Oxford. It furthers
the University's objective of excellence in research, scholarship, and education
by publishing worldwide. Oxford is a registered trade mark of Oxford University
Press in the UK and certain other countries.

Published in the United States of America by Oxford University Press
198 Madison Avenue, New York, NY 10016, United States of America.

Library of Congress Cataloging-in-Publication Data
Names: Kaimal, Girija, author.
Title: The expressive instinct : how imagination
and creative works help us survive and thrive / by Girija Kaimal.
Description: New York, NY : Oxford University Press, [2023] |
Includes bibliographical references and index.
Identifiers: LCCN 2022027313 (print) | LCCN 2022027314 (ebook) |
ISBN 9780197646229 (hardback) | ISBN 9780197646243 (epub) |
ISBN 9780197646250 (online)
Subjects: LCSH: Creative ability—Psychological aspects. |
Creation (Literary, artistic, etc.)—Psychological aspects.
Classification: LCC BF408 .K2236 2022 (print) | LCC BF408 (ebook) |
DDC 153.3/5—dc23/eng/20220712
LC record available at https://lccn.loc.gov/2022027313
LC ebook record available at https://lccn.loc.gov/2022027314

DOI: 10.1093/oso/9780197646229.001.0001

3 5 7 9 8 6 4 2

Printed by Sheridan Books, Inc., United States of America

For Miu and Lails

Contents

Figures

Foreword

When Mel Brooks was once asked to explain why a joke was funny, he replied, "Explaining a joke is a little like vivisecting a frog. You may understand afterwards how it works, but the frog dies."

In fact, at least in the first years of the Arts and Health program at the World Health Organization (WHO), I was prepared for the skepticism the work sometimes received from public health professionals and colleagues, but was somewhat surprised at the resistance shown by some artists: "Why do I need to measure what I do? I know if it works or not; I can feel it with the audience." Of course the simplest response to that is to remind the artist that when policymakers are deciding where to place taxpayers' money in national budgets, an individual's feeling is probably not going to be enough justification. Part of my job at WHO is to help artists understand that measurement and evidence is not an unnecessary distraction; particularly when applied to health care settings, in the home, the community, or the health facility, measurement is essential. On face value, why would an insurance company pay for a clown in a hospital? Well, what if we could show that that clown improved recovery time from pediatric surgery, saving significant amounts of money the insurance company would have had to cover?

Yet at the same time, if we feel joy in experiencing the anticipation of a piece of music building to a climax, and feel the awe and exaltation of reaching that penultimate moment in the performance, with an extra delight in that it wasn't exactly what our minds were expecting, but still a complete fulfillment, does that joy lessen the experience if we know that each of these emotional states within this performance can be linked to specific biochemical reactions in the brain, as outlined in Chapter 5 of this book on the neurobiological outcomes underlying self-expression? Does Dr. Kaimal's discussion at the beginning of the book on the philosophical underpinnings of the health benefits of the arts create too lofty a pedestal for something that was so commonplace in our lives? Her chapter on the primeval origins of these set of creative and therapeutic practices, and their continued use by indigenous populations, aligns with the WHO which always has had a special focus on serving the excluded and marginalized, and often indigenous populations. In our contemporary society, in this particular case, we are not bringing solutions to them, instead that they are reminding us of what we have lost and they have continued practicing. And lastly, her discussions on how arts can support childhood development, as well as recovery from traumatic experiences, physical, mental, or social, as well as its use for older populations, speaks to immediate needs today. Even if an artform is something we cannot relate to personally, we all know someone who could benefit, and eventually, inevitably, we will too.

But, still, given this, why is there often resistance? Many of us grew up in the age of psychoanalysis, in which we believed that speaking about something out loud, understanding the inner mechanisms, could resolve neuroses, hidden conflicts, and uncontrolled emotional reactions. But the downside, we might think, is this: What if we actually liked those uncontrolled emotional reactions? What if they gave us pleasure? We fear that understanding something may lessen our spontaneous enjoyment of it.

Back in the day, when I was a fledgling actor at the American Academy of Dramatic Arts, I had a teacher whose ultimate criticism of a student's performance was a single stinging phrase: "You're thinking." We were hammered with the notion that if we became consciously aware of what we were doing, it would feel artificial to the audience. In hindsight, I understand this approach. When they are growing up, children naturally live "in the moment" and "spontaneously" react, and every situation is charged with urgency and commitment, good, bad, or indifferent. Even when they are bored, children are REALLY BORED. And throughout our upbringing, in almost every culture around the world, this spontaneity and energy is systematically drummed out of us to prepare us for the adult world. It is thought that if we reacted truthfully, fully, and in the moment in all situations, we would not be able to function in adult society. So, in a sense, the process of learning to act is actually a process of unlearning the accumulated suppression of these abilities we had naturally as a child.

Now, many decades later, after a life spent fully exploring both artistic expression and evidence-based health in resource-poor settings around the world, I no longer see knowledge and spontaneity as mutually exclusive. Nor do I see arts and health as mutually exclusive. Being aware of how something works is not the same thing as being self-conscious about it. One can be aware of a dopamine trigger in the brain but still be so fully immersed in the flow of deep aesthetic engagement that the magic is not lost. Indeed, for us arts and health geeks, the arts and science are both forms of magic, rooted in the same two common concepts.

Seventy thousand years ago, at about the midpoint in the brief (so far) lifespan of our species, a cognitive revolution took place. We had already for many millennia been painting figures and symbols in caves, we had mastered fire and simple tools, and we had organized into social groupings and bands.

But 70,000 years ago, two things happened that changed the course of our evolution. The first was the "magic what if," as Stanislavsky called it: the ability to imagine something that does not exist in nature or has yet to be proven to exist. This creative leap led to the first imaginative art but also was the foundation of the hypothesis, the beginning of the scientific method.

The other change that happened was the emergence of caring for the injured, unwell, and vulnerable, a trait unique to humans on the scale we have practiced it since then. The two innovations are not unrelated. For the clan to put itself at risk by caring for the vulnerable members, it had to imagine a positive outcome and realize why it was beneficial to the clan to invest the time, skill, and organization to nurse the unwell back to health. This notion of defining the group by the care of the vulnerable is the essence of compassion. The birth of health care was made possible by the creative act we call hope.

In this volume, Dr. Girija Kaimal has put together an impressive collection of the current state of play of the neurology of the aesthetic experience and effective practice of arts used for health. For those of you who worry that learning how and why the arts might be beneficial to our well-being might spoil the magic, I say, "Don't worry. The frog lives!"

Christopher Bailey
Arts and Health Lead, World Health Organization
Geneva, Switzerland, February 2022

Introduction

Premise

The premise of this book is that creative self-expression is the foundation for mental health and well-being just as physical exercise and nutritious food are essential to the body. My aim is to explain why the human instinct for creative expression exists, what happens when we cannot express ourselves effectively, the sublimating role of creativity, how it aids healing, and how it can help us thrive. My four goals for writing this book are as follows:

1. **To dispel the idea that creativity is the domain of a select gifted few.** I highlight how creativity is a defining feature of the human species. Living with the reality of uncertainty in our human lives, our inherent creative capacity, which can manifest itself in many ways in our lives, is the source of our ability to survive and thrive. The desire to express ourselves is an innate need that serves as a safety valve for health and well-being. As humans we seek to share what we know in order to maximize our survival and enable a sense of belonging of our unique selves in an accepting community of peers.

2. **To democratize the idea of creative self-expression and share evidence from neurobiology and neuroscience on how creating, innovating, and bridging from the intangible of the imagination to the concrete of objects promote well-being.** Most scholarship about art has tended to be about viewing art or experiencing it, especially the works of famous artists. We cannot live out every life scenario, and therefore receptive artistic expressive experiences such as encountering the stories embedded in artistic works of paintings, fiction, poetry, drama, and dance help us learn vicariously about life and all that it can be. Expressive artistic works enable us to add the stories of our own experiences to this pantheon of creative works.

3. **To share evidence on how creative self-expression helps us cope adaptively when faced with adversity and trauma.** Beyond literal self-expression, creative self-expression is especially relevant because it

The Expressive Instinct. Girija Kaimal, Oxford University Press. © Oxford University Press 2023.
DOI: 10.1093/oso/9780197646229.003.0001

gives us an outlet, a perspective, and thus a sense of agency and control. When faced with challenges that threaten our own capacity to function, working with someone like an art therapist who can serve a facilitative role can help us develop a sense of belonging and function adaptively in the world again.

4. **To provide suggestions on how the results of research on creative self-expression and well-being can be integrated into our lives.** We have evolved arts practices over time, and the future promises to bring new tools for research and self-expression.

These four ideas make up the structural foundation of this book, with each idea covered in a dedicated part. In the chapters included in this book I explore questions like: What is the purpose of art in our lives? How does creative expression help us learn about life itself through stories embedded in the metaphor of the art form such that we learn how to respond to or to know of the human condition without having lived through a particular experience? Do we instinctively create, seek, and replicate that which resonates with us? Is art and beauty essential like food, drink, and social connection? Could the desire for beauty, to be surrounded by elements of nature, be an innate need? Are art and creative expression essential for a good life? What can we learn from the stories embedded in fiction, drama, dance, poetry, music, and visual art?

As with any scholarly and creative effort, this book is defined by my worldview and expertise. My choices of material to include are necessarily connected to my interests and expertise. The focus is primarily on the therapeutic and health-promoting aspects of visual art-making, which is the lens through which I wrote this book and the lens that is present as a through-line in every chapter. Most of what I share relates to my own developmental and professional history: my Indian heritage, being a woman, a mother, an artist, a scholar, and an educator, deeply interested in the landscape of art-making in our lives. It is necessarily derived from and built on the intersection of my understanding of the world and the role of art within it. I integrate my interpretation of the meaning of creative expression in our life by connecting it to evolutionary theory, human development, and the human capacity to cope and respond to threats and adversities in our everyday life. Relatedly, I include anecdotes to exemplify a particular idea as it relates to lived experiences and personal applications of some of the research and theory.

I invite you on a journey with me. What sort of journey is it, you ask? Is it a quest? A hero's/heroine's journey? A treasure hunt? A journey of discovery or a trip to a vacation? What might you expect? Should you prepare for high drama, conflicts, and battles to be fought, or should you expect a trip where you sit back, relax, and enjoy the ride? Is it a yarn: a story of a journey? All great questions, and all I can say is that I hope it is a bit of all of the above: that you encounter a journey that traverses time and space, forwards and back. Perhaps you might see some of your own story in here and learn about some others. As with all journeys there are things we might prepare for and expect, but no matter how well predicted our needs be, we will encounter surprises. I hope this book and the journey through it fulfills the best purposes of journeys: to travel, to learn, and perhaps to see the familiar anew.

In terms of logistics and structure, each chapter can be considered a stand-alone essay, like a site/town visited on the journey. But each chapter/essay is also part of my overall goals, which are to share the motivation and foundational ideas underlying the value of creative self-expression as an evolutionary adaptation of the human imagination to help us survive and thrive every day. I use visual and verbal metaphors especially inspired by nature throughout this book because they connect to our evolutionary history, biological processes in response to external threats (physiological and psychological), as well as my very personal human journey through places and time.

Guide map for this book

You are here. And this is your map. To guide us on this journey, I have for us a big-picture contour map of the terrain (Figure I.1). You will see that this book is divided into an introduction and four main parts based on the goals outlined above in the "Premise" section.

As you can see from Figure I.1, the book begins with a foreword and introduction, which includes the premise, guide map, and origins of the ideas and research included here. Part I presents the first part of the big-picture contour map of the terrain, focused on the landscape of the field, spanning historical and theoretical perspectives on creative expression. It comprises three chapters. Chapter 1 presents an overview of the importance of self-expression, how it is related to our evolutionary need to imagine the future, and the role of metaphor as a bridge between self-expression and artistic expression. Chapter 2 summarizes a range of theoretical and philosophical perspectives on creative self-expression and why we need to democratize the idea of creativity. Chapter 3 focuses on our collective heritage and roots in indigenous practices and our connection to nature. This chapter includes research on being in nature, which serves as a bridge to Part II.

Part II provides the next section of the big-picture contour map of the terrain. Building on the conceptual foundations presented in Part I, Part

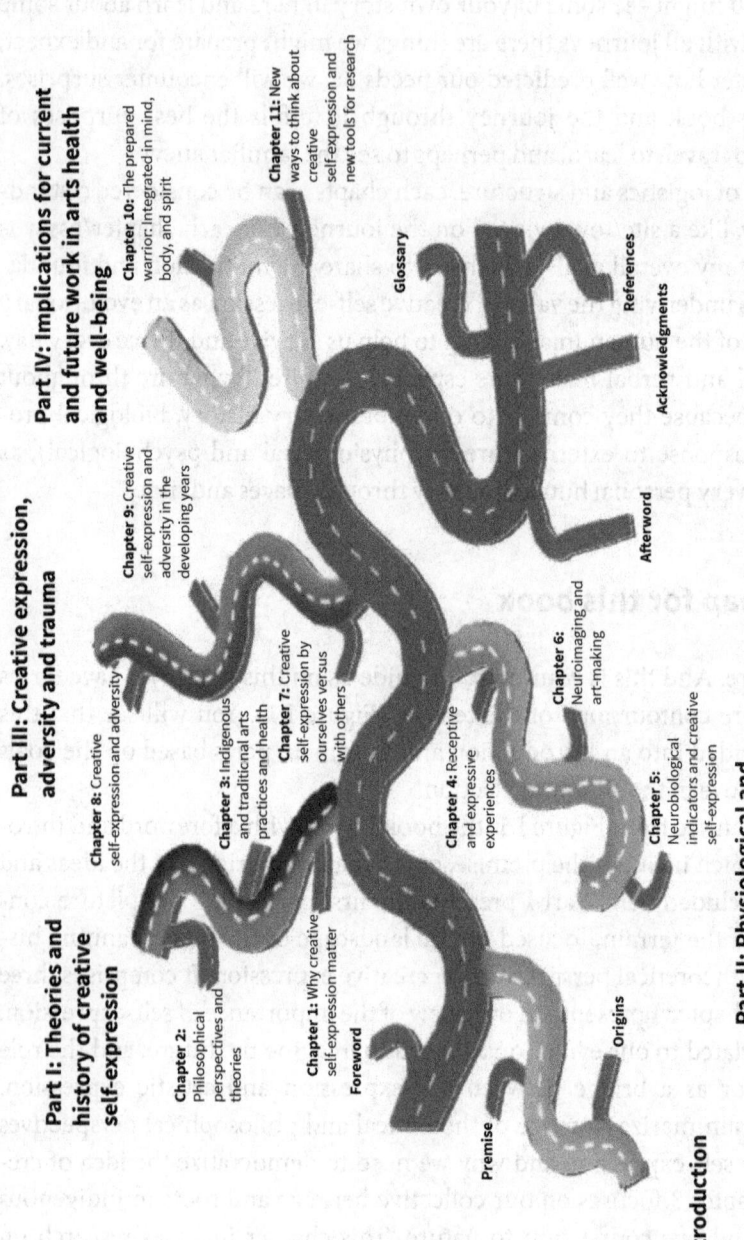

Part I: Theories and history of creative self-expression

Chapter 2: Philosophical perspectives and theories

Chapter 1: Why creative self-expression matter

Foreword

Premise

Origins

Introduction

Part III: Creative expression, adversity and trauma

Chapter 8: Creative self-expression and adversity

Chapter 9: Creative self-expression and adversity in the developing years

Chapter 3: Indigenous and traditional arts practices and health

Chapter 7: Creative self-expression by ourselves versus with others

Chapter 4: Receptive and expressive experiences

Chapter 6: Neuroimaging and art-making

Chapter 5: Neurobiological indicators and creative self-expression

Part II: Physiological and psychological processes and outcomes

Part IV: Implications for current and future work in arts health and well-being

Chapter 10: The prepared warrior: Integrated in mind, body, and spirit

Chapter 11: New ways to think about creative self-expression and new tools for research

Glossary

References

Acknowledgments

Afterword

Figure I.1. Terrain map for the book

II focuses on current research and the peer-reviewed evidence base on the health outcomes of creative visual self-expression and art-making. Chapter 4 provides an overview of receptive and expressive experiences: namely, how our brain processes sensory input and how viewing/receptive experiences differ from making/expressive experiences. Chapter 5 focuses on the neurobiological aspects of self-expression, including neuroinflammation and biomarker-based evidence of outcomes of art-making. The human body's immune system maps well to the warrior metaphor: It responds to external threats (biological [e.g., viruses] and psychosocial [e.g., stress]) that activate the body's defense mechanisms. This metaphor does not represent violence but rather a form of self-defense to help one tackle the challenges and stressors that are an inevitable part of life. Chapter 6 includes evidence on what we know from brain imaging studies of visual self-expression and the outcomes seen in the human brain and body.

Building on the findings of Part II, which mostly involve normative processes, in Part III I present the unique strengths of the arts in times of adversity. Chapter 7 provides an overview of the arts, health, and human development professions, including art therapy, and how they differ from each other in serving individuals in need. Chapter 8 includes findings related to creative expression among children. There is an imperative on us adults to offer tools to developing children and youth for self-regulation which in turn is essential for their well-being. Chapter 9 focuses on how the arts help us manage and cope with trauma and adversity across the lifespan, including examples from the military and medical settings. I share evidence on this topic, including the unique intersection of arts education and arts for health for this population.

Lastly, in Part IV, all the chapters covered so far are linked to effective practices and directions for the future. Chapter 10 includes ideas on how to integrate creative practices into our lives in meaningful ways. Just like diet and exercise, managing our inner lives is key to leading a healthy and meaningful life. To be engaged in artistic practices is to face, confront as needed, process, and manage our emotional lives. Chapter 11 offers ideas on what remains to be studied and better understood in the realm of arts and health, including the use of new technology and tools. I conclude with an afterword, a reflection on the journey and a concluding message to the reader.

My aim in writing this book was to make the research on arts and health meaningful and relevant to anyone interested in the topic. This includes scholars and practitioners in arts and health as well as the reader interested in the interplay of arts, science, and human development topics. Many metaphors emerged for me throughout the process of writing, including those of hunting, gathering, discovering, challenging, giving birth, and dying: Like life and nature itself, creative activity is an ongoing dynamic interplay or battle of life and death and regeneration. The journeys of our lives can be informed and enriched with a deeper understanding of our capacities and the opportunities to express them meaningfully.

Origins

For as long as I can remember, art-making has been a friend through life. It was my armor, my shield even before I knew it to be so. As a child growing up in India, I was sickly and frequently had to stay home. At one point I experienced

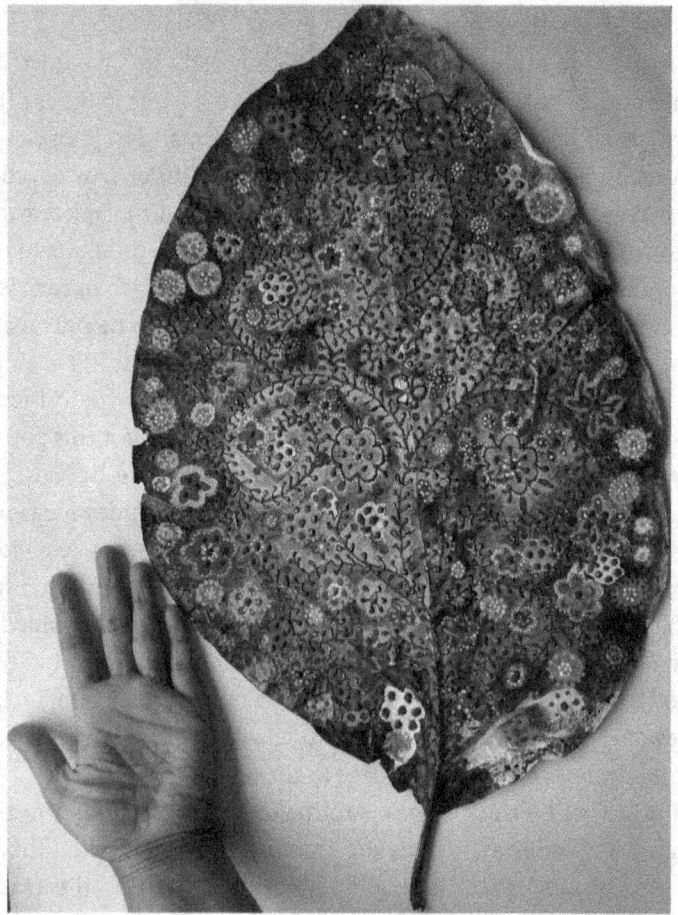

Figure I.2. Extraordinariness of the ordinary (Kaimal, 2019). Mixed media: Teak tree leaf, henna, paint pens, and ink. Dimensions: 15" X 8"

febrile convulsions, and consequently my health status was monitored closely through much of my childhood. In fact, in pre-K and kindergarten I probably went to school for barely half the year. I do not remember much of the time I spent at home or what I did. I vaguely remember the concerned looks of adults around me and frequent checks of temperature. Despite my frequent illnesses, what I remember fondly from that time was the reactions I got for my drawings made from the sickbed. I spent hours creating scenes with crayons and paper and would paste them on the door for family members returning home at the end of the day. I loved to draw at school, too. My artwork would appear in school exhibits, even when I was absent. Art was my proxy, my companion, and an early expressive option that eventually played a large role in my own journey for coping, fun, purpose, meaning, making sense of the world, and gaining insight and perspective.

During my school years in India, I learned many traditional forms of expression, including classical Indian dance, and several forms of art-making were introduced to me through festivals and community celebrations. My mother engaged in many creative activities around the home, and I went on to learn many of these traditional forms practiced by her. Life circumstances limited some of her professional aspirations, and she found outlets for creative self-expression around the home. She wrote little narrative notes and stashed them away in her jewelry case, embroidered pillowcases, sewed clothes, and knitted sweaters for my brothers and me.

Among her many pragmatic creations, she had one project that has always stayed in my mind: She would place the tops of carrots that were being prepared for cooking in a shallow bowl with just enough water to cover the tops. Slowly the carrot tops would sprout the most beautiful leafy structures that would grow to be a few inches tall: fine, bright green leaflets that contrasted with the orange carrot tops and looked particularly stunning on the kitchen windowsill as the sunlight filtered through. This art installation, although aesthetically beautiful, served no practical purpose. It was simply an expression of creativity: an upcycling through creative re-creation of kitchen vegetable waste. These early exposures to creative acts taught me that art could be a part of everyday life, an outlet for self-expression, and that aesthetic beauty generated from the simplest of natural sources could bring joy.

My father introduced me to narrative writing. In his books and articles over time, he wrote of his travels, ideas around sustainable agriculture, low-cost housing, civil engineering, and satire related to Indian politics. He was raised in a home marked by clinical depression and a series of traumatic deaths. Writing, I imagine, served as an instinctive way for him to manage and process the experiences, stressors, and challenges of everyday living. Although he was a civil engineer by profession, my father introduced me to the possibility of being both a scientist and an artist. He personified ways in which analytic and logical thinking could coexist with imaginative and narrative expression.

Although I never had much formal training other than standard art classes in school, I pasted my own work around the walls of my room. Along with my diary, my artistic creations helped me make sense of the world around me. Creative self-expression was thus intertwined with my developmental years and was an outlet even though I did not really have words for it or fully understand it at that time. I had the vague sense that this was somehow my "thing," a way to channel all sorts of complicated emotions and thoughts into things outside of me: a way to externalize.

After I completed secondary school, art assumed a central place in my life. I went to design school and spent a good part of the 1990s studying to become a professional textile designer with expertise in woven and printed fabrics, prints, and patterns. In India, I worked in the vast, rich landscape of the artisanal traditions. But in the 1990s, with globalization and the disappearance of longstanding local markets in India, many artisans were despairing and committing suicide. In order to redress this tragic circumstance, a group for designers developed an initiative to help the artisans adapt their exquisite craft traditions, such as fine-thread weaving and mud-resist block printing, to a modern market. As a result, through my work as a designer working with many indigenous crafts, I developed a deep love of making art inspired by nature, community history, and places. I also learned firsthand how our well-being was connected to our everyday lives, meaningful work, and the cherished quality of personal fulfillment. I remember often my formal first introduction to the societal impacts of the constructs of arts and mental health in the time I spent working with them.

From artistic practice to art therapy, arts, and health

In 1998, I moved to the United States. I came with two suitcases and some art supplies. For a while, my art supplies were the only things that helped me feel worthwhile in a new and unfamiliar country, serving as reminders that I had something to contribute to the world. In this new country, I started experimenting with a range of art media and began painting on any surface I could find. I found a chest of drawers in a dumpster and painted over that. I found a table and painted over that. In focusing on the art and painting on surfaces with abandon and having no real plan other than to decorate, I allowed myself to be the colorful being that was struggling not to sink into despair. Connecting my interest in psychology with a history in art-making, I serendipitously found the field of art therapy and decided to get a master's degree in it. This new field combined my interests in human behavior with artistic expression.

Art now took on a different role: It expanded in scope from artistic practice for personal wellness to promoting psychological wellness in a range of populations, including inpatient psychiatric units, alternative high schools for adjudicated youth, and an HIV/AIDS clinic. In all these settings, art-making with child and adult clients helped me better understand them. I found that when we create or witness the creations of another, we get to know them much better and much faster than we would with words alone. Art therapists refer to this as an expression of our unconscious: the part of the brain that controls most of our behaviors and actions. Art therapists guide people in connecting or reconnecting with the creative practices that support mental health and help people grapple with life's challenges and uncertainties. My interest in the connection between artistic practices and human well-being deepened, and as I worked with clients, I continued to wonder how humans could best work through traumatic experiences and grapple with adversity. I eventually pursued my current work—that is, studying creative expression in a range of human populations.

From clinical practice to research and scholarship on art therapy, arts, and health

Nothing is more fulfilling than the satisfaction and fulfillment of supporting and being part of the journey of an individual with mental and physical health challenges. To be part of a fellow human being's journey toward wellness is a privilege and a deeply cherished honor. As I met with patients, I increasingly was drawn to the questions of the "why" and "how" of creative self-expression. With the intention of better learning how to study and understand human expression, I went on to get my doctorate in human development and psychology. I learned how to examine and understand the construction of human life story narratives as it relates to all aspects of human development.

In my research laboratory now at Drexel University, where I focus on arts, health, human development, and well-being, I am systematically trying to understand what I might have implicitly sought and experienced in my earlier years. Many of my studies and my overall approach to research have developed from my own initial artistic practices and insights (e.g., Figure I.2 artwork made from natural materials like teak leaves). Sometimes drawing helps us master an idea immediately; other times it needs layering and reworking. My own art at this time is inspired by memories of people, places, events, and things that sparked joy or intense emotion: Art has helped me create, celebrate, remember, and cherish. In particular, making art helps me learn. Through the process of what emerges when my hands work with different media, the resulting image serves as a reflecting mirror that provides perspective and insight.

Research in the arts and in the area of health and art therapy has taught me that different art media correspond to our mental states. Some are better suited to capture and support particular emotions. Oil pastels and scratch art are well suited for expressing anger and aggression. Instead of punching and scratching someone, the person can release aggression on a foam board and scratch off everything. One of the potentially democratizing aspects of art is the possibility that at the individual level there is no right and wrong in art. It is always a representation of ourselves and of who we are in the moment. When we dissipate our expression, we might look at what we have created and find in that externalization other feeling states, complexity, and nuance that we might not have held in the moment when we were led by a blinding overwhelming emotion. What we create may sometimes be constructive and at other times destructive, but when shared it becomes an extension of ourselves open to interpretation, projection, and representation (Gussak, 2021).

Art has provided me the space for sense-making through various life stages and phases: My doodles reflect back my current state of mind, my confusion, my questions, my efforts to make sense of the unknown or of confusing mental and emotional states (see Figure I.1). Sometimes, making art, releasing energy, dissipating it through my hands, helps shift my mood. I become less angry—more compassionate and kinder toward others—once the expression has left my hands. It sometimes feels like a process of mourning, grieving, and letting go. Once it has traveled from my brain through my hands and into an external object, it is literally externalized: It is outside of me, allowing for perspective-taking and distancing from the mental states that are internally distressing. The externalization also can break the cycle of rumination: a repetitive loop that reworks and rewires the same thoughts, ideas, or compulsions. Art-making can be ruminative, too. We might make the same thing repeatedly.

At times, art alone may not be enough. Although art might capture a perhaps nonverbal primal mental state, writing poetry, prose, or other kind of narrative offers a different expressive option. Writing has its own options for reworking but is less forgiving of abstractions and meaninglessness. Writing allows for resequencing, re-storying, changing details, and anonymity. It does, however, have a core structure of words with specific meanings that cannot be broken down further. Poetry is closer to the free drawings I might create. They are a distilled personal representation of an inner story or an inner feeling state. Metaphors and analogies might help hold the ideas in place. Writing offers a more organized sequencing of thoughts and ideas in a way that is different from drawing. Drawing can give perspective, but writing can help problem-solve and organize thinking. The quality of paintings holding multiple experiences and ideas concurrently likely allows for the freedom of ambiguity, non-linearity, multilayered realities, and options to rework and redo (depending on the art media). Each of us also has our preferred self-expression, like sports, culinary arts, horticulture, music, or movement, that might be more in sync with our interests.

It is a conundrum of human existence that we can never know what goes on in the mind of another. We can only make conjectures based on the actions, words, behaviors, and other bodily signals we might pick up (including with neurobiological mapping tools). A friend once said, "Forget others; we barely even know what is going on in our own heads." In that statement lies the rationale for our expressive instinct: our innate desire and drive to express ourselves. Our desire to express ourselves is part of our deep primal need to be part of something, to belong, to be accepted, and to truly feel we get to be who we are. I have come to believe that to be an artist, one must be able to hold and confront one's perceptions, perspectives, and emotions every day. If you can make it work, there is no better way to manage yourself. Which leads me to the motivation to write this book. My personal imperative to write this book was to share what I have learned and known over the years.

It has been my dream to write this book over the last several years. I hope you find it useful as you travel on your own journeys and grow your own trees of life. Be sure to let me know what you think.

PART I

UNDERSTANDING THE LAY
OF THE LAND

*Theories and historical perspectives on creative
self-expression*

I begin this book with Part I, wherein I share theoretical and historical perspectives on the interconnections between arts, health, and well-being. This section has three chapters. Chapter 1 offers an overview of why self-expression matters at a very fundamental human level of survival. Chapter 2 is a summary of different theoretical and philosophical perspectives on creative self-expression. Chapter 3 reflects back in time to examine indigenous and traditional arts practices and what they might tell us about the value and purpose of artistic expression in our lives. The purpose of this section is to set up a review of the lay of the land and the many different ways creative and artistic self-expression have manifested in human lives.

1

Why does creative self-expression matter?

> My mission in life is not merely to survive, but to thrive; and to do so with some passion, some compassion, some humor, and some style.
>
> **Maya Angelou**

> Communication is truth; communication is happiness. To share is our duty; . . . if we are ignorant to say so; if we love our friends to let them know it.
>
> **Virginia Woolf**

Terrain map: Why does self-expression matter? What pushes us humans uniquely toward imagination and expression of this instinct? In this chapter I provide an overview of why creative and artistic expression is fundamental to our survival and to our desire to thrive. I introduce the ideas of evolutionary perspectives on human self-expression and creativity and innate attributes, including how they relate to narrative storytelling and art-making. You might well say, "I am not an artist, so this does not apply to me." That is a fair argument, and I would say to you that as a human being you are inherently creative and capable of tremendous imagination and the desire to share that imaginal perspective in a range of ways with the world around you. Still skeptical? Allow me to explain.

Being human and living in an uncertain world

A few years ago, in response to the news of a catastrophic earthquake on the news, my then six-year-old asked me if we would all face the same end. I reassured her that we would not, but inside me I knew that was an unrealistic promise. As living beings, each day could potentially be our last. And yet, we live every day with optimism, and the paradox of this essential reality of our existence as human beings is, namely, that of our *uncertainty* regarding

The Expressive Instinct. Girija Kaimal, Oxford University Press. © Oxford University Press 2023.
DOI: 10.1093/oso/9780197646229.003.0002

Figure 1.1. Imaginal Naturescapes. Media: Repurposed photo paper and gel crayons. Dimensions: 2 ft. × 3 ft. (Kaimal, 2018)

the future. The structure of human life can be constructed and understood with a past, present, and future that we all experience. As the Danish philosopher Søren Kierkegaard said, "Life can only be understood backwards, but it must be lived forwards" (Cappelorn et al., 2008). We each have a past we have known, a present we live in, and an as yet unknown future. We can as human beings look back in time, but we can never know what lies ahead each day or each minute. The past is a constellation of our memories and meaning associated with events: a repository of triumphs, challenges, people we have known and loved over time. The present is fleeting and processed every moment and filed away in our memories (some experiences more deeply and effectively than others). More on this when we talk about adversity, but I get ahead of myself.

Why are we here? What lies ahead? The structure of human life and the unpredictability of the future has been the source of human innovation over millennia. Throughout history, humans have tried to explain human life cycles and predict the future, often by using patterns and trends in natural phenomenon to determine the future. Many religious rituals and fortune-telling endeavors around the world are based on the hope that investing in certain activities will result in hoped-for outcomes. Sometimes these predictions have been problematic in that patterns were seen where none actually existed. For example, astrological signs are built from astronomical phenomena but are not necessarily related to any credible patterns of human life.

With the advent of scientific knowledge, previously unpredictable things are increasingly foreseeable through computational models and improved technological tools. Geosciences help us with weather predictions. These in turn help us prepare and plan for changes that may keep us safe during inclement weather, natural disasters, and other emergencies. In the past, we might have prayed to the weather gods or relied on priests to tell us what lay ahead. To some extent, scientific advancements help us learn more about the world around us and what changes can be expected. Striving to predict the future remains a struggle: It is essentially, by definition, an unknown. Nevertheless, it drives our curiosity and the pursuit of novelty that is ingrained in our instincts (Farahbaksh & Siciliano, 2021).

Now you might say, "Well, I am not that unsure of my future. I have science, technology, education, and a job to help me plan for this uncertain future. I work hard, I invest in my retirement funds and buy insurance to protect me from unforeseen adversities." These are all valid points. In many ways, in modern society with the abundance of information around us, we have the tools to predict the future based on prior experience or by closely observing and learning from the experiences of others. We might be able to predict and plan based on the inescapable realities of illness, aging, and death that lies ahead for us all. We might invest in education and skills training for ourselves, put away money in college funds for our children, come up with a mortgage plan, save for retirement, disability and/or adversity. If we value human connection and community, we might also invest in social capital and ensure a community of support for us over time.

Scientific advances increasingly give us more answers about what to expect in the future. As we learn more about genetics, we can determine the probabilities of our developing a specific disease. Knowing our risks for certain conditions, we might prepare to delay their onset with diet, medications, exercise, and so forth as best we can. If you knew you had the BRCA gene, you might even take extreme measures like getting an elective mastectomy, like a famous movie star did recently. Or you might have a history of certain genetically linked mental illnesses and, being concerned about the probable risk of transmission, might choose (not without controversy) not to have children, like as a well-known author with diagnosed bipolar disorder did (Jamison, 2015). Alternately, you might have hit the genetic lottery with excellent genes, but you are just as likely to die any minute from a range of conditions, including weather, accidents, or injuries.

Does all this sound terribly pessimistic and depressing? Bear with me. I assure you, it leads to some exciting possibilities.

The essential and irreplaceable purpose of imagination

Now that we have established the reality of uncertainty and our ongoing efforts over human history to manage it as best we can, it is important to highlight how our brain works. The main point here is that as humans, our future, however probable or predictable, is essentially always a surprise. Importantly, this uncertainty that defines us is the very thing that inspires and motivates our brain to constantly assess and the scan the environment and context for its impact on our lives and, most fundamentally, whether or not we will survive. This is the basic mission assigned to the brain: to maximize our chances for staying alive each day.

A transformative finding in recent years has been that our brains are not computers that gather and process information and produce an output. Rather, our brains are *predicting machines*. The brain works to gather information through the senses and to combine this information with existing knowledge to determine how best to prepare the person to survive what the brain thinks lies ahead. This process is a combination of conscious and unconscious processes (Bubic et al., 2010; Friston, 2005). This predictive capacity seems to be part of all living things since it helps ensure survival by anticipating dangers and predators at an almost reflexive and instinctual level.

To maximize survival options, the brain is inherently wired to imagine possibilities for the future that enhance safety and resources and minimize risk and danger. Thus our actions are led by what we know and how we might respond to stimuli and information around us to make choices that help us survive and then thrive. As a result, we can also conjecture that we as human beings are not just prediction machines; rather, we have the potential to be imagination machines. Because we are wired to be predictive, we are inherently imagining possibilities. Just the anticipation of predictive capacity is enticing to us. Our brain cannot help but imagine and foresee. It literally activates our dopaminergic reward pathway (Kandel, 2012, p. 427). The imagination is not just visual imagery; rather, it is the ability to generate abstract ideas and thoughts. Even the small percentage of the population with aphantasia (inability to visualize imagery) can engage in imaginative activities (Zeman, 2021). Even our dreams are working to process experiences and predict the future (Wamsley, 2021). In a study examining dreams throughout the night, the dreams closest to waking were found to be the most future-oriented because that is when we awaken and move into action. Dreams prepare us by creating scenarios that help us make sense of our memories and experiences. The capacity to imagine is in all of us, perhaps as an antidote to the challenges of uncertainty.

Why is this relevant? This is where I believe the human creativity comes in: as way to connect imagination with action. Creativity in our imaginative processes helps us manage and prepare for possibilities (our uncertain future). Experiencing positive emotions is a big part of the contribution of creative self-expression and of the arts in particular (See figure 1.1). Seneca (as translated by Gummere, 2013) is purported to have said that we suffer more in our imagination than in reality. Might it then be that creative self-expression, particularly through art-making, helps us experience positive emotions, since they are few and far between in everyday life? Perhaps that is what connects us as humans to creative expression.

The philosopher Maxine Greene was one of the first theorists to suggest the idea that imagination is fundamental to life. According to Greene (1994), many of the entrenched challenges of society (particularly those of schools) could be addressed through active engagement with the arts. She asserted that no encounters released the imagination in the way that thoughtful engagement with works of art or aesthetic enactments did. Imagination is the capacity that enables us to move through the barriers of the taken-for-granted and summon up alternative possibilities for living and being in the world. It permits us to set aside (at least for a while) the stiflingly familiar and the banal; to suspend judgment and, for a time, live in wonder. It opens us to visions of the possible rather than the predictable. It permits us, if we choose to give our imagination free play, to look at things as they otherwise could be. Greene (1994) further argued that artistic inquiry and engagement was a means to achieve the democratic ideals of equity and inclusion, offering us the option to think in terms of open possibility, in terms of freedom, and in terms of the power to choose. She refers to this aspect of the imagination as "social imagination." She acknowledged the skepticism associated with the arts: that the arts are isolated aesthetic experiences and are intrinsically valuable, but that they do not have to lead to specific goods or measurable outcomes to be justified. She countered that argument with the creative possibilities offered through the arts and said that "wide awakeness" (the sense of the unexpected associated with such experiences) may be precisely what is needed to stimulate the kinds of reflective practices and reflective learning all of us hope to see. She maintained consistently and convincingly that the arts provided to the human imagination a sense of possibility and hope (Greene, 2007).

It is important to note that imagination works both forwards and backwards in time. Although looking toward the future helps us survive, thrive, and prepare for possibilities, re-imagining and reworking our pasts are important too. When we engage our natural imaginative capacities, we can transcend space and time and rework our stories. McAdams (2001) asserted that psychological disciplines have increasingly accepted the role that stories and narratives play in structuring our lives, including how they intersect at the societal level and in cultural contexts.

To be human is to be uniquely self-aware. It is our special gift and our curse that, unlike other mammals, we are reflective and carry an inner story of our selves (Monti et al., 2021). If we look further into individual temperaments, we find that some of us are relaxed and laid back and move forth with the expectation that everything happens for the best and that things will work out. Alternately, others are more anxious about an uncertain future, worrying about every negative eventuality. Similarly, if we are unable to look ahead or see only hopelessness, we might lean toward depression. If we are developmentally younger, we tend to consider children and youth invincible, choosing to be in denial of our mortality and approaching all risks and dangers with a sense of invincibility. Uncertainty itself has elements of privilege associated with it. The very things we strive to do in order to minimize adversity are indicative of the privileges afforded to us.

How do we live with and take charge of the many frailties and uncertainties as humans? Could creative expression and the arts have a role? Even though the oldest handprint on a rock is that of a Neanderthal ancestor from almost 65,000 years ago, and even though Neanderthals gave humans many adaptive advantages such as the ability to live in colder climates and immunity from diseases different from those in Africa (Gibbons, 2021), the creative capacity of humans is distinctly different from even their closest species relatives. There is something that is uniquely human in creative works. Zwir et al. (2021) examined the DNA of *Homo sapiens*, chimpanzees, and Neanderthals and found that creative abilities (i.e., being able to conjure new solutions to problems and challenges) are what advanced humans compared with other primates. The authors assert that although emotional reactivity is common to all primates, it was self-awareness and self-control, which are unique to humans, that helped them generate solutions and tools to deal with problems. Self-awareness allows for autobiographical memory and imaginative capacity. This advantage of creative problem-solving led humans to take over from the Neanderthals and all other species as the dominant one on the planet.

There is evidence of this emerging cognitive complexity in simple drawings of triangles imagined as a sort of early graffiti on rocks (Helm et al., 2019). The expressive and "making" capacity of animals is different from humans. Other animals can create exquisite, visibly creative works, such as when birds build nests or beavers create dams. These are, however, considered instinctive evolutionary protective features, the goals of which are to procreate and propagate their species. Moreover, in observations of primates and mammals engaging in human activities like painting, English et al. (2014) found that animals that create things like paintings do not necessarily gain any personal benefit or use imagination as we know it to mean; rather, they are primarily responding to positive reinforcement from their trainers.

In contemporary society, attitudes toward the arts are complicated. Several scholars have examined the purpose and role of art in human life. Some evolutionary theorists (Gould, 1997) have argued that art is simply a byproduct of the human brain's expanded processing capacity, a spandrel that is created simply as a result of improved cortical abilities. This hypothesis is rejected by most scholars, who argue that art has several specific roles in society. Dissanayake (2000, 2001) has referred to arts engagement and art-making as a process of *making special* the everyday and the ordinary by commemorating special events, milestones, and landmarks in the life of an individual or community. Based on observations of traditional communities and viewing art from an anthropological perspective, she argued that art-making is part of human development and history and is not separate and distant, like considering the modern artist as an individual expert with works placed in museums (Dissanayake, 2003, 2015).

In examining the historical context and role of art-making, Dutton (2010) further argued that art-making is not a cultural artifact; rather, it is part of human evolution and a means to capture the imaginative qualities inherent in human functioning. He referred to art not as a technical concept confined to a cultural context but rather as a universal phenomenon of human evolution like language, tool-making, and kinship systems. He defined a piece of art as having 12 essential qualities: (1) direct pleasure, (2) skill and virtuosity, (3) style, (4) novelty and creativity, (5) criticism, (6) representation, (7) special focus, (8) expressive individuality, (9) emotional saturation, (10) intellectual challenge, (11) art traditions and institutions, and (12) imaginative experience. He argued that the arts are different from activities like sports where there is typically no imaginative experience because the end result of a win or loss is what guides interest in the game. It can be argued, though, that this is not necessarily a valid critique, because games and plays can also be demonstrative of imaginative variations within the core construct of a winning score or a loss.

Dutton (2010) further asserted that art is embedded in a context but is not necessarily always reflective of that context; rather, it is the creation of individuals or communities who happen to live in that moment. Recent scholars of human development and education (Hetland et al., 2007) suggested that working with the visual arts helps us develop a craft (learn to use and care for tools); engage and persist (stay with a task and persevere to complete it); envision (imagine possibilities not yet seen); express (convey ideas nonverbally); observe (learn to see effectively); reflect (learn to think through with self and others); stretch and explore (learn from mistakes); and learn about artistic practice and arts professions.

The philosopher Catherine Watson argues that philosophy and art serve the same purpose (Horgan, 2019). And both philosophy and the arts say, essentially, "you are not alone. Others have thought and worried about this, too." They connect you to your species, theoretically and emotionally, which can give you encouragement and consolation. To experience art is to both belong and to learn. It is not humanly possible for each of us to personally live out every human experience, which is why we read poetry and fiction, watch art and dance, listen to music, watch drama, and seek out any other art form that offers insights on the human condition.

These ideas are not unique to Western philosophy, nor are they modern. In the book *Vasistha's Yoga* by Swami Venkatesananda (Namoh Narayana, 2004), the author cites ancient life stories that highlight the role of self-mastery and self-regulation as the key to living well, including recognizing the value of sincere effort, serving the needs of those in your care, and finding purpose in life, which can vary from person to person. Knowing oneself is defined and presented as a goal that is achieved through thoughtful action and/or meditation. The *Bhagavad Gita* also suggests that the way to live a productive life is to focus on the generative effort itself and not worry about the fruits of one's labor.

So how do we connect our inner imaginative lives to expression, verbal and nonverbal? What is the entry point of self-expression, and how is it related to art?

From imagination to self-expression: Intangible to tangible

Self-expression is the manifestation of our innate imaginative capacity. It is action; it is concretization and externalization of what we see and foresee in our mind's eye. We might verbalize via words of speech, physical movements, sounds, or visual expressions. It can be a form of communication to ourselves and other. Self-expression helps us step into our imagination, perhaps in a concrete and manifested way. Kandel (2012) referred to this as being compelled to share our stories (p. 404) to share what we know. We are a deeply social species, curious and eager to share what we think can help ourselves and each other. To be unable to share our inner lives has been found in studies to negatively affects our physical health (Slepian et al, 2017). This drive to express ourselves is deeply ingrained. It is a part of who we fundamentally are as human beings.

In his landmark studies Pennebaker (1997a) demonstrated how being unable to express ourselves makes us physically unwell: Conversely, being able to express ourselves, even if in the solitary act of writing, promoted health. Sapolsky (2003) found in studies of mammals across species that a sense of agency and control helps provide an outlet in times of distress. This can involve simple physical acts and behaviors that help the mammals cope. In humans this expression can happen in words, physical movements, musical expressions, drama, poetry, and visual expression. These are conscious expressions of our presence in the world. It is our expression of the desire and willingness to step into and take up our space in the world. Even simple acts like walking and moving are forms of making choices and of depicting agency in the world. Our bodies also actively express our experiences. Biological changes, hormones, brain activity, and pheromones are all expressions of our identity. We are concurrently both entirely unique and yet entirely just like every other human being who has come before us (see Chapters 4, 5 and 6 on neurobiological aspects of self expression). The idea that our creative pursuits can help us find our way through trauma and challenges led to the emergence of regulated mental health professions like art therapy. The role of a facilitator or therapist who helps us through adversity is not new but has existed in different forms throughout time (more on this in Chapter 7).

Self-expression, creative self-expression, human connection to belonging

As human beings, our ability to imagine possibilities links us directly to our ability to construct stories. We are both storytellers and lovers of stories we hear. Our lives are structured around the lifelong story we have of ourselves and the stories we create about others we might meet. So far, we have identified uncertainty, imagination, and life stories as essential aspects of the human condition at the individual level.

We do not exist in isolation. We are parts of a larger whole. We are deeply social beings with an innate need to communicate with each other and to belong to our own tribes. Even at the level of brain cells, we have mirror neurons attuned to reflect and recreate what we see in others, setting the foundation for empathy, morality, and intersubjective mutuality (Iacoboni, 2009). We are structurally made to connect and respond to each other as human beings. Yet one of the great mysteries of human life is that we can never truly know the internal thought processes of another human being. Einstein (1930) once said, "The most beautiful thing we can experience is the mysterious. It is the source of all art and science." We are forever trapped (until such time as we can read others' minds) in not knowing the true intentions, thoughts, feelings, and perspectives of another human being. We can guess at these aspects of others from observing and listening closely, asking for responses, and tracking their bodily fluids, biological indicators, and brain functions. But still we are always guessing. We can never truly know. It is the ultimate protection of privacy, in a way. It is our own mind and brain to protect and share as we wish. Yet within each individual human being lies this great desire to connect. Dan McAdams (2001) referred to these feelings as our twin and opposing forces of agency and connectedness.

Our stories and our human lives are an interplay of the harmonious and the disharmonious, of perhaps both a desire to differentiate ourselves and be all that we can be as individuals and a desire to be connected to each other so that, in all our uniqueness, we also belong to a community that supports and values our unique self. How do we find this magical sweet spot? We might spend our lifetimes in pursuit of this combination. Our need to experience, understand, and express ourselves is deeply intertwined with our connection with other human beings. We are influenced and impacted by those we encounter just as they are by us. Notably, our stories are helped not just by us but by those who know and have known us. For example, our stories as babies and toddlers before our first memories are held by our parents, siblings, and their family members. The tales they have told us enter our past as a version of who we are. Friends and peers we have met in life hold stories of time spent together and anecdotes that we might have forgotten over time. These narratives from others are ongoing edits and additions to our own story. We are constantly re-imagining and refining our tale as new experiences and information enter our lives. This interplay of intersecting storylines is the connective tissues, our collective DNA of the storylines of our human tribes. Self-expression is about being able to shape and contribute to our own storyline while understanding and recognizing the contributions of others. We cannot go back in time or change the past as we lived it. We cannot erase trauma and hardship. What we *can* do is change our personal narratives: change how we interpret events, reexamine them, perhaps learn new details and rewrite them, changing in the process ourselves and our lives.

But what if our story is not of words, or if words alone do not capture it? The connecting bridge is the metaphor. Along with imagination, our narratives can be shared, expressed, and understood through metaphors. These metaphors are the bridge that connects our desire for expression beyond raw output alone to distilled creative works: The ability to work with metaphors is our gift, our magical portal to connect, learn, express, and communicate. Especially when we delve into creative forms of self-expression, metaphors are the salient building blocks and mirrors to invite others to understand us just as we strive to understand them.

Metaphor as the bridge between the verbal and nonverbal expression and creative self-expression

A metaphor is a figure of speech or a symbol that we use in our interactions and expressions that denotes a similarity between two unconnected or un-likely things (Killick et al., 2016). A metaphor is a symbolic, abstract tool we use to understand the world, and a unique and creative way to allow us to project and communicate our inner experiences, be they emotions, ideas, or a combination of life experiences and perspectives (Lakoff & Johnson, 2003). Metaphors allow us to learn new things and make connections that in turn help us expand our understanding of a topic or experience (Hayes, 2014). Metaphors connect the familiar with the unfamiliar and help us see connections in ways that were previously not possible. Metaphors allow us to engage with a concept or idea at multiple levels and to unpack and delve deeper as needed. In a broad sense, metaphors represent our inner states and include analogies and similes, beyond the limitations of the literal. When we represent our condition in an abstract metaphorical form, we allow it to be interpreted in a range of ways. It provides many pathways for others to un-derstand us. In talking about what artistic expression embodies, Suzanne Langer (1953) referred to the quality of abstraction through metaphors. She said that metaphors allow us to expand beyond literal thinking by enabling many aspects of our imagination to connect with the image. Art allows us to represent our lives symbolically: for us to retain our experiences beyond the time of their actual physical manifestations. An example she cites is the phys-ical experience of crying. When we can evoke the emotion in the viewer that the individual felt during the time the tears flowed, that is a manifestation of the abstract representation of the human experience. No other being except a human being can understand another human and communicate through symbols and metaphors.

Thus, if I say that my life is like a tree, you can interpret the metaphor of the tree in many different ways. It can be tree as in feeling rooted, or it can be tree as in being outdoors; it can be tree as in having leaves and branches and sustaining life; or it can be any other association you have with a tree. By offering our inner state as a metaphor, we allow for a range of ways in which to present our state and a range of ways for someone else to interpret it. This ability to engage in abstract thinking helps us to move with agility between symbols and words, both of which intersect to facilitate our expressive potential and our ability to generate our stories and to link our stories with others. With a metaphor we allow for seemingly isolated individual experiences to be feel included within the vast landscape human experience and to see our unique experiences as being part of the greater whole. Relatedly, at the societal level, we might think of mythological stories as metaphors of their times. For example, as a child growing up in India, the stories we absorbed were mythological tales that were connected to stories for entertainment as well as community festivals. One such was the story of Goddess Parvati, and one of the unique aspects of her identity was that she had a thousand names and selves. I never quite understood what that meant or represented until much later.

In human society and communities, we process and express ourselves through words and speech. But what if we did not have the words to communicate, or if words could not capture the entirety of our experiences? What if experiences that were difficult and challenging left us bereft of skills in the traditional forms of communication? Creative works serve this very need; they help humans to manage their lives and themselves. Scholars have spoken about the anthropological and evolutionary role of art in our lives—the purpose of art as making special, memorializing, and remembering, of how art represents our pre-literate oral historical times. As humans, when we make things, speak of our experiences, or move our bodies, we both express and hold the many ambiguities and stories within us. Less is written about the healing, creative life-enhancing aspects of art-making. That is what I seek to highlight in this book: the role of voice, authenticity, viewer, viewers, creating with others, creating with a therapist, creating with peers, creating for an unknown audience. In this book I build on the works of past scholars and offer a range of ways in which self-expression helps us understand ourselves, manage our emotional lives, and practice ways to cope.

Works of art, especially those we create, help us connect with ourselves as well as feel seen by others in our communities, our orbits, or our tribes. It becomes this external self that is both part of ourselves and also connected to stories of others. Through expressing ourselves in this visual format, we invite perspective-taking from ourselves as the creator and viewer as well as others who see it. The artwork becomes a vehicle for communication and sharing our inner life beyond what words alone could capture. If I had to create a visual, it would be Figure 1.2.

I propose that the human emotional experience is best captured over time through the arts. Artforms help hold both the center and the margins of human experience. It is the form of expression that helps us feel less alone and isolated in our experiences, including across time. To experience art is to feel a sense of belonging, but to create art is to invite others into this new symbolic and metaphorical space, which is an important theme of this book. Through the symbolic connections, we get to feel connected in the shared experience, sometimes even centuries or millennia after the original work was created by the artist.

Viewing art can help us see meaning, reduce loneliness, feel a sense of belonging, see new ways of being and new perspectives, and see ourselves in a mirror. Even if we are by ourselves without the opportunity to engage with another, we can channel our need for expression by creating visual artworks or written pieces. (See Chapters 7 and 10 for in-depth discussions of art-making by ourselves versus art-making with others, including facilitators and therapists.)

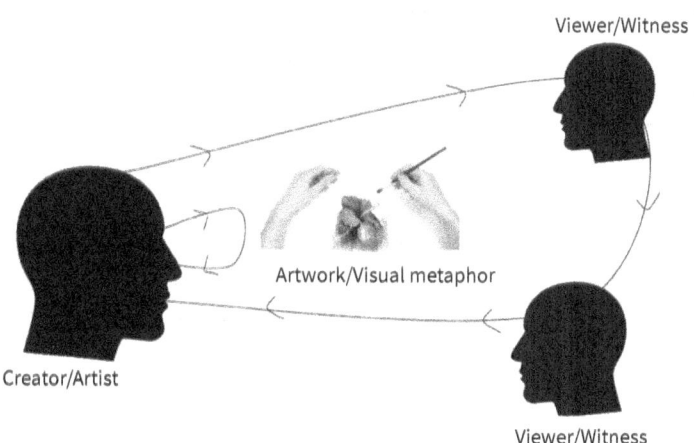

Figure 1.2. Art as the visual metaphor that connects to ourselves and to others

The creative process can be a repetitive meditative practice that helps us manage anxiety or that distracts us from distress (Figure 1.1). It can be a way to gain new knowledge, learn about ourselves and others, and imagine new ways of being. When we create with others, either in a therapeutic setting or with peers, we further multiply these outcomes with additional support, insights, perspective, and a sense of belonging. Even when people are physically impaired such that they cannot use their hands, they can still use their mouths and feet to paint. That desire to express ourselves is a natural process and analogous to all other aspects of taking in, processing, and letting out. This topic is covered in more detail in Chapters 4, 5 and 6.

Key takeaways

Uncertainties are a fact of human life. Our predictive brains allow us to counter that vulnerability with the power of imagination. To survive and thrive, we have a deep, innate desire to communicate, express ourselves, and connect with others. The instinct to express ourselves creatively is innate: It is our natural response to the desire to make sense of the sensory stimuli we receive every day. It is how we manifest our unique journeys and experiences within the collective of our communities and relationships. Through metaphors in artistic expression, we channel this imagination into creative self-expression. The expressive instinct manifested through art-making is an extension of the many ways we communicate through creative sense of mastery (creative agency, self-efficacy). It is sublimation: the successful mastery and externalization of an inner state of distress/confusion, discomfort that can be emotional or cognitive. Art allows us to access nonverbal aspects of our experiences. Not everything is experienced or expressible in words. Arts allows for this type of communication when words are not enough and/or if our experiences prevent us from expressing ourselves in words (e.g., trauma, language or cultural barriers).

This chapter introduces ideas related to different aspects of human self-expression: the neurobiology of self-expression; the role of narrative; differences between art-making by oneself versus art-making with others; insights from indigenous and traditional art forms; developmental aspects of self-expression; trauma, adversity, and self-expression; contemporary perspectives; and, finally, reflections on the future. I elaborate on these ideas in the upcoming chapters.

2

Philosophical perspectives and theories about creative self-expression and well-being

No man has the right to dictate what other men should perceive, create or produce, but all should be encouraged to reveal themselves, their perceptions and emotions, and to build confidence in the creative spirit.

Ansel Adams

Man is least himself when he speaks in his own person. Give him a mask and he will tell you the truth.

Oscar Wilde

Terrain map: In Chapter 1, I proposed the idea that creative expression is a natural extension of our brain's innate wiring to imagine an inherently uncertain future. This uncertainty and how it manifests in our social, emotional, and relational options and choices sets us on our journey of discovery about self-expression, creative self-expression, art-making, and what it means for us as human beings. Self-expression through metaphor becomes the artistic way to externalize and connect with ourselves and with others (Figure 2.1). This chapter presents some salient theoretical and philosophical perspectives on creativity as it relates to self-expression, well-being, and exercising the imagination. Included in this chapter are relevant philosophical and theoretical perspectives of creative expression and how they have been conceptualized over time as part of human development.

The Expressive Instinct. Girija Kaimal, Oxford University Press. © Oxford University Press 2023.
DOI: 10.1093/oso/9780197646229.003.0003

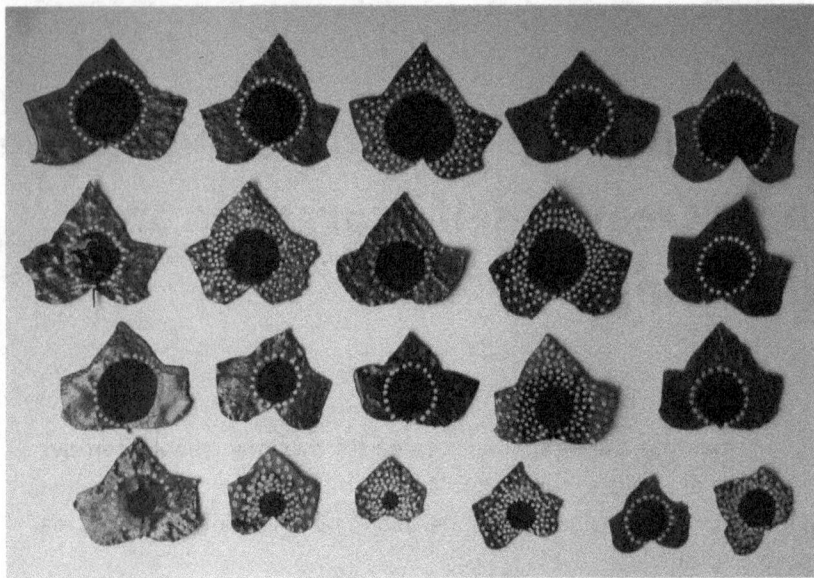

Figure 2.1. *What if Black holes can "hold" everything* (Kaimal, 2021). Media: Pressed and dried ivy leaves, resin, and ink

If you are human, know that you are inherently creative

In the past several decades of being an artist, designer, art therapist, and researcher, I have regularly heard adults lament their self-perceptions of not being creative. It is an unfortunate assumption that I would like to dispel from the outset. As I mentioned in Chapter 1, human beings are, by default, creative. We have the unique ability among all living beings to be able to "imagine," and we all do so every single day. We also have the additional skill of being able to translate that imagination into creative actions/products. The unfortunate misconception that only a select few are truly creative arises because we mistakenly equate creative expression with expert-level skill. Let me explicate.

What if we do not perceive ourselves as creative or even deem creativity essential? Consider the suggestion from the World Economic Forum's report on jobs of the future: It lists complex problem-solving, critical thinking, and creativity as the top three skills needed for the future (Whiting, 2020). In fact, Dance (2021) argued that the arts help us to stimulate creativity, boldness, and tenacity by giving us the courage to fail without repercussions. This practice of learning by working through failed creative efforts with our hands gives us tools for innovation as well as for resilience. Creative potential can come from a range of activities, but, as Dutton (2010) would argue, the arts provide an ingredient, the active agent of human imagination, that make it particularly potent as a tool. As the world continues to delegate skills to artificial intelligence systems and robots, the human capacity to innovate and create remains unmatched. Creative capacity gives one the confidence to address challenges—that is, the knowledge of how to solve problems as needed when faced with obstacles. Sometimes this ability comes as a sudden insight and at other times as a result of deliberate reflection and problem solving (Kounios & Beeman, 2015). Sometimes these obstacles require time-tested solutions that call for specific skills and knowledge, but at other times a new and divergent approach might be needed. **Being empowered with creative skills is therefore a way to reduce the panic of the uncertainty** and threats that we know will come our way: to allow for uncertainty and ambiguity as a time to distill, process, and incubate for an optimal solution or resolution in time.

But Van Gogh cut off his ear! How can creative expression be related to health?

It is hard to argue for the healthful aspects of artistic and creative self-expression when pop culture examples of questionable behaviors by artists abound. In popular culture, the common perception is that artists live on the margins or outside of social virtues and norms. There is the tale of Gaugin, who abandoned his family and treated Tahitian girls poorly in the pursuit of his artistic practice. There is justifiable concern about Picasso's abuse and mistreatment of the women in his life (Dixon, 2019). How might we refer to "arts and health" when the now-beloved painter Van Gogh was known to cut off his ear in a fit of fury? Who has not, at some time, considered artsy individuals to be overly emotional, insubordinate, licentious, unpredictable, and/or flaky?

A recent example of the precarity between creative expression and mental illness is that of the psychosis experienced by Yayoi Kusama. Kusama suffered many challenges, including being plagiarized and unrecognized in New York as an artist in the 1960s and 1970s. By her own admission, her despair at being rejected by mainstream artists, her emotional breakdowns, and her suicidality were contained through channeling her work into painting. Her visions and hallucinations became part of her externalized artistic works. She was eventually supported by a fellow woman artist, Georgia O'Keeffe. No doubt you see the irony of moving from the margins to the center as these artists are now valued and revered, with their works selling for millions of dollars. Interestingly, going back in time, there is speculation that the artists who made some of the rock paintings deep in the recesses of caves did so in order to experience hypoxia, a condition that results in dopamine release and hallucinogenic out-of-body experiences (Kedar et al., 2021).

True to pop-culture conceptualizations, many well-known artists lived their personal lives seemingly outside of social norms. Their art too reflected advances in artistic expression for their times, and the risks in their art were often an extension of their personal lives. Gussak (2021) wrote extensively about the interconnections between destructive and creative drives, especially among individuals with a proclivity to violence (mostly men). He argued that to be creative and to succeed in the art world, one must maintain plentiful doses of self-promoting narcissism and audacious and impulsive risk-taking.

Artistic practice could potentially lead us out to exploration and innovation as well as invite us back into the fold of safety and belonging in the landscape of human experience. Yet, living outside the norms of society, due either to life circumstances (adversity, trauma, loss) or to personal conditions (illness, disability), is lonely, and the arts have the potential to connect us back: To be able to feel a sense of belonging and safety is a requirement of the human condition (more on this in later chapters on adversity). Kusters (2020), however, warns against the romanticization of artistry, philosophy, and madness. Thinking on the edges of human cognition might be challenging but is not directly associated with mental illness or psychosis. Focusing specifically on philosophy and his own challenges with psychosis, he argues that all human exploration is an effort to examine and understand our existence, which can lead either to despair or action.

Another argument made for artistic engagement is that of promoting excellence in other disciplines. In Western society, we might revere superstars in any discipline, but art is also considered by many to be disposable, one of the first items to be cut from school and city budgets in times of financial crises. This is the case despite the evidence that the arts help with all other aspects of our functioning, even if at high levels of excellence and functioning. In a study comparing all the 21st-century Nobel Prize–winning scientists with other scientists of the same period, the breakthrough scientists were significantly more likely to be involved in the arts than the latter: They were twice as likely to play a musical instrument, seven times as likely to draw or paint, 12 times as likely to write fiction or poetry, and 22 times as likely to perform as dancers, actors, or magicians.

Jacobus Henricus van 't Hoff, winner of the first Nobel Prize in Chemistry, noted the connection between artistic hobbies and scientific brilliance as long ago as 1878. Van 't Hoff pointed out that a large fraction of famous scientists had "artistic inclinations." Newton, for example, was a painter; Galileo was a poet. This made sense, he said, because science is fundamentally creative. Anyone can make rote observations, but it takes leaps of imagination to come up with original hypotheses and the experiments to test them. Moreover, the most successful scientists were those who integrated their artistic and scientific endeavors rather than using the arts just as a distraction (Root-Bernstein et al., 2008). Psychologist Grant (2017) attributes creative expression among groundbreaking individuals as an extension of their curiosity and ability to think differently. This curiosity leads to seeking out new experiences (including with travel) and allows highly creative individuals to make connections across a range of life experiences.

So what about everyday imagination and creative actions? Where do the rest of us fit into this world if we are not world-famous artists?

Democratizing self-expression

As both a clinician and a researcher, a refrain I hear often is "I am not creative." A patient once told me that he stopped making art in school when his teacher told him, "You are no Leonardo." This was a man in his early 70s who had held this belief almost his entire life. I felt incredibly sad when I heard that. Why do we hold these heartbreaking self-perceptions when we know that we are all capable of creative and adaptive problem-solving on a daily basis? More importantly, why do we let these stereotypes of creative expression diminish our spirit of curiosity and exploration? If we are not a Leonardo or a Picasso, does that mean we are not permitted to make art and engage in creative play and exploration? This attitude is not fair or democratic to the human spirit and certainly not reflective of the history of human creative expression.

As we have seen in some of the examples and literature cited above, creativity is not always about famous artists—or even about art at all. Creativity applies to all disciplines. One way to think about it is the conceptualization of "Big C" and "small c" creativity.

Big C and small c creativity

Some of the framing of creativity research might help with our understanding of the many facets of creativity. Scholars like Runco (2014) and Csikszentmihalyi (1996) have referred to "Big C" creativity in reference to transformative events and acts of groundbreaking innovation and novelty. "Big C" creativity refers to genius-level innovation, and instances are necessarily few and far between in human history (Kaufman & Beghetto, 2009). Think about landmark artistic works, scientific discoveries, and innovations as well as transformative new knowledge or technological advances. These endeavors are often the works of teams or are romanticized as the work of a lone genius, especially in artistic practices. Think about those whom we perceive as geniuses in society: the Einsteins, the Curies, the Leonardos, the Wollstonecrafts, the Aryabhatas. These are individuals recognized for discoveries that transformed human society.

In "Big C" creative works, novelty is further complicated because too much novelty is often rejected by society until adequate repetition makes it familiar (Schubert, 2021). The initial rejection of new and revolutionary artworks is sometimes the hallmark of transformative change. For example, it is hard to believe now that Impressionism was first considered too novel an approach, too different from the previous traditions of realistic artworks, or that Van Gogh in his time was rejected for having an artistic style considered too stark. In viewing creativity as an individual trait, there is a danger in distorting it as somehow unattainable and limited to only a select few (Plucker & Beghetto, 2003). Runco and Jaeger (2012) further defined the characteristics of creativity as novelty and usefulness. As human knowledge has advanced, being an individual creator becomes more difficult. Much of what is now considered "Big C" creativity tends to be the product of groups of people working together collaboratively.

In opposition to "Big C" creativity is the idea of "small c" creativity. "Small c" creativity represents a humbler, less grandiose version of creative expression, opening up the possibility for all of us, genius or not, to engage in and benefit from the creative expression inherent in all human beings. Although I personally still find it offensive to minimize everyday creativity as somehow "smaller" than "Big C" creativity, it still allows for the construction of the idea of individual experience: approaching everyday challenges and experiences through subjective and innovative responses. In our daily life, we might engage in and enjoy the many delights that result from creative expression. The Runco and Jaeger (2012) definition is just as valid in "small c" and "Big C" if the implications are viewed at the level of individual insight and transformation. Things we create can be novel for us in terms of expression and content and lead us to use this insight in effective and useful ways in our own lives. "Little c" creativity can be cumulative in contributing to well-being in society. Beghetto and Kaufman (2007) described "mini-c" and "pro-c" creativity: "Mini-c" refers to intrapersonal learning from the creative process and "pro-c" refers to the innovations we make in our professional lives. "Pro-c" innovations might sometimes become "Big C," but if not, they still advance the profession.

"Small c" creativity is what a lot of this book focuses on: not necessarily the world-changing ideas and innovations (even though they might) but the smaller acts of exploration and imagination that we generate as we negotiate the challenges of life. This democratic perspective on creative self-expression and artistic exploration is what I explicate extensively throughout the book: the therapeutic aspects, the self-regulating aspects, the problem-solving aspects, the power to distract as well as to experience joy in discovering new ways of doing and seeing things, the power inherent in having a sense of mastery and confidence in developing and practicing skills of making and doing.

In the early 2000s there was a push toward this goal with the "maker movement" (Dougherty, 2012). The idea was to take ownership of the human ability to physically make and fix rather than delegate or digitize. The "making" could be any aspect of the home (e.g., cooking, gardening, tinkering, car and appliance repair), with the aim being for us to become agents of the human ability to create and sustain our environments. It harkened back to a time when fewer machines were around to support human needs. Dougherty (2012) referred to this as emerging from "people's need to engage passionately with objects in ways that make them more than just consumers" (p. 12). Dewey (1923) extolled the virtues of learning by doing. Relatedly, the maker movement emphasized the importance of tactile engagement, the importance of our hands as essential to the learning process.

The maker movement did not distinguish between art, science, or engineering. The main goal was to explore the actions of making in dedicated maker spaces such as in schools and colleges or in creating one's own maker space. It was intentionally not defined as anything goal-led, like an invention; any discoveries would happen as a byproduct rather than as the main goal. The maker movement is related to the idea of "small c" and "Big C" creativity and to connecting us to the idea of the innate human desire to be active agents in our environment. This movement was challenged in some ways because the maker movement did not clearly define the context and beauty of possibility and imagination beyond working with the hands alone. Humans are inspirational beings; in addition to making, we also are uniquely able to imagine possibilities in ways that no other species can.

Philosophical worldviews on creative self-expression, health, and well-being

To understand philosophical perspectives and stances is to understand the underlying structure of our thinking, our approach to learning and perceptions, and how we come to our conclusions (Shraim, 2021). This process helps us uncover our assumptions, values, and ethics surrounding topics related to arts, health, and creativity, and, perhaps even our blind spots and the inherent subjectivity of our perspectives. Philosophy and art are similar in that they remind us of the humans before us who struggled with the same questions that we struggle with today. This association leads us to feel connected to the continuum of human existence (Wilson, 1984). We are reassured that we are not alone, yet not saved from the challenges of being human. Our perceptions as well our creative outputs are founded on our worldview: Our beliefs, values, preferences, and habitual patterns of responses shape our perceptions of reality. It is a self-organizing process that includes assimilation of experiences and expressed manifestations of this view. When we create, we express our view of our own reality as interpreted, understood, and integrated from our own unique personal experiences. This view can transcend art forms such that each person develops his or her own unique style across different domains, including visual and written forms (Gabora et al., 2012). Through this expression we gain clarity and perspective on our own inner states.

Philosopher Martha Nussbaum (2001) connected worldview with the stories we tell. She asserted that how we view and experience the world is embedded in our language. Moreover, she asserted that our own stories are mirrored in the mythologies of our cultures and that through the stories our cultures hold, we negotiate our own moral challenges and conflicts. Our capacity to be open and trusting through our shared stories while living in an uncertain world defines us as humans. Art makes tangible that which was previously shapeless and held within us (Langer, 1957). She refers to art and craft as revealing aspects of ourselves in form, either in instrumental practical value (craft) or with symbolic meaning. The aim is symbolic representation and communication of insights, all of which is abstracted either in images, sounds, or words. This abstraction can hold different levels and types of meaning and insight. It is sensuous, wordless abstraction (Langer, 1957).

The artist Shirin Neshat refers to artistry as being able to accept uncertainty (Crook, 2021). Our ability to imagine and balance assumptions and manage uncertainty is our unique strength and perhaps our burden as human beings. We are endowed with this superpower of imagination through our highly evolved brains. Our imagination can lead to undreamed-of new possibilities, but it can also hinder us by focusing on the dangers of the future.

Conceptualizations of artistic pleasure and well-being: Hedonism and eudaimonia

Historically the arts have been considered from different philosophical perspectives. *Hedonism* is defined as the pursuit of pleasure and the active avoidance of pain (Moore, 2013). It is associated most commonly with short-term sensory rewards or fleeting feelings of joy, ecstasy, pleasure, gratification, love, relief, satisfaction, and awe. The underlying idea is that the pursuit of pleasure and the avoidance of pain are what motivates us. Hedonism tends to be associated with the pursuit of the fulfillment of human desires at the individual level. As can be seen by the words associated with pleasure, some have a more fleeting and negative valence than others. Hedonism, taken to the extreme, raises questions around selfishness and vice in the pursuit of pleasure. These associations add an ethical dimension to hedonism and to considerations of when and how pleasure is destructive to the individual and society and when it might be of value.

Moments of joy are few and far between in human existence. According to a hedonist, experiencing joy in ethical ways allows one to live happily. But do we really feel good when we pursue hedonism? Our moral codes and values can be the determinant of that for each of us. There is evidence that a diversity of experiences in the physical environment helps us feel good (Heller et al., 2020). It literally feels good to move about and explore in different physical locations. Are we being hedonistic or are we connecting to our historical and evolutionary roots in symbolic, meaningful, and metaphorical ways that are deeply valuable to our being?

This leads to a second philosophical stance related to well-being, namely that of *eudaimonia*. Eudaimonia originates from the Greek idea of happiness and welfare and is associated with flourishing, well-being, and blessedness. Broadly, eudaimonia refers to living well, but living well can be interpreted in different ways. In modern psychology, eudaimonia emerges in positive psychology and work around gratitude and quality of life. All of these approaches are attempts to define a virtuous yet meaningful life. A similar construct is that of ikigai from Japanese philosophy; ikigai refers to a state of being where a range of personal desires are aligned with societal good. Flow might also be potentially centered here as a eudaimonic state.

Perhaps there is a continuum from hedonism to eudaimonia in art; perhaps both the fleeting pursuit of pleasure and longstanding, sustained meaningful joy can be present in art-making. If art is in the eyes of the beholder, perhaps the hedonists perceive the sensory and emotional components and the eudaimonists extend the feelings further to encompass emotion and meaning-making. Figure 2.2 shows a visual representation of this formulation.

In what ways are these examples indicative of health or well-being? The artists and their lives used in the examples above were associated with hedonism, volatility, and perhaps selfish interests and emotionality. If an artist lives a hedonistic life outside the norms of society and yet contributes to its well-being

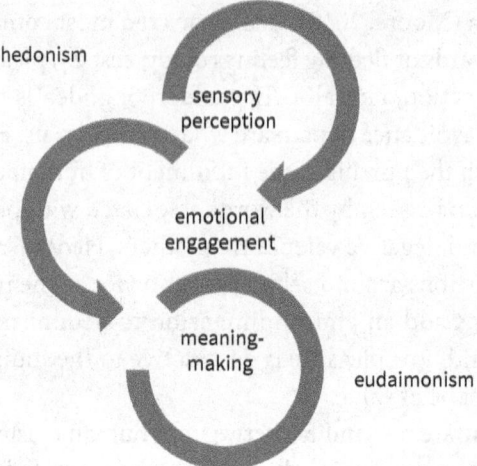

hedonism

sensory
perception

emotional
engagement

meaning-
making

eudaimonism

Figure 2.2. The continuum from hedonism to eudaimonia in creative works

through the exploration and quality of artistic innovation, who then decides what is the joy of art: the person who views or the person who creates? When, then, are our experience with art hedonism and when are they eudaimonic? Researchers in the current field of neuro-aesthetics grapple with some of these questions.

Neuro-aesthetics and creative expression

Contemporary theorists of art and aesthetics suggest that there are many ways to consider the idea of pleasure in art. Rolls (2017), in a unique evolutionary take, argues that beauty is seen in (a) aspects that promote survival (including sexual mate selection and environments that are likely to be safe for thriving); (b) in the parsimonious and novel design aspects of things that indicate patterns and problem-solving; and; (c) in the learned positive emotional responses related to cultural and genetic variations that such that we grow up becoming attuned to enjoying and appreciating that aesthetic. Aesthetics is anything that appears interesting, engaging, or beautiful to us (Rolls, 2017). Thus, even appreciation of luxury goods is a way to signal to potential mates that they have resources and therefore value in the human world. As one would expect, this response varies by individual; for humans it extends beyond mammalian instincts to appreciation of novel ideas and creative and imaginal works, including art.

Neuro-aesthetics scholars postulate a three-stage model for experiencing art-making and art-viewing. In referring to the aesthetic triad (Chatterjee & Vartanian, 2014), the authors identified three elements of aesthetic experience: sensory motor connection, emotional valuation, and knowledge/meaning-making. Extending this, Coburn et al. (2017) suggested a three-stage experience for interacting with spaces as well: (1) formal elements like color, composition, and contrast; (2) personalization and affective association; and (3) deep meaning-making and learning from the viewing experience. Similarly, Tinio (2013) suggested that both viewing and making involve a first exposure called initialization, followed by adaptation and expansion, and lastly finalization. Both viewing and making involve an initial act, followed by deepened engagement, and completed by a sense of closure and understanding.

As Tinio (2013) highlighted and as seen in theories of art therapy, this approach again involves multiple levels of engagement, from the superficial to the meaningful and the personalized. Dixon (2019) offers that to know of the personal or moral failings of an artist is to see their works in greater complexity and context. Art thus offers a range of experiences, both perceptual and challenging and deepening our thinking and understanding of society and what constitutes mores and acceptable morality at different times in history. Dixon (2019) argues, for example, that we must not ignore the personal lives of artists. To know of the abusive treatment of women by Picasso is to struggle with that to which we are drawn visually in his artworks while being repulsed by the inspiration for those works, and this ambivalence is a mirror to our own lives and moral choices.

Matthen (2017a) argues that pleasure in art is a conscious evaluation and that engagement with the work is reinforced with motivation. He further argues that aesthetic pleasure, as defined by facilitative pleasure, requires active mental engagement, action, and alignment with that which we inherently find beautiful or engaging. He is referring to viewing artifacts but recognizes that active meaning-making is key to the aesthetic pleasure derived from the object. Kneller (2017) suggested that art can communicate pleasure and enjoyment through a facilitative process with directed activity where we derive inspiration and motivation from our engagement with the work. It serves to move us prospectively. He also referred to a passive experience, "relief pleasure," which tends to be equated more with simpler sensory relief (akin to alleviating thirst or hunger or relieving sexual tension via orgasm) or listening or watching passively, knowing that you are in the presence of something that is providing a known pleasurable experience. These pleasures are enhanced and defined by that which we are exposed to: culture, experiences, familiarity.

There is a recognition here of the value of aesthetic connection with art as a multilayered and multidimensional experience.

Building on this idea, Guyer (2017) and Doran (2017) proposed the rejection of value-laden assumptions and opened the potential of art to engage the imagination and play as productive outcomes of aesthetic engagement. Kneller (2017) offered the argument that nature is an example of facilitative pleasures. Our experiences are deeply related to our natural surroundings (see Chapters 3 and 10 for more on this). Similar to an appreciation of the elements of nature, this experience can be at multiple levels of engagement and appreciation.

If we look at the conceptualization of creative practices from a historical perspective, we see that Indian philosophical traditions and cultural practices have linked the role of contemplative, reflective, and spiritual practices to self-expression. Puligandla (1998) highlighted the non-dualistic philosophical approach in Hindu traditions of Advaita, which considers individual consciousness to be part of a universal consciousness such that art, science, and spiritual practices exist in harmony rather than in dissonance. Using the example of sleep, where the brain is active despite the individual being asleep, the perspective is that human functioning is layered and includes unconscious intuitive processing as well as conscious expression.

The concurrent role of mundane everyday practices and the intersection with creative joy is highlighted consistently. Yoga and meditation come up often in the Hindu tradition. Indian philosophers and artists have reflected on the role of art and the ability of artistic practices to gain depth and meaning over time (Roy, 1945). In an interview, Romain Rolland suggested that art must at some level appeal to the spiritual needs of all human beings whether or not they are able to appreciate the nuances or aesthetic appeal of the form. Referring to the fact that Indian musical traditions were shared orally, Roy (1945) argued that the same artistic approach can be interpreted and represented in infinite ways and that these traditions have survived and been adapted over time because of these creative possibilities. The Indian philosopher and mystic Sri Aurobindo referred to human consciousness as existing on a lower plane, while creative practices allow us to transcend these limitations and reach into what he refers to as a higher universal supramental consciousness. Creative expression, especially as practiced through yoga, is a practice that is at once authentic, transcendent, and transformative without being led or defined by egoistic drives. He refers to descending into a deeper understanding of self as being paradoxically also an ascent to the divine. He further argues that intellectual reasoning can only take us as far as our minds will allow and experiencing transcendence from the human condition: that to better understand reality we need to be willing to look beyond and sense beyond the immediate context of our lives and pursuits.

Art and love can be expressed in simple human interactions or can be representative of larger connections across humanity:

> Art, poetry, music, as they are in their ordinary functioning, create mental and vital, not spiritual values; but they can be turned to a higher end, and then, like all things that are capable of linking our consciousness to the Divine, they are transmuted and become spiritual and can be admitted as part of a life of yoga . . . for there is only one thing essential, needed, indispensable, to grow conscious of the Divine Reality and live in it and live it always. (Roy, 1945, p. 296)

According to Roy (1945), Aurobindo suggested that the measure of a person was not what he or she said or did but what he or she became. Is not that the eventual purpose if our lives: to transform, transmute, and transcend who and what we thought we could be?

Sensual aspects of creative expression

Given that our artistic practices engage several of our senses, it is inevitable that the sensual aspects of our selves are activated. It is easy to see how sensory activities can be conflated with artistic works and the inherent joy in them. But limiting these experiences to relief pleasures is where our perception falls short and also connects to the limited perception of art-making as simply sensual and explosive unfiltered expression. Matthen (2017b) recognized the overlap between the aesthetics of beauty and physiological responses like sexuality. He noted sexual attraction and culinary pleasure in physical hunger but attributes these to the relief pleasures such as those obtained through orgasm and satiety after eating as these desires are fulfilled. But delighting in and contemplating aesthetically pleasing objects are different activities. He defines this engagement as a pleasure nexus that includes mental engagement as well as cultural connection such that, through the facilitation of the artist, the viewers learn to find the diverse ways to experience pleasure.

In terms of physiological changes (more on this in Chapters 5 and 6), the hormones released during sensual and sexual experiences are not unlike those activated by art-making. They engage our reward pathways, release "feel good" hormones, engage our senses, especially those of touch, and connect us to each other in the human experience. Sexuality and artistic practices are perhaps connected via the hormones in our body. It is inevitable that when we examine the process of art-making and the haptic qualities that engage our senses, memories, identity, and reward pathways, the process becomes sensual and perhaps sexually arousing. The hormones released during sexual acts and those activated with feelings of attraction and pleasure are the same regardless of activity. Betty Dodson (1987), the guru of pleasure and sexuality, especially for women, wrote and spoke extensively about how art-making was arousing for her, and she interspersed intense art-making with sexual exploration with self and others. Much of her art was representational (not abstract) and as such might have aligned more with hedonistic or the relief pleasure processes described by Matthen (2017). Authors Lorde (1978) and Baldwin (2013) recognized the power of the love and eroticism in bringing forth our deepest truths, love for each other, mutuality, reciprocity and growth. To equate sensuality with loving, caring, and making/creating thus deeply intertwines these processes. To create is to step into experiences and imaginings past, present, and future and sometimes at the edges of human cognition and human experience. Many societies and colonizers who sought to control the populace thus limited creative expression for fear of where it might lead. As a testament to the power and fuel of creative energy, interestingly some of the most ruthless leaders, including Nazi leaders, were known to have been failed artists (Hoffer, 1951). The desire to channel our expressive and creative urges can lead to both constructive and destructive possibilities. To not know what art activates is to fear the release of primal forces and urges. To control and restrict artistic practice is to limit our life force and sense of agency. Colonizing forces in India banned traditional art forms like dance by shaming and wrongly associating them with prostitution; they destroyed martial art forms like Kalaripayattu by killing the gurus and banning its practice. The shaming of artists by demonizing them and associating them with lifestyles of promiscuity and licentiousness minimizes and delegitimizes the message and purpose of art (see Chapters 4 and 7). How might we conceptualize the layers and associations with artistic practices?

Aristotle said that the purpose of art was to evoke empathy for expressed emotion: a shared catharsis for both the person expressing and the person viewing. In his research on violence and art-making, Gussak (2021) argued that art-making is an externalization of our inner mental states. The outcome can be in the form of catharsis or sublimation. Catharsis is pure expression; sublimation is a more processed form of expression beyond simply acting out mental states through physical actions. Sublimation is the expression of inner states, including emotion and cognition, in ways that feel authentic to the self and are constructive in the world (and not destructive). Gussak

(2021) offered an example of vandalism as catharsis, whereas graffiti converted to art on canvas exemplifies sublimation: One is expressive but destructive, whereas the other is expressive and creative. Building on Aristotle's conceptualization of catharsis as a purgation of pity and fear, Kearney (2007) suggested that through the narratives of others, we are invited to revisit our own life and perhaps live it out differently and see a new future for ourselves. Aristotle meant that art and narrative evoked empathy in us as an initial reaction. This was followed by fear that if we over-identify with the characters, our own lives might be deluged akin to the drama of the protagonists. Our challenge as viewers, then, is to purge our emotions without losing ourselves (Kearney, 2007). This form of catharsis allows us some release from our pain by helping us see cause and effect and ways out, but it is not yet art: It is only self-expression. Connecting this concept to the ideas presented in Chapter 1, what distinguishes our expressive instincts from creative self-expression is the additional ingredient of metaphors that embed meanings and creative associations.

My friend and poetry therapist recognizes this power of expression in her own work and once shared that to be creative/expressive was overwhelming and to numb ourselves through times of stress is an adaptive choice: Expression can only flow out when we are relaxed and willing to engage in expression and what it reveals (personal communication, Anjana Deshpande, June 20, 2021).

Dynamic aspects of creative expression and human development

The dynamic influences "creative capacity" and "creative expression" merit a mention. Art and culture are dynamic and changing all the time. Our stories, our forms of expression, and our understanding and representation of the world itself are also changing all the time.

A feature in the *New York Times* (Farago, 2021) challenged some assumptions about the cultural constructions of human expression. A miniature painting (8 inches high) from the time of the Mughal Emperor Shahjahan included examples of artistic styles spanning Christian frescoes, Persian calligraphy, and Hindu iconography, along with the grandeur that the Mughal emperor sought to portray. The painting further inspired European artists like Rembrandt, indicating how deeply receptive sensitive artists are to each other's styles and forms of representation.

The author Rilke (2021) asserted that the ability to be with our thoughts and in solitude was an essential aspect of creativity that highlighted the paradox of the need to be alone in order to better connect with others. Zadie Smith (2020), in her essays reflecting on the time of COVID, asserts that there is no great difference between novels and banana bread: They are both just something to do. They cannot be a substitute for true human connection and love and experiences that help us through. She implies through this analogy that by doing and making we take an indirect road to addressing the basic needs of human longing.

Human expression is an exquisite dance of calibration such that our primal drives are our fuel, with our cognitive capacities containing and channeling these powerful forces. Both our scientific endeavors and our artistic endeavors engage our imaginations to either advance innovation and technology or advance new cultural assets (Loeb, 2021). Both stand the risk of going against public opinion in promoting new ways of seeing, being, or making. Scientific innovation now requires a lot of education before new technological innovation can be introduced, but the process of gaining insight or discovery is not different from that of producing a cultural or artistic product. They both expand our imagination into new realities experienced by our senses. As human beings, we have our preferences in the realm of art and aesthetics, which is a combination of both evolutionary instincts that promote survival as well as learned cultural preferences.

Key takeaways

This chapter provides an overview of how we might see creative self-expression as a part of human history and civilization. My main point here is to emphasize the evolutionary and inherent value that creative self-expression has in our lives. I hope this foundational assumption invites you to appreciate this space of creative self-expression, health, and well-being as a non-hierarchical realm, democratic and open to all. I highlighted some leading theories around creative self-expression and the need to democratize these artistic practices. I provided an overview of different aspects of creative self-expression, including examples from both Western and Eastern philosophical traditions, and how we might think of pleasure, satisfaction, and joy as they relate to creative self-expression. Moving past self-defeating and derogatory perceptions of art-making and artists, I suggest that artistic practice is a doorway to multisensory engagement. Although artistic practice can be conflated with socially marginal experiences, it can also be a way to engage in holistic awareness and well-being. Creative expression is thus potentially a way back to ourselves and our communities when we feel lonely, isolated, or thrown into experiences outside of the realm of perceived normal life. It is a way to create a land for the lonely; a tent for the dispossessed; a vast landscape of human experience where we see our isolated experiences as part of the greater whole of the world.

3

What our ancestors knew

Indigenous and traditional arts practices and health

> To action alone hast thou a right and never at all to its fruits; let not the fruits of action be thy motive; neither let there be in thee any attachment to inaction.
>
> **Translation of** *Bhagavad Gita* **2:47, Sarvapalli Radhakrishnan**

> An artist is an emotional and spiritual historian.
>
> **James Baldwin**

Terrain map: As we map our journey across time, it is increasingly clear that creative self-expression in art forms is as old as human history itself. Examples such as prehistoric rock art are reminders that artistic expression has been a part of all human communities and civilizations. To fully immerse ourselves in the current contexts of creative expression, we must examine the role of indigenous and traditional artistic practices, particularly as they relate to promoting health and well-being. Beginning with ancient rock art, in this chapter, I will share how indigenous and traditional artforms have elements that connect seamlessly from ancient to modern life as reminders of the timeless aspects of the human condition. Many of these art forms have survived to this day, and each of us could trace back to a community of origin. The unfortunate and oppressive history of colonialism and imperialism minimized the value and importance of these practices. Contemporary efforts in research and revitalization of indigenous practices to better understand the value of these deeply integrated creative practices could offset some of these irretrievable losses. In particular, the aspects of storytelling and narrative, contemplative and meditative practices, connection to nature, and sustaining a nurturing community are reminders from these arts practices that can be deeply relevant to current times.

The Expressive Instinct. Girija Kaimal, Oxford University Press. © Oxford University Press 2023.
DOI: 10.1093/oso/9780197646229.003.0004

Figure 3.1. Floral floor decoration called pookalam made during the harvest festival of Onam (Kaimal, 2018). Media: Leaves and seashells

Rock art as the origin story

When we think of ancient artistic practices, the references commonly cited are of cave drawings and prehistoric artwork preserved on stones. Further adding to this shared history is the well-established fact that rock artwork has been found all over the world. These visual expressive renditions emerged in different parts of the world independently of each other. Rock art made in caves has been found from 40,000 years ago in Europe to the most recently discovered evidence of art made approximately 45,000 years ago in Borneo (Aubert et al., 2018). There is evidence that some symbolic representations occurred among Neanderthals up to 60,000 years ago and that images of hand stencil prints, geometric shapes, and marks on cave walls were found in Spain

(Hoffmann et al., 2018). The rock art found in caves is considered the earliest representation of figurative art. Rock art in Colombia that is estimated to be almost 12,500 years old includes representations of figurative works with depictions of simple indications of landscapes, human hands and figures, as well as scenes of animals, hunts, and nature (Mosley & McMahon, 2020). The depictions are those of life itself as it must have been experienced by the artists in those communities. The symbols in the artwork and handprints are considered to have been an attempt to represent conceptions of the world at that time, including those of religion, cosmology, activities of everyday living, and social interactions: fundamental expressions of their culture through visual art. The evidence indicates that they perhaps represented key events like group hunts or landmark social milestones. There is evidence that children made marks too (Cooney, 2011). And these are only the examples that have survived to this day. It is possible that many works were also transient and/or eroded without record over time.

What do these endeavors tell us? We can only speculate on the purpose of the expressions, but the desire, the compulsion, the wish to create or leave a mark was somehow present in communities of hunter-gatherers who lived tens of thousands of years ago. Some suggest that the human/animal hybrids represented in some of the images that have survived were precursors to spiritual stories and concepts (Aubert et al., 2018). Perhaps these represented the hopes and dreams of these events or ritual prayers to ensure successful hunts. We cannot know for sure if these visual documentations or visual creations were accompanied by music, dance, and drama; they could just as readily have been ways to while away the time during long waits or periods of extreme weather that prevented foraging and hunting. In a newspaper article, Jones (2021) makes an evocative humanistic point on the significance of cave paintings in understanding human history. Although our current scientific understanding of evolution is based on fossil records and documentation of the remains of animals and plants, once humans started painting on cave walls, they were documenting the world around them in a new way. They were representing their stories and histories: animals they hunted and fished, handprints and human forms related to their experiences. Cave paintings were in many ways abstractions from hundreds of thousands of years ago of exquisite renderings representing so-called modern discoveries of formal elements like perspective and composition. We see it thousands of years later as part of our shared legacy. We know some of these practices only through the indigenous and traditional art forms that exist today.

Indigenous and traditional perspectives on creative expression, health, and well-being

A question that emerged for me while working as an artist and art therapist is whether and to what extent art-making historically has played a therapeutic role in human lives and how it can inform the modern interpretation and profession of art therapy. What can they tell us about the role of art in our everyday lives? In previous chapters, I proposed that art-making serves to activate our imagination and that it aligns naturally with our brain's predictive capacity. We can go backwards in time chronologically to explore how art-making has served human needs and therefore how we might understand its role in the present and possibly for the future.

It is well established that artistic expression has historically and simultaneously evolved in all civilizations around the world (Dutton, 2010; Kaimal, 2019). All communities around the world have their own traditions of art-making, music-making, dancing, movement, drama, and literary traditions (oral or written). These traditions are deeply intertwined with the rituals and rhythms of life (Crowe, 1995). A noted voice on the topic has been the independent scholar Ellen Dissanayake (2000), who proposed that art-making was integral to humans in establishing rituals and communication as well as in "making special" key events and milestones in the lives of individuals in communities. She identified the roots of artistic practices as an extension of the nonverbal communication between infants and their mothers. This initial nonverbal interaction sets the stage for lifelong striving to communicate verbally and nonverbally with others. None of these theorists have, however, explicitly addressed the therapeutic role of the arts in helping individuals cope in response to challenges, including deriving strength from one's individual creative capacity and a sense of community.

There is also increasing recognition that mental health issues are a worldwide challenge: The World Health Organization (2014) indicated that lack of mental well-being is a leading cause of disease burden around the world, with one-fourth of the global population at risk of developing a mental health challenge in their lifetime and one-fifth of children and adolescents having mental health problems. Wars, adversity, discrimination, illness, and natural disasters further exacerbate these unmet needs for psychosocial support. Most parts of the world have extremely limited resources and few skilled professionals to support mental health and well-being. Research on the health implications of traditional artistic practices is also extremely limited, but these practices may potentially represent culturally responsive and potent means to advance overall health.

Connecting the historical universality of artistic practices and the mental health needs of our modern world, therapeutic approaches grounded in creative self-expression are embedded in our evolutionary survival instincts, including our responses to threats and the choices we make to ensure safety and belonging (Kaimal, 2019). Recent scholarly and artistic endeavors are beginning to explore indigenous knowledge and insight developed through generations of observations and deep understanding of nature and natural processes (Langlois, 2018; Whiting, 2018). There is increasing awareness of the value of traditional healing practices, including narrative storytelling (Duff, 2019; Gotschall, 2013) and integrating cultural practices like sweat lodges in medical hospitals (Center for Mental Health, 2019). Huotilainen et al. (2018) highlighted the role of arts and crafts in building community and feelings of wellness through flow states (Csikszentmihalyi, 1990) induced during art-making. James (2019), for example, highlighted the return to traditional artistic practices like embroidery as a means to cope, for example among migrant women facing adversity and despair. In this example, women who were part of the migrant caravan escaping violence in Central America created evocative pieces that retained and sustained their textile heritage and likely offered a productive creative distraction and outlet during a time of adversity.

At the same time, it is important to recognize how knowledge about human development and the conceptualizations of traditional art-making relate to contemporary society and an understanding of therapeutic art-making and arts for health and well-being (Joseph, 2006; Pascoe, 2015). Smith (2020) called for the recognition of scholarly inquiry and systematic understanding and valuing of traditional and indigenous knowledge, which she referred to as ethnoscience. Citing examples from the seafaring Polynesians to the discovery of the zero in India, Smith (2020) called for a recognition of embodied and oral knowledge systems that preceded current research methods and to recognize their contributions to human epistemology. This indigenous knowledge (Chilisa, 2012; Pascoe, 2015) highlights the importance of traditional wisdom and insight, including the close interaction of artistic practice with natural materials, creative agency, and contemplative and spiritual meaning-making (Franklin, 2018) while recognizing our interconnectedness with other living beings in nature (Nagarajan, 2018; Pascoe, 2015).

We need to be better informed so that cultural forms of expression are not appropriated incorrectly; so that efforts to use them are respectful of local cultural and spiritual traditions; and so that they are incorporated into materials, media, and art therapy approaches as sensitively and ethically as possible (Fincher, 1991; Iyer, 2018; Kaimal, 2015). Similarly, the storytelling and the connection to nature that are inherent parts of indigenous knowledge have been found to strengthen aspects like memory. For example, Australian aboriginal communities have a distinct oral history tradition that integrates stories and landscapes to remember things. Reser et al. (2021) found this method to be more enjoyable and more effective for retention compared with modern methods of improving memory and recall. Many such powerful techniques exist to enhance memory, understanding, and interconnections with our surroundings. Yet, the role of art-making in our lives and its purpose in supporting human development are not adequately understood. Traditions have value when their rationale and origins are understood and founded on longstanding knowledge and wisdom, often earned through careful observation and understanding of the world around us.

In understanding the role of indigenous practices in health and well-being, an example of note here is the hierarchy of needs that was developed and made famous worldwide by the humanistic theorist Abraham Maslow. Maslow spent several weeks in the company of the Blackfoot elders (Michel, 2014) and learned about their conceptualization of self and community. In the Blackfoot belief system, self-actualization is the foundation, not the pinnacle, of human needs. Self-actualization is deeply intertwined with the needs of the community and actualization and perpetuation of the culture broadly. Maslow, rather inexplicably, took these ideas and inverted them such that self-actualization was placed on the pinnacle and physiological and psychological needs formed lower tiers of this pyramid of needs.

This inversion unfortunately could be dangerous in that it minimizes purpose and meaning as higher-level human needs, regardless of whether our physiological safety needs are being met. A more meaningful way to conceptualize needs might be as a network or weave wherein lack of one need might be fulfilled in the presence of others. Thus, lack of home and shelter might be offset by a caring community and a sense of feeling useful and valued by loved ones. Similarly, the absence of a sense of belonging might be offset by physiological needs and self-actualization needs being met. A helpful example was provided by Wordsworth (2017), who noted that we run the risk of dehumanizing refugees when we focus only on the Maslow hierarchy such as food and shelter without recognizing the need for feeling valued and fulfilled in the world. The author shared an example of a Syrian family who chose to remain in Syria despite the physical hardships and left the county only when the prospects of higher education for their children were found to be in jeopardy. The Blackfoot beliefs and recognition of the interconnected aspects of human choices, needs, and ideas around well-being seem more attuned to the reality of human lives than the more widely known ideas around the hierarchy of human needs.

There is increasing awareness in the worlds of psychotherapeutic practice on the need to develop approaches to diversity and to deepen our understanding of the role of visual expressive traditions in health and well-being. By inviting discussion, dialogue, and awareness of the role of the arts in human development and evolution of the therapeutic role of the arts, we can expand the scope of traditional approaches to creative expression and promote an understanding of the role of integrating the arts and the profession of art therapy worldwide with traditional knowledge and wisdom, as well as reduce the likelihood of culturally misinformed or Western imperialist approaches to treatment that would be ill suited (Kleinman, 1981; Whitaker, 2002) and misaligned in relation to the needs of the patients.

What we know about the purpose and role of indigenous and traditional arts practices

I refer to "indigenous arts practices" as those that are identified and associated with a specific community located in a geographical region, including those with a heritage of artwork that might be sacred with depictions of belief systems, spirituality, and community history. Examples include artwork by aboriginal communities in Australia, totem poles in North America, or rice powder kolams in India: artworks defined by the place and the materials of that physical space. I define "traditional practices" as broader in scope; they do not need to be connected to a specific community but could be practices taught over generations, such as knitting and woodworking. These are less defined by a community and more around a heritage or traditions in a family handed down over time. The distinction I make is that indigenous art practices are connected to a specific community and have historical, cultural, and spiritual relevance. Traditional arts practices might span a range of communities and might not be tied to a specific group and thus might be more open to cultural interpretation and modification without fear of appropriation. Both are, however, connected in that they have historical significance and likely are deeply intertwined with the valued practices of an individual or community (Arslanbek et al., 2022).

Nagarajan (2018), in her book *Feeding a Thousand Souls*, connects the everyday practice of kolam-making in southern India with a spiritual and environmental role. Kolam is a form of morning ritual artistic practice where women first clean out the front of their homes, sprinkle the ground with water to settle the soil, and then create beautiful patterns with rice flour. The rice flour is meant to feed ants and bugs and is a way to give back to the earth and compensate for the many ways in which the human being through the course of the day takes back from the earth and its beings. The elements of kolam are simple and traditionally consist only of dots and lines, but these dots and lines can be connected in infinite ways to create aesthetically pleasing patterns. I would argue that this aesthetic practice helps the householder gain a sense of pride and accomplishment in starting the day in a meaningful way, enjoying the effort-based reward of creating and viewing a beautiful piece of art every day. Figure 3.2 shows a contemporary group kolam/rangoli made with a combination of natural media, paper, and rice flour.

Similar traditions of floor decorations abound in many parts of India. In Kerala, every year during the harvest festival of Onam, Malayalis decorate the entrances to their homes with circular decorations of flowers and leaves. Each day of the festival includes a time to create a rangoli (a decorative design made on living room and courtyard floors during Hindu festivals) with freshly picked flowers and leaves. People create variations with a range of items, and the whole region comes alive with decorations. The use of natural materials enables easy clearing of withered decorations and allows creation and related joy of a new work every day (Figure 3.1). Here again the elements are simple: They use concentric circles of repeating elements that are automatically aesthetically pleasing in their repetitive predictability and variation. Working with culturally familiar arts practices like Rangoli can be way to connect and communicate (Redwood et al, 2018).

The practice of textile art is an example of the intersection of traditional and indigenous practices. In her book on using textiles in therapy with women, Futterman-Collier (2012) wrote about the role of textile arts in the

Figure 3.2. Contemporary group kolam rangoli made by art therapy students in India (2018)

development of women. She referenced the different stages of a woman's life and how textile arts can help support the psychological needs of each stage through the qualities of the medium. For example, she referenced making quilts as a metaphor for the psychosocial needs of community, building, and restoration. Similarly, creating knitted clothing provides protective, generative, and comforting pieces. The repetitive actions that result in fiber and textile work could reinforce a sense of safety. She referenced examples of how the process of making induces a sense of mastery and confidence. The process itself is transformative in that it helps us see the world differently even as we leave our mark on it.

This view echoes Lambert's (2008) suggestion that repetitive actions promote the production of serotonin, a neurochemical that reinforces a sense of joy and belonging. In addition, Collier (2012) suggested that even the act of choosing what to create, even if one is using premade designs, indicates a level of psychological investment and choice, be it to make products for oneself or for others. The textile works are then metaphors of human lives, particularly those of women, who have historically had domestic roles that did not allow for time to create clothing and items of everyday use in the home. Many activities are also communal. For example, bridal embroidery trousseaus were historically made by women as part of a group among the Rabari nomadic communities of Gujarat. The time to create the trousseaus was also a time for women to gather and be a support group for each other.

In a later chapter, I speak about working together with my daughters on a quilt to manage and reduce the stress of the coronavirus (COVID) lockdown. We used a simple India running stitch technique called kantha embroidery. In times of stress we returned instinctively to the familiar and the known, which for me was traditional Indian arts and crafts methods and esthetics. An interesting, related connection with indigenous and traditional art forms is the idea of being interdependent and respectful of sustainable practices and natural cycles. Kantha embroidery was a method to recycle and perhaps upcycle old, worn-out sarees into quilts and bedspreads. The old fabrics thus became reimagined in new roles rather than being discarded as waste. This reimagining and valuing of material objects and integrating them into our lives and community practices is a recurring theme in indigenous practices.

Drawing on the lessons learned from his American Indian grandmother, Lakota writer Marshall (2001) wrote about the gentle ways in which his grandmother taught him to creatively respond to and manage fear and stress:

There was a time when I wondered why old people were so wise. I do not anymore because now I know that wisdom is life's gift. Life demands that we face adversity with courage, demonstrate fortitude in the midst of temptation, tell the truth no matter how painful, walk in humility, sacrifice for our families, practice generosity to be truly rich, respect all who are part of the great circle of life, choose honor above personal gain, act with compassion toward the needy, strive for harmony in personal relationships and otherwise demonstrate the virtues that give meaning to life. (p. 202)

Through the act of creating he highlights how indigenous wisdom connects well-being to the act of making, social relationships, and intergenerational exchanges.

This wisdom is imparted through lived experiences and stories, the analogy or metaphor for handling challenges. The lesson might be in vicarious learning through the story or through actual action. For example, he shared how he was frightened once by a storm and instead of dismissing his fears, his grandmother taught him active strategies to cope. She did not name them as such but taught him how to manage his fears by channeling that nervous energy into actual pragmatic, creative tasks. She asked him to pile the firewood effectively so each log would burn and to balance the rest as each log turned to ash. She then asked him to sort and count beads and string them for a beadwork project. Through both these tasks, he stayed distracted and focused, both of which are the natural strengths of the arts in promoting resilience and the regulation of emotions. Not only did she teach him to manage his fears, but she also actively taught him how to gain agency and self-efficacy through doing and responding to frightening situations. Lakota wisdom, like that of most indigenous traditions, highlights further the deep interconnectedness of humans with the natural world and the humility and respect needed to thrive sustainably: to be thankful and respectful of the land and animal food sources. Similarly, the stories and myths of every community are a reminder that the human condition remains fundamentally unchanged over time and that we have much to learn from stories because they both hold the sequential structure our brains understand and also cycle through time, because the ideas at their core are about the range of human experiences.

Lévi-Strauss (1950) in fact referred to mythological tales from around the world as the original therapies because they provide us with symbolic representations of struggles and the ways in which imaginary humans have responded to and overcome them. Indigenous community stories from the Indian myths of Mahabharata and Ramayana, although outdated in many ways around contemporary ideas of equity, are still metaphorical sources of insight about how to respond to and cope with life's uncertainties, challenges, and adversities. Through specific characters and their choices, we see ways to align in terms of values, choices of responses, and ways to derive strengths. Most importantly, we see human foibles, vulnerabilities, and the essential quality of humility in accepting and learning through our experiences (personal communication, Manoj Kaimal, July 4, 2021).

Contemplating traditions and art-making

Indigenous practices include several dimensions of artistic practice, such as meditative approaches, pragmatic products for everyday living, and processes as well as recognition of the interconnectedness of all things in the known universe. In contemplative and meditative traditions, "mindfulness" is a term we hear often in society today. Derived mainly from the contemplative and meditative practices of Buddhism, the idea is to stay in the moment and to use the senses to become present and not be distracted and distressed. Exhibiting patience and being present and at peace with all events around us, Kongtrul (2020) argued, is a way to manage ourselves effectively. In particular, he referred to accepting life events as a gift if we receive it and a blessing if we do not. Given the struggles with distraction and the inability to focus in our current day and age, Kongtrul (2020) in particular highlighted that the arts are a way to stay present and focused. They allow us to engage our senses and direct our attention to tasks that we can control rather than feeling like we are dealing with those that we cannot control. Having creative practices to turn to then becomes a way to reflect, a way to regain a sense of connectedness, peace, and belonging.

One of the first people to actively connect art-making and contemplative traditions was art therapist, yogi, and leading scholar of contemplative artistic practice Michael Franklin. He drew the link between individual creative expression as a form of and the idea of the creation of the universe. Interpreting the teachings of Sri Aurobindo, Franklin (2018) said, "The Creator with the artists as creator and that which is created are all one and the same. Form and formless are steered by the spanda impulse," the vibration of creative energy. Franklin (2018) articulated the link between creative and reflective practices by drawing the connection through contemplative activities integrating art media. Art-making and creative practice thus serve as a space in which one can engage in meditative and reflective work. He refers to the Hindu principles of dharma or ethical action as exemplified in the studio and the spiritual practices of seeing the divine through art-making. By referencing art-making as spiritual, he sees creative works as a form of karma yoga, a form of yogic practice that involves service.

If meditation is about learning to discipline one's mind and manage attention, then there are many ways to do that. Focusing on breathing and breathwork is one way. Being attentive in creative practice can be another. Akin to being quiet in meditation, karma yoga can be about being attentive in any aspect of the work we do. Creative practice thus involves working with all our senses, with intention, and being attentive to the sensory aspects in the moment. Being responsive and fully present with the art media helps us understand our interactions with the external object and, by extension, our ability to interact with and understand others in our world. Franklin (2018) cited in particular his work in the studio with clay and how he sees being able to explore the potential of a medium and its limits by understanding its unique qualities. This practice of contemplation in action and of sensitivity and understanding in the creative process helps provide us with practice with multiple aspects of functioning. It provides discipline, reduces reactivity by keeping us in the moment, and builds skill through repeated practice. All these aspects contribute to well-being through the contemplative and "making" traditions.

Such formulations of caring and being detached are not in contradiction. An example of this reflective role of mandala designs lies in the Tibetan Buddhist monks' practice of making elaborate designs that are then swept away. The process is meant to both encourage focus, reflection, and discipline while also helping reduce attachment in the sweeping away of the ephemeral art. In Hindu and Buddhist traditions, mandalas represent aspects of self and spiritual journeys of exploration and awareness (Liu et al., 2020). The artistic practice then becomes a way to control unhealthy attachment and works of the ego. Mandalas as a symbolic and therapeutic tool were popularized in the West in the works of Carl Jung and were representative of the process of individuation. They are used extensively in art therapy practice and research (Potash et al., 2016). Hindu and Buddhist traditions, for example, propose detachment as the solution to all misery. That appears to be the exact opposite of Western attachment theory, but really they are not. Both promote unselfishness and caring. Secure attachment is the capacity to care and to let go.

Reflecting on the value of art, Mahatma Gandhi considered its role in life to be direct in its expression of the language of nature (Roy, 1945, p. 76). I imagine this includes nature as it manifests in human nature. He considered its value to be that of bringing joy and inspiration (p. 71). Decrying the pretensions of modern art, he refers to the greatest artist as the person who lives the finest life. To that end, manmade art was not of interest to Gandhi: Rather, nature itself was his perception of art, and he kept his walls bare for this reason. In extending this idea of contemplative practice, Gandhi encouraged spinning yarn on the charkha (hand-cranked Indian spinning wheel) as a symbolic act of making the very unit of fabric, namely the threads. Interestingly, this "making" of yarn and the fact that it needed both hands and some amount of focus and developing skill served as an excellent method to focus attention while being productive and active. I think of this meditative and productive practice of spinning thread as an act of making and of the repetitive skilled process of making thread for weaving as the embodiment of contemplative altruistic artistic practice.

Implications of colonial destruction and addressing appropriation

Given the history of the colonial erasure, imperialist oppression, marginalization, and trauma inflicted on indigenous practices worldwide, there is expectedly a distrust of outsiders who want to learn or appropriate traditional practices. It is imperative that anyone interested in indigenous practices approach them with deep humility, be led by the community, and ensure that the context and history of the practices are respected, not appropriated or misrepresented. In 2020, we saw the global movement to recognize societal injustices in the callous public killing of George Floyd in the name of policing. The nation and the world erupted into protests. There is also increasing recognition of the problematic ways in which heritage arts have been stolen or co-opted.

In times of distress, especially for marginalized and oppressed communities and individuals such as Black, Indigenous and People of Color (BIPoC) or those from historically excluded religions and ethnic groups, indigenous practices can be a source of strength and inspiration. Migrant women in Mexico used traditional embroideries to capture and create their journeys (James, 2019). An African child soldier artist from Sudan referred to creating his own creative restorative practice that included dance traditions and yoga (Donato, 2020). Similarly there is increasing recognition and concern that many artifacts and representations of indigenous art forms found in museums and other collections are reminders of colonial theft and war crimes (Güner, 2020). These concerns raise questions around the exploitative appropriation of arts practices without a deep understanding of or respect for indigenous and traditional art forms. How often have we heard outrage around the use of attire or designs that are sacred to a community but are mere adornments to a culture unfamiliar with the imagery? Weinberg (2018) highlights the need for sensitivity to the justified mistrust that indigenous communities have toward outsiders given the histories of exploitation, an-nihilation, and colonization. Working together with indigenous community members and recognizing intergenerational and historical trauma (Comas-Diaz, 2021) becomes then our moral and ethical imperative in any arts practices and therapeutic efforts.

In our effort to unpack the therapeutic aspects of indigenous and tra-ditional artistic practices, my students and I have been examining them through our own history and heritages as well as by talking with artists and art therapists working in authentic and close partnership with indigenous communities. Given our personal experiences with artistic practices in Turkey and India (Arslanbek et al., 2022; Kaimal & Arslanbek, 2020c), we were interested in what practitioners in the field of art therapy have learned from traditional and indigenous arts practices. In fact, given the many op-pressive colonial actions that damaged indigenous arts forms worldwide, this distrust and reluctance on the part of indigenous communities to engage with researchers is valid.

As such, the use of indigenous approaches runs the ethical risk of appropri-ation. Appropriation means the copying of practices and traditions without understanding, crediting, or valuing the roots of the practice and its meaning to the community of origin. In Chapter 2, I wrote about the dynamic aspects of creative expression. Unlike dynamic creative exchanges and learning, ap-propriation is an experience of disrespect, marginalization, and exploitation of cultural traditions for socioeconomic gain. Appropriation of art forms and practices without an understanding of context is a concern. We have appro-priated artistic practices at times, and research tools need to be adapted to deepen our understanding of the value and impact of traditional practices handed down over generations. In a review of nine peer-reviewed papers, we found (Kaimal & Arslanbek, 2020) that the therapeutic aspects of indigenous art forms for visual arts practices are deeply interconnected with spiritual traditions, narrative storytelling, counseling, and wisdom for the community, respect for all things living and non-living in nature, using natural and locally available materials and creative products that are sustainable. Traditional practices integrate natural materials from the environment; all natural media have their life cycles, and the practices are sustained by the need to remake them (Crowe, 1995). Arslanbek et al. (2022) offer the analogy of a tree to ap-proach and better understand and work with indigenous approaches. In this analogy, the artistic practice or art form represents the fruit of the tree, which was nourished and created through the collective efforts of the invis-ible roots, branches, pollinators, weather, and nutrients from the soil. To rec-ognize all that came before, including the roots (history) and environment (sociocultural context), is to better value the fruit (the indigenous art form). To approach with this respect allows us to recognize what we need to learn if and when we seek to incorporate any scared arts practice into our personal or professional practice.

Alter-Muri (2020) similarly identified the therapeutic value of the art of tattooing found in many cultures and communities, where the human body itself becomes the canvas: the surface for creative expression. In contemporary society tattooing can serve as a way to commemorate an achievement, milestone, memory, or loss or to reinforce a desired identity. In the choice of the tattoo's imagery and placement, Alter-Muri (2020) argues, lies a narrative, a story of the individual and salient aspects of the self, recorded on the skin.

Figure 3.3 shows how we can consider the emergence of modern applications of therapeutic art practices with traditional art forms. Traditionally, artistic practice was facilitated by a master healer and/or elder in the community, and the practice itself was embedded in the life of the community. These roles have become differentiated in relation to the facilitator (often a therapist) and the client. The artistic process and art product stay consistent. The goals are potentially different in that the therapeutic aspect likely lies in mastery, learning, and sharing while creating together. The facilitators likely also had a more active teaching role than a witness role.

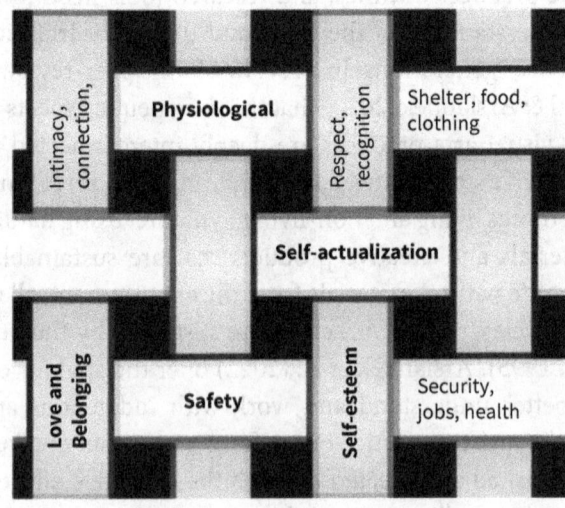

Figure 3.3. Conceptualizing human needs as interwoven aspects rather than as a hierarchy

Nature as central in indigenous communities

Indigenous and traditional art forms manifest this connectedness to nature in a range of ways. Kopytin et al. (2019) examined the elements of ikebana and how it relates to expressive therapies. Ikebana is a traditional Japanese art form that has existed for over 600 years. It began as a Buddhist tradition of offering flowers to the dead in temples. Unlike flower arrangements, ikebana represents efforts to connect creativity and harmony with nature, inspiring humility and reverence for natural materials. Similar to the Japanese practices like calligraphy, the tea ceremony, and haiku, ikebana is a means for meditation and body–mind training, to train for spiritual immersion, which is in turn expected to lead to humility, empathy, and skillful action. These diligent practices are expected to result in self-transformation, discipline, and a deeper understanding of the essence of all that we encounter (Hovane, 2017; Kopytin et al., 2019).

Because they inherently use natural media and materials, many indigenous artistic methods have embedded health benefits. For example, indigo clothing was used by samurai warriors as an antibacterial agent to protect against wounds (Great big story, 2018). *Indigo naturalis* (natural indigo, not the synthetic version) has a variety of pharmacological activities, such as anti-inflammatory, antioxidant, antibacterial, antiviral, immunomodulatory, and so on. It is said to have a very good clinical effect on psoriasis, leukemia, and ulcerative colitis (Qi-Yue et al., 2020). Natural indigo takes a long time to make, but when used as a fabric dye, it improves in quality and color over time compared with synthetic indigo (which is brighter but fades and provides no health benefits). The creators of rock art from places around the world used natural media for colors; red ochre, for example, has been found in Australian and Colombian rock art.

This idea of humility and ongoing skill-building practices as a means to self-mastery is not unlike the goals of therapy. In therapeutic interactions involving arts practices, the therapist helps clients/patients use art media to express themselves while also reflecting on both the process and the product. In a global environment with increased distancing from access to natural materials and media, these intentional practices connect us back to our roots.

Scientific evidence and the biophilia hypothesis

Modern scientific inquiry further validates what indigenous communities have known about being close to natural environments. Our interconnectedness with nature and the affiliation of humans with other living beings have been referred as the "biophilia hypothesis" (Kellert, 1993; Wilson, 1984). This hypothesis suggests that humans derive esthetic intellectual, spiritual, and cognitive meaning and sustenance from other beings and that, through evolution, our sensory systems derived heightened sensitivity to living and lifelike stimuli of the natural world. As humans who have spent millions of years living in close proximity to the natural environment, we are inherently fascinated by visual stimuli in natural landscapes, such as vegetation, wildlife, and "the motion of leaves in the breeze" (Kaplan, 1995, p. 174).

Current research supports what our ancestors knew about the benefits of being in nature. For example, even 15 minutes in nature has been found to reduce cortisol levels and improve health. Despite the many opportunities of access to jobs and resources available to those living in urban environments, urban dwellers who lived near a park had better health outcomes that those who did not. We inherited from our hunter-gatherer and settled agriculturist ancestors a desire for and familiarity with the healthful benefits of natural surroundings. Even exercising is proposed to have benefits when conducted in nature rather than in the sterile, non-stimulating indoor setting of a gym. Researchers have found that walking or running in the outdoors tends to activate many parts of the brain because it alerts us to be responsive to spatial aspects and sensory inputs that are not present in the predictable indoor space of a gym (Raichlen & Alexander, 2020).

Being in nature has been found to reduce stress (Kabisch et al., 2017) and to improve creativity and problem-solving skills (Atchley et al., 2012) as well as to decrease anxiety and rumination and improve working memory (Bratman et al., 2015). The acts of walking and being in nature were found to improve cardiovascular health, reduce blood pressure, and enhance self-esteem (Barton et al., 2012). Hospital patients reportedly recovered faster when they were able to view a nature scene (Brown et al., 2013). A randomized crossover study explored whether viewing different scenes prior to a stressor altered autonomic function during the recovery from the stressor. The two scenes were (a) nature (composed of trees, grass, fields) or (b) built (composed of manmade, urban scenes lacking natural characteristics) environments. Autonomic function was assessed using noninvasive techniques of heart rate variability; in particular, time domain analyses evaluated parasympathetic activity, using the root-mean-square of successive differences. During stress, secondary cardiovascular markers (heart rate and systolic and diastolic blood pressure) showed significant increases from baseline that did not differ between the two viewing conditions. Parasympathetic activity, however, was significantly higher in recovery following the stressor in those viewing the nature scenes compared to the built environments ones. Thus, viewing nature scenes prior to a stressor alters autonomic activity in the recovery period, and viewing nature scenes had a greater effect than viewing built scenes. Overall, this result suggests that nature can elicit improvements in the recovery process following a stressor.

Forest bathing is another Japanese idea that is rooted in this construct of experiences in nature. Richardson et al. (2016) proposed that being in nature such as forests helps us in three distinct ways: We experience a sense of joy, contentment, and management of threat, all of which are deeply ingrained evolutionary responses. To be in nature is to remember our roots as living mammals in an environment where the majority of our evolution took place. It is a reminder of what we find joyful in the pursuit of pleasure, what we find calming in a sense of contentment, and what we find safe in the absence of threat. Of course, all these aspects of a forest can turn threatening if we become prey and get lost, but ideally, forests can provide these tremendously restorative experiences. Li et al. (2010, 2011) found that walking in forest environments reduced levels of stress hormones such as adrenaline and noradrenaline and showed relaxing effects in both male and female participants compared with walking in a city. On both trips, the participants they walked for 2 hours in the morning and afternoon on a Sunday. Blood and urine were sampled on the morning before each trip and after each trip. The day trip to the forest park significantly reduced blood pressure and urinary noradrenaline and dopamine levels. Taken together, habitual walking in forest environments was found to have sustained physiological benefits.

Biomorphic features are also prevalent in human construction. Builders throughout history have often endowed their structures with nature-like visual qualities by drawing inspiration from the "monumental design model" (Kellert, 2003, p. 36) of plants and animals in the design of ornamentation, scaling, and proportionality. This observation is reasonable if we consider that all of the known universe of 98% of living matter in living beings is made of five elements: carbon, hydrogen, nitrogen, oxygen, phosphorus, and sulfur (CHNOPS as it is fondly called; Newton et al., 2000). Thus, the idea that we are made of stardust is technically accurate. Although we might think of things known through our senses as discrete objects, we are deeply interconnected. Even trees are now known to communicate through microscopic signals and spores (Wohlleben, 2016). Our bodies communicate with each other through invisible microscopic pheromones and secretions through our very porous bodies. These communications are essential to our survival in that they signal safety, distress, and the desire for affiliations and allies. My favorite example of this human-to-human communication is the breastfeeding mother. The infant connects and communicates with the mother through the suckling action. That suckling action deposits saliva on the mother's skin. The mother's skin then responds to the message from the baby's saliva by providing nutrients and creating antibodies, embedding them in the breast milk, and providing them to the baby in the next feeding. How brilliant is this natural pharmaceutical process?

Most of these experiences and the preceding examples of receptive experiences indicate the benefits that accrue from being in or responding to nature as a stimulus. Natural environments like pathways and walkways, including those in forests, might encourage movement, but it is unclear how and to what extent they enhance creative self-expression. Much research remains to be done to better understand the deep-rooted connections and impacts of being in and expressing ourselves through natural materials and media. In addition, many indigenous practices are deeply rooted in local history, context, and often oppressive memories of trauma, dispossession, and marginalization. Attending to, respectfully reviving (without appropriating), and learning from the insights of longstanding traditions, which often are born of close observations of characteristics of our natural environment, can only enhance our collective knowledge of the world and its contributions to our health and well-being.

Key takeaways

In this chapter we reviewed the essential interconnectedness of art-making, nature, contemplative practices, and practices of the community. Indigenous practices remind us to be generative, reflective, and compassionate and to recognize the interdependence of all living things: how the simplest of methods through repetition, creative engagement, and a sense of sustainable connection can advance our health and well-being. Traditional and indigenous practices remind us of the inspiration and well-being provided by being in and using natural materials and media in our creative explorations. Many indigenous traditions have been destroyed over time through colonization and oppression. Expectedly, these experiences have led to a distrust of outsiders and justified concerns around appropriation. That said, each of us has heritages from which we can draw inspiration in terms of how our ancestors lived in harmony with nature.

PART II

EMBODIED EXPRESSION

What we know about the human body and its physiological and psychological responses to expressive experiences

Most scholarship about art has tended to be about viewing art or experiencing it, especially the works of famous artists. One of my aims with this book was to do away with the way we minimize and negate our creative capacities and instead to empower ourselves with this secret superpower that resides within us all. This idea of a democratized perception of creative self-expression is increasingly supported in research evidence from neurobiology and neuroscience. Making things, innovating, and bridging from the intangible of the imagination to externalized creative expression is associated with physiological and psychological health outcomes.

In this section, I will focus on what goes on within our minds and bodies as we view and create. Chapter 4 provides an overview of what we know about receptive and expressive experiences as processed through our sensory systems and the different parts of our brain. Chapter 5 provides evidence on neurobiological processes, including evidence from studies that demonstrate the impact of visual self-expression and art therapy on the outcomes of inflammation, the body's natural defense mechanism. I share an overview of different neurotransmitters such as dopamine, serotonin, oxytocin, and endorphins and how they relate to artistic expression. Finally, in Chapter 6, I review studies using brain imaging technologies and what they reveal to us about the functional and structural impacts of art-making.

4

Receptive and expressive experiences

How we see, create, and make narrative sense of it all

> No two human beings ever experience two sensations, experiences, feelings, or thoughts identically . . . I am interested in making art to be experienced and explored by as many individuals as possible with as many different individual ideas about the given piece with no final meaning attached. The viewer creates the reality, the meaning, the conception of the piece. I am merely a middleman trying to bring ideas together.
>
> **Keith Haring**

> The intuitive mind is a sacred gift and the rational mind is a faithful servant. We have created a society that honors the servant and has forgotten the gift.
>
> **Albert Einstein**

Terrain map: *Receptive* experiences are those whereby we observe and sense something, whereas *expressive* experiences refer to our acts of actively creating something. Both aspects are expectedly interconnected and involve sensory engagement and meaning-making as we associate the experiences to our own memories, emotions, and life story narrative. In this chapter, I will share how both these aspects work together with implications for significant positive health outcomes. To that end, I include relevant descriptions of the human body, brain, and sensory systems and how they all relate to our experiences of viewing artistic works as well as creating them.

The brain, body, and sensory processing

At a simple level, all human instincts can broadly be categorized as "approach" or "avoidance" (Kandel, 2012, p. 325). These "instincts" of approach and avoidance are primed for activation intuitively (p. 385). Our unconscious processes

The Expressive Instinct. Girija Kaimal, Oxford University Press. © Oxford University Press 2023.
DOI: 10.1093/oso/9780197646229.003.0005

Figure 4.1. *Unfurled* (Kaimal, 2020). Media: Polymer clay and pins. Dimensions: 6" X 4"

led by the amygdala decide whether or not whatever is in our sensory field is safe, desirable, and approachable (seeking pleasure) or to be avoided as potentially threatening or dangerous (avoiding pain). Our feelings and emotions are then layered on this initial perceptual triaging as additional nuances of our experiences, including naming and expressing these felt sensations, reactions, and responses. Rolls (2017) further asserts that these emotions are simply states related to punishments and rewards that connect to how we respond to aesthetic triggers, including those in art. In art and in life, these experiences are often not that distinct, which means that considerable conscious effort is needed to distinguish and make choices about experiences such that they turn out to be adaptive rather than maladaptive.

How do these systems work together for us to make sense of the world? In general terms, the cerebral cortex has four lobes: frontal, parietal, temporal, and occipital. The frontal cortex includes the prefrontal cortex (PFC) and the motor cortex and is involved in executive functions and decision-making, whereas the others are involved more in perceptual processes. The parietal cortex is involved with processing sensory information, including touch pressure, heat, cold, and pain. The temporal cortex mainly processes auditory information and encoding of memory. Within the cerebral cortex lies the limbic system, which includes the thalamus, hippocampus, amygdala, hypothalamus, and basal ganglia. The thalamus serves as a relay station, with specific areas that receive information from different sensory systems that it then conveys to the cerebral cortex. The amygdala primarily modulates the fear response, while the hippocampus leads the processing of learning and memories. The basal ganglia coordinates information from the cortex to help with planning and executing movements (Lusebrink, 2004).

Thereafter, the PFC serves as an orchestrator, the control center of cognition, particularly for difficult tasks that require attention and focus, and works in coordination with the rest of the brain to facilitate fast responses to stimuli (Haller et al., 2018). These response times vary, and the extent of self-control through the PFC can also vary, as we well know from our own and others' impulsive and at times un-self-regulated responses.

How does this all relate to creativity, imagination, and art-making? I will provide first an overview of the visual system, then the somatosensory and motor cortex, and finally how we come to make meaning and narrative constructions through creative self-expression.

Dominance of the visual systems in the human brain

Human beings have relied on the visual sense more than any other, because over millennia, the sense of sight has helped us survive by alerting us to danger and leading us to resources that could help us thrive. It is well established that the visual and aural systems are the most developed of our senses: more so than those of smell, taste, and touch (Dutton, 2010). Visual systems are hypothesized to have become a dominant sense especially because human beings evolved to be upright and could see considerable distances. As a result, visual processing became the leading source of information about human experiences and mental states and now consumes the largest proportion of brain resources.

Processing of visual data inhabits a dedicated area of the brain (occipital lobe) that has specialized cells and pathways that track and process visual information (Ripley & Politzer, 2010). It is estimated that 70% of all of the human sensory receptors are in the eyes (Merieb & Hoehn, 2007), and approximately 55% of the entire cortical area in a primate brain is dedicated to visual processing (DeMoraes, 2013). For comparison, only 3% of human sensory receptors are associated with the auditory system and 11% with the somatosensory system (DeMoraes, 2013). In addition, humans can get a sense of a visual scene in less than 0.10 seconds (Semetko & Scammell, 2012). It takes only 150 milliseconds for a symbol to be processed by the human brain, and only 100 milliseconds for humans to attach a meaning to it (Holcomb & Grainger, 2006; Thorpe et al., 1996).

The challenge for the visual system is to make sense and meaning of the information coming through the eye (Albright & Stoner, 2002). Our visual system interprets the image based on a range of inputs, including filling in and imagining incomplete parts of images, recognizing that we have literal physiological blind spots (Albright & Stoner, 2002), and interpreting color, size, and angle along with attributing meaning to these perceptions. "We separate things out and put them together in our perception and understanding of the world" (personal communication, Christianne Strang, May 22, 2021).

In terms of the mechanics of visual processing, there are two levels: the level of the descriptive properties of the visual input and the level of making meaning based on the relevance and evaluation of the input in order to determine the appropriate behavioral response (van Rullen &Thorpe, 2001). Information travels from the eye through the retina and optic nerve to the occipital cortex, such that an image is perceived and then connected with other parts of the brain associated with the somatosensory and the auditory systems (DeMoraes, 2013). Light is perceived by photoreceptors, which include the rod and cone cells and eventually the first neurons, which are the retinal ganglion cells (RGCs). They converge thereafter at the optic nerve head for each eye. The two optic nerves converge at the optic chiasm, which is located near the pituitary gland. From the optic chiasm the same axons that originate in the RGC layer continue through the optic tract until they synapse with neurons in the lateral geniculate nucleus (LGN). In the LGN, only about 5% to 10% of the synapses are from the RGC neurons. The rest are from regions connecting to other parts of the brain, such as the thalamic reticular nucleus and the visual cortex. From the LGN, neurons connect through optic radiations to the visual cortex, where there is a 300- to 400-fold increase in neurons compared with the RGC layer. Here is where information is processed. Images are understood in terms of first-level descriptive attributes like luminance, color, movement, depth, memory, and contrast, and then later at the level of meaning-making and associations with memory and preferences (Chatterjee, 2004).

Color is processed milliseconds faster than movement. This sensitivity to subtle variations in color perception and interpretation deeply affects our responses to visual stimuli and how we respond to them. Moreover, color enables us to discern patterns and objects by enhancing figure–ground discrimination (Kandel, 2012, p. 341). Interestingly, the majority of the cone-shaped cells for color perception in the eye are responsible for the perception of the color red, and less so for blue and green (Lanza, 2020, p. 87). This is likely because in our evolutionary history, the color red usually signified danger such as blood, injury, fire, and potential toxins, all requiring immediate and prioritized attention compared with blues or greens, which typically implied vast swathes of vegetation, clear skies, or water bodies. Lanza (2020) further suggests that this physiological predisposition to perceiving the color red is why in modern contexts it is used for symbols and imagery that demand our attention (e.g., stops signs on roads, symbols of caution).

Visually, our brains also prefer order, symmetry, and contrast and patterns (Ramachandran & Hirstein, 1999), elements that help us better prepare for, map, and understand the world around us. In fact, Kragel et al. (2021) found that the visual system is constantly scanning the environment, checking with both our short-term and long-term memory. Our eyes and visual systems appraise the environment to determine what might potentially happen and as such prepare us through all this spatiotemporal learning to make sense from a survival perspective of what we need to see.

Neural underpinnings of somatosensory and motor cortices

The human sensory processing system, although initially disparate, is deeply interlinked. The other relevant sensory systems for receptive and expressive visual art are the somatosensory and motor cortices. Interestingly, given that the visual system is so dominant, simple shifts such as lying down and being blindfolded enhance awareness of other sensory systems and in fact represent a cue to the body to deactivate external awareness and focus inwards (Unwalla et al., 2021).

Somatosensory cortex

The somatosensory system tells us about objects in our environment through the sensation of touch and the position of our body in space (proprioception). The somatosensory system also provides information on experiences of pain, itchiness, temperature, and tickling. Somatosensory neurons are sensitive to mechanical pressure, temperature, tissue damage, and chemicals. The sense of touch or haptic perception is especially relevant to those who "make" or create with their hands (or even feet and mouth in the case of some artists) because we perceive qualities of a material through that sensory engagement (e.g., pressure, feel, vibration, responsiveness in terms of softness or hardness, warm, cold, soft or hard to the touch). Touch is deeply connected with the limbic system and the occipital cortex and further activates responses, reactions, and meaning-making (Lusebrink, 2004).

Motor cortex

The motor cortex consists of the primary motor cortex, the premotor cortex, and the supplemental motor area. The primary motor cortex controls movements and sequences of movements. The premotor cortex is sensitive to the context of a behavior and movement and guides the response based on the action needed for the task. It sends axons to the spinal cord as well as to the primary motor cortex. The supplemental motor cortex is involved in programming complex sequences of movements and coordinating bilateral movements. The association cortex is the fourth layer of the motor hierarchy and, although not strictly part of the motor cortex, it includes the PFC and the posterior parietal cortex. These areas ensure that the movements are targeted adaptively to the needs of the person and are appropriate to the behavioral context (Knierim, 2020).

Tactile sensory information from the world is gained through active exploration with the hand (primarily). During voluntary limb movement, the central nervous system is continuously inundated with both somatosensory signals arising from changes in the external world and those from our actions. Human psychophysical experiments showed that voluntary limb movement decreases sensitivity to tactile stimulation on the moving limb (Umeda et al., 2019). Furthermore, we have associative pathways connecting sensory perception and meaning-making as well as extensive networks of mirror neurons facilitating fast processing and mutuality, making for efficient evolutionary choices (Iacoboni, 2009). Moreover, the findings around mirror neurons highlight how innately attuned we are to feel empathy and experience intersubjectivity with others (Iacoboni, 2009). Heyes and Catmur (2022) further assert that mirror neurons contribute to low-level processing of observed action, which is especially relevant to visual-motor associative learning, indicating a strong connection between the visual and motor systems (see Figure 4.2).

Other senses of sound, smell, and sense of our bodies and being in spaces are all relevant to receptive and expressive experiences, including activating memories and feelings of safety relaxation and processing of layered and complex emotions. The sense of smell or olfactory perception is well known to have strong connections with the amygdala and activates brain areas that regulate emotions, such as the orbitofrontal cortex, hippocampus, and amygdala

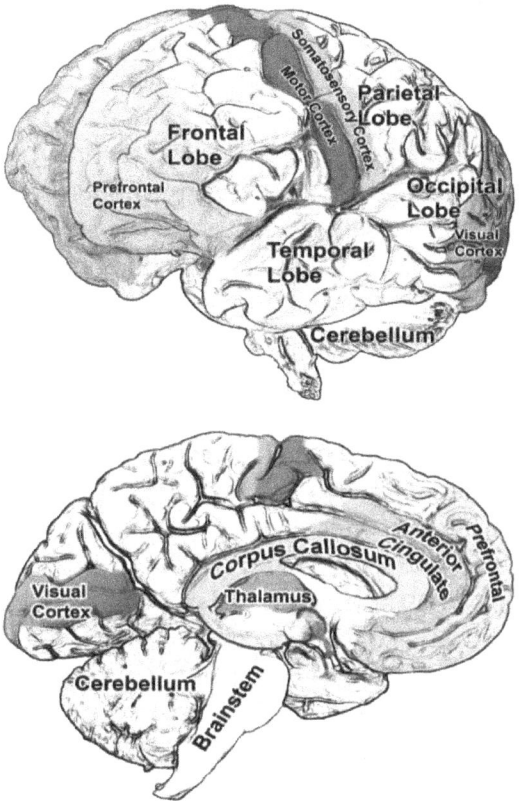

Figure 4.2. Parts of the cerebral cortex and key inner brain structures
(Artwork by Christianne Strang, PhD, ATR-BC)

(Kadohisa, 2013; Wilson & Stevenson, 2003). Willander and Larsson (2006) demonstrated that memories induced by olfactory stimulation were associated with stronger feelings compared to other visual and auditory systems, including relaxant effects and impacts on mood (Chen et al., 2020; Genc & Saritas, 2019; Krusemark et al., 2013; Xiang et al., 2016). Recent research shows that the existence of pleasant fragrances resulted in improved creativity (Baron & Thomley, 1994; Ehrlichman & Bastone, 1992). Zhu and Mehta (2017) in fact concluded that improved mood can be the reason explaining improved creativity under pleasant olfactory stimuli (though they also point out the need for future evidence-based research). Interestingly, across the lifespan, there is evidence that women are on average more sensitive to odors (Sorokowski et al., 2019) and that the sense of smell declines with age (Doty & Kamath, 2014).

From perception to imagination and expression

Halligan and Oakley (2021) asserted that the human mind can be described as comprising conscious and nonconscious aspects, both of which ultimately depend on neural processes in the brain, and that the executive functions typically attributed to the experience of consciousness are carried out competently, backstage and outside subjective awareness, by a myriad of fast, efficient nonconscious brain systems. Perception begins with our senses, and most of it is unconscious. It is only when these perceptions come to consciousness through words and images that we can make sense of them and integrate them into our individual experiences and personal identity narratives (Kandel, 2012, p. 18).

Kandel (2012, p. 500) further highlights that our brains are wired to respond to social connections, information, and meaning. As discussed in Chapter 1, as humans we are innately wired to try to learn about the world we perceive, respond instinctively and intentionally, and share what we know with others. As humans, we are constantly sensing and learning. As we perceive the world around and within us, parts of our motor cortex intuitively respond, as seen with the mirror neurons that reside in many parts of the brain and that react rapidly to the world around us (Kandel, 2012, p. 435). Biederman and Vessel (2006) suggest that our perceptual systems are set up to enhance learning such that we constantly seek out new and novel information to better learn, with the eventual goal of having survival advantages in any given environment.

Our brains are wired to notice human faces, movement, contrast, patterns that promote an understanding of science, and the wide natural landscapes that provide a vantage point of safety. According to Kandel (2012, p. 350), the visual artistic experience is encoded perceptually through our primal brain instincts of approach and avoidance and then interpreted into feelings and emotional experiences through our conscious processes. Dutton (2010) further asserted that "the greatest works of art are not necessarily the most novel or unusual. They do tend to be somehow the most personal: those that evoke a strong sense of individual personality" (p. 247). These assertions illustrate to me the implications of authentic self-expression: to encourage creative self-expression that represents the authenticity of the individual in the visual representation of the artwork and encourages sharing and re-storying the personal narrative toward health through the facilitative therapeutic relationship. (There will be more on this facilitative aspect in Part III, where I delineate the different ways in which self-expression can effectively be guided.)

Art can generate both responses, such that initial responses may be instinctual—aversion or attraction—and later reactions might work to combine, refine, or better understand the initial reactions. The more we are pushed to engage with new experiences and information, the more likely we are to learn, change, and feel like we are responding and growing in the world. Art serves both to help us understand and make sense of novelty in a distinct and specific way: through its boundaries of a temporary transport to playfulness and an invitation to a novel imaginary circumstance. In addition, artistic works and viewing help us direct our attention. Novel experiences, including those in the physical environment, help us feel better (Heller et al., 2020). For example, using geolocation tracking, experience sampling, and neuroimaging, these researchers found that daily variability in physical location was associated with increased positive affect in humans, as seen with greater functional coupling of the hippocampus and the striatum. Diversity in real-world daily experiences leads to learning and keeps our brain challenged and aroused. Interestingly, according to some measures, our brain wanders up to 70% of the time (Baldwin et al., 2017), though we are typically not aware that this occurs most of the time. Our brains constantly scan the environment, reviewing inner streams of thinking and planning and also resting from conscious activity.

What distinguishes receptive from expressive experiences is the active engagement of motor and somatosensory cortices along with the inner brain regions of memory and emotional associations. Although mirror neurons are activated in expressive experiences, the actual physical act of making things has significant impacts, including activation of physical activity related to reward pathways (Lambert, 2008). As seen in previous chapters, the human brain's predictive capacity is related to our imaginative abilities and to the construction of personal stories. We are wired to understand things in sequences of cause and effect, including what actions might lead in the future to preferred outcomes. Recent work has shown that the brain's default mode network (DMN) is active when people imagine the future (Lee et al., 2021). The authors tested participants (both sexes) to see whether imagination of the future could be decomposed into two dissociable psychological processes linked to different subcomponents of the DMN. While measuring brain activity with functional magnetic resonance imaging (fMRI) as subjects imagined future events, they manipulated the vividness of these events to modulate the demands for event construction, just as we manipulate the valence of these events to modulate the demands for event evaluation. They found that one subcomponent of the DMN, the ventral DMN or the medial temporal lobe subsystem, responds to the vividness but not to the valence of imagined events. In contrast, another subcomponent, the dorsal or core DMN, responds to the valence but not the vividness of imagined events. This separate modifiability of different subcomponents of the DMN by vividness and valence provides strong evidence for a neurocognitive dissociation between (1) the construction of novel, imagined events from individual components from memory and (2) the evaluation of these constructed events as desirable or undesirable. This finding indicates that the approach and avoidance mechanisms function by reflecting on the future and how important it is to have both the part that imagines possible scenarios and the part that imagines responses.

The experiences of engaging in self-expression concurrently include multiple parts of the brain and body. Creative expression is considered a whole-brain process and engages our executive networks, salience networks, and the DMN (Beaty et al., 2015, 2018). The executive attention network is associated with the prefrontal cortex and helps us focus on tasks and conscious decision making coordinating with other parts of the brain. The salience network helps with deciding what to focus on in the array of sensory information that the brain in bombarded with. The DMN is associated with daydreaming, brainstorming and creative tangents of imagination, and restful, unfocused functioning. The DMN includes the ventromedial prefrontal cortex, posterior cingulate cortex, and regions in the medial temporal and parietal lobes, such as the hippocampus. It decides which sensory signals to pay attention to and links the DMN and executive networks in dynamic ways to approach solutions. Creative expression is the result of the simultaneous activation of multiple brain systems and structures. These include the sensory and motor systems, the limbic system, and the conscious processing of the executive systems.

Does this mean that artistically trained individuals have superior visual processing abilities? Chamberlain et al. (2019), in a study of 79 college students, found that artists had superior processing abilities in attending to and having control over higher-level processing, including representation in drawings, but found no difference in lower-level perceptions of visual illusions and spatial perception. Glazek (2012) suggested that, overall, expert artists might differ from novices in activation of the PFC but that fine-motor activities involved in drawing and sketching allow for improvements in visual cognition and interhemispheric connectivity.

The implications of these studies are that observations, perceptions, and meaning-making can all be learned, and we can be sensitized and derive adaptive benefits regardless of skill levels. In addition, our aesthetic preferences are shaped by the environments we grow up in and the colors, textures, patterns, and art forms we are exposed to throughout our early years. I, for example, love details and color reminiscent of Indian textiles. I can appreciate other art styles, but my brain definitely lights up with joy upon seeing beautiful lines, colors, and designs rather than the modern minimalistic aesthetic. In a study of children in India, Lilly and Venukapalli (2021) found that children aged 13 to 15 preferred representational images (lifelike imagery) to semi-representational and abstract images, indicating that some artistic preferences take time and experience to appreciate compared with images that most resemble life around us.

The story as the connector: Visual, motor, and narrative

How does it all come together? Clark (2014, p. 35) argued that predictive processing is a multilevel model such that sensory processing and meaning-making occur in sequential or concurrent ways. Sometimes we respond quickly and instinctively to things we see or sense, and at other times we engage with deliberation and reflection. Our brains try to be efficient (Clark, 2014, p. 245) and conserve energy if possible through responding with heuristics to the unknowns and novel experiences and incidents that come our way. For example, we might have an initial gut reaction to someone and later discover that they are someone or something completely different. Our reactions are thus a constant combination of new information that we receive filtered through the sieve of our prior experiences and knowledge.

As seen in the preceding chapters, the life story narrative is deeply embedded in our brain processes and human functioning. D'Argembeau et al. (2014) referred to life stories as consisting of autobiographical remembering and reasoning. Autobiographical *remembering* relates to facts and concrete contents of events, whereas autobiographical *reasoning* is related to the broader meaning and implications of these memories. They examined the differences between these two constructs using fMRI; participants were invited to engage in reflection related to both of these aspects. Autobiographical memory was associated with the frontal, parietal, and temporal regions of the brain whereas autobiographical reasoning recruited the left-lateralized network involved in conceptual processing, including the dorsal medial PFC, the inferior frontal gyrus, the middle temporal gyrus, and the angular gyrus. Depending on the participant's level of personal/affective meaning-making, the ventromedial PFC was differentially activated.

Thus, autobiographical reasoning in the larger autobiographical memory network likely mediates the retrieval, manipulation, and integration of the conceptual understanding of ourselves and our lives in order to derive meaning and value from past experiences. The regions may play a key role in the creation of personal narrative, contributing to a coherent and stable sense of self and identity. To have a story is to be able to construct it forward and backward, to be able to both remember and imagine possibilities. In a study on human imagination, Lee et al. (2021) found this process to be highly connected to the DMN. The DMN itself includes the ventromedial PFC, the posterior cingulate cortex, and regions in the medial temporal and parietal lobes, such as the hippocampus. It is aptly associated with reflection, daydreaming, and unfocused attention when the brain is not doing anything purposeful.

We create a personal story that helps anchor our identity over time (McAdams, 2001). The structure of our predictive brains and our capacity for imagination set us up naturally to have this ongoing story of our lives. I use the words "narrative" and "life story" interchangeably here because I think of them as essentially the same thing. "Narrative" sounds technical, but really it is just a story that has a beginning, a middle, and an end, has characters, and has a coherent message. A narrative is a coherent sequential representation using words that tells us something about a person, event, or thing. Habermas and Bluck (2000) proposed that truly coherent life stories only emerge in adolescence. A coherent life story has four kinds of coherence: temporal, thematic, cultural, and causal. Temporal coherence is the organization of events and experiences on a timeline; thematic coherence is an overarching principle or quality of the individual life that includes deeply held values or beliefs; cultural coherence relates to the community context of the individual; and causal coherence is understanding the cause of an event or experience. Our entire life is a dialogue between our inner narrative and how it integrates and adapts to the events of our lives. James Baldwin (2013) referred the acceptance of one's past as not the same thing as drowning in it rather learning how to use it.

Our ability to create a self-narrative develops through childhood and adolescence. As adults we are able to construct an ongoing evolving narrative about who we are, what we want, and what the people and events we encounter might mean for us. If in the absence of data we create stories, Bruner (1986) referred to life stories as the vicissitudes of human experience organized across time. We add pages to these stories each day of our lives as we integrate new experiences into our storyline, either by modifying our tale or adding to ongoing themes with new information. McAdams (2001) asserted that stories are a fundamental part of our identities. We integrate life experiences selectively as we continually add to and refine our personal storylines. These include cultural values and norms that we might have imbibed from our community and developmental history as well as personal narratives and schemas based on our own evolving sense of self.

Fundamentally as humans we are innately storytelling animals (Gotschall, 2013). Brené Brown (2015) said that in the absence of data we create fictional stories. I would add that with data we create nonfiction and without data we create fiction. Either way, we create narrative and stories all the time. Without data, we might create a fictional imaginal story and with data we would create a nonfiction storyline. No matter what we say, we always tell a tale. We tell a tale to our imagined reader. Winner (2018) argued that viewing artwork makes us feel like we are connecting with the artist, like we can peek into the inner life story of the person whose work we are drawn to. For this same reason, we also have a hard time with forgeries or copies of art because that feels like a betrayal of the trust in the belief that we were seeing the representation of a fellow human being's inner world.

If I had to visualize how we live with and take charge of these uncertainties, it would look something like Figure 4.3, which shows the structure of our stories and how we remember our struggles, our triumphs, and our interactions and relationships with others as they are filed away into our life story narrative.

As can be seen from Figure 4.3, our inner life stories and our expressions are constantly impacted and refined over our lifetimes by those we encounter and those who add to and hold our stories. Our stories are refined both in future orientation as well as with the past. We are a curious species, eager to survive

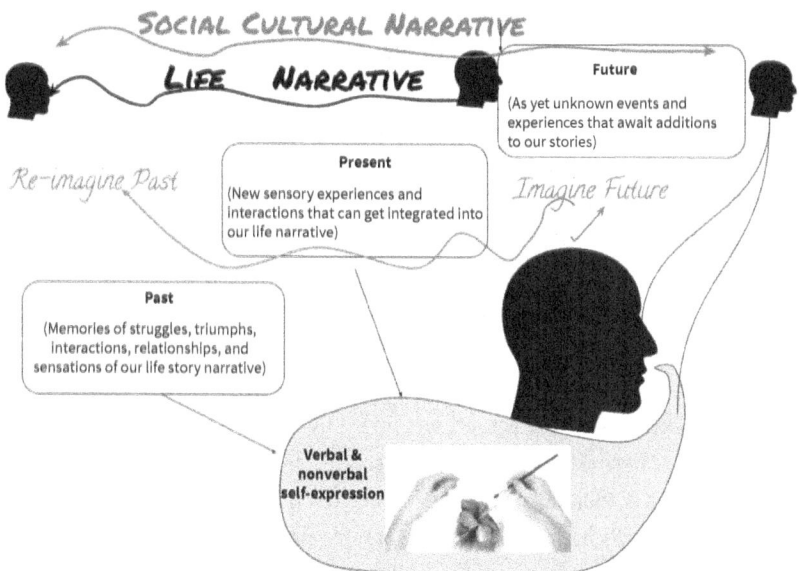

Figure 4.3. Imagination, expression, and the human life story

and thrive. Just as we have tried to determine and prepare for the future, we also strive to understand each other. Our view of the future can change over time because we learn something new every day. In addition, we imagine the underlying reasons for why other human beings say and do what they do. This represents a reciprocal process whereby our actions are also interpreted by others. Recent viral videos of people sharing their creative works and singing and playing improvisational music in neighboring apartment buildings during the COVID-19 quarantines highlight our essential interconnectedness with each other. We have words and systems for communication, but, in reality, we remain bound within our own thought processes and bodies. The fact that the brain is a curious predictive machine would, then, make sense because it works to process information from our sensory systems. This process helps alleviate the anxieties surrounding the essential mysteries of human existence: We strive to connect with other human beings, and we can never really know the future.

Bruner (1986) referred to the beauty of human connection in its specificity. In the individual details of our lives, the unique specificity lies in the universal. This paradox is indeed at the heart of human connection and conditions. We assume that things are different and that we might be alone in our experiences. Those unique aspects are the points of vulnerability and connection. To be able to share those vulnerabilities is to be human: to reach out and hold each other. Stories live to be told and shared and remade and reworked in our social contexts and worlds (McAdams, 2001). The tales we tell get especially complicated when we encounter adversities and traumas that challenge our sense of coherence. We might be unable to integrate these experiences into our stories when they challenge our values, morality, and physical reality, which is when a facilitated external support system comes into play. Moreover, even to find words for our stories becomes a challenge. Being able to create the story and being able to say the unsayable in these settings become the tasks and the goals (more on this in Chapters 8 and 9 on adversity in childhood and adulthood). When we connect our predictive capacity with an ongoing ability to change, according to Kandel (2012, p. 427):

> Learning occurs when an actual outcome differs from the predicted outcome. Many kinds of behaviors are affected by rewards and as result, undergo long term changes when actual rewards are different from predicted rewards. When actual rewards are exactly as predicted, behavior remains unchanged.

The brain cannot help but imagine and foresee. Through art viewing and seeing we can perceive possibilities: new possibilities and new ways to see our world. And, even if we do not perceive new possibilities, perhaps we find a sense of familiarity that helps us belong. In this way dopamine release is deeply intertwined with prediction an learning (Fadelli, 2021). Learning occurs when prediction does not equal reality

Brain → prediction ← dopamine release

We have established the uncertainty of our lives, the predictive and imaginative nature of the brain, and our attempts to counter the negativity bias with creative works. So we return to our question of why self-expression matters in our lives. I propose that self-expression is a natural process of output processing from the senses akin to all other processes in the body. William James (1890) delineated distinct layers of the self, namely the material self (the concept of oneself as a material being), the social self (the concept of oneself as a member of society), and the spiritual self (the concept of oneself as a moral person). These, he proposed, constituted the idea of pure ego (the concept of oneself as a thinking and acting subject as an individual). These aspects of self connect to the idea of expression since each aspect manifests in our interactions with the world in different, distinct, yet deeply interconnected ways. For our material physical self of the human body, we know now that the human body is an integrated set of systems for input, processing, and output. For example, the human body breathes in oxygen, absorbs it into the body, and breathes out CO_2. Similarly, it takes in solid and liquid foods, absorbs nutrients, generates an immune response as needed to respond to threats, and eliminates toxic waste from the body in the form of urine, sweat, mucus, and feces. As with all processes that involve an intake, the stimuli we receive require processing and expression outward in regular and effective ways. We express outward in all our body functions that connect to our sense of self.

Similarly, the brain is constantly responding to and taking in stimuli through all our senses (sight, smell, sound, taste, and touch) as well as the perceptual senses of neuroception (sense of safety), proprioception (body in space), enteroception (sense of inner body organs), and interoception (internal sense of self). Interoception in particular as a sense has been associated with our sense of selfhood (Monti et al., 2021) because it helps us connect our personal identity with the sensations of our body states, both physical and emotional. This embodied sense of self is uniquely human (Vaisvaser, 2021) and connects us with our memories, our experiences, and our sense of stable identity; it is hindered in individuals with disorders of identity such as schizophrenia and dissociative identity disorder. Interestingly, those with a stronger, more stable concept of self are more in tune with their inner bodily signals, particularly their heartbeat and breath, and are less prone to sensory illusions (Monti et al., 2021). Our social and spiritual selves invite us to relate to others in our human species and enable us to construct intangible constructs and ideas together.

The role of the viewer/witness: Being the audience and seeing ourselves and with others

One of the things we do when we create is to be fully present in the moment, engaging our senses and aware of how we are both part of and witnessing the creative work in a specific moment of space and time. The viewing/witnessing individual goes through the process of receptive engagement. Receptive engagement meditative and reflective actions that engage all our senses to perceive and regulate our mind from distracting worries and concerns (more on this in Chapter 10). To be in the moment is to be fully present and attentive to messages gathered by our senses, fully aware of one's surroundings, safety, and opportunities. When we are creating with our hands, we are paying attention with our motor functions, with our tactile senses, with our sight, and, if there is sound, that as well. To witness and to be seen goes to a fundamental part of who we are. Through the externalized creative work, we share parts of our story that did not or could not fit into words and invite those who see it to in turn "see us." To witness the art thus is an act of evaluation as well as acceptance; depending on who accepts the work and who rejects it, it gives us information on where are stories belong and might be accepted (Figure 4.4.

Our instinctual desire to express our inner states compels us to externalize with or without audiences and witnesses (other than ourselves). If there is even one audience member or witness who understands what we are trying to convey, then our responsibility as an expressive artist is complete. In this movement from the person expressing to the audience member lies the completion and fulfillment of the artistic process and journey. An expression is perhaps incomplete without a witness even if the first audience/witness might be ourselves. In visual and written art, the first audience is inevitably oneself. We see our writing and our art first. We appraise, we critique, we decide whether to preserve or destroy that which we have created. Once we have chosen a medium and externalized our creation using that medium, the product is then available for further review, analysis, new learning, and discussion. If we have created a similar artwork or written piece before, then the response might be predictable: We already know if it is something we like and want to preserve. When we create something outside of our regular

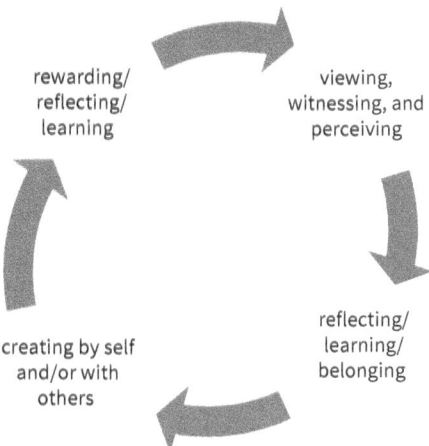

Figure 4.4. Cycle of receptive and expressive experiences

expressive range, however, we are compelled to examine its meaning. It might reflect back to us something we do not like, or it might highlight an aspect of ourselves that was not yet available to our consciousness. The popular figure from *Mister Rogers' Neighborhood* referred to this as the process of making our experiences "mentionable". He rightly identified that when we mention (express) our inner states and emotions, we take the first step to making them manageable. To mention/express what we are going through helps us name and therefore understand and manage ourselves more effectively.

The role of artistic media

A key element in the expressive experience lies in the choice and characteristics of the art media. They can range from those used in the fine arts such as paints and pencils, or those used in folk arts and craft forms, including clay and fabrics (Moon, 2011b). Each artistic medium has its own unique quality that the person working with it must truly understand. Franklin (2018) refers to working with clay as a process of understanding the limits of its malleability; this requires tactile, temporal, and visual sensitivity because clay changes over time and with temperature (Figure 4.1). Fabrics have their own qualities of softness and changeability, characterized by the tools and texture of the yarn or core elements (Collier et al., 2013). More structured media like pencils and crayons bring the artist closer to the surface of the paper and allow for variations in force and pressure as well as greater control over representational imagery (Haiblum-Iskovitch et al., 2018). Paints come with their own unique attributes. Acrylic paints allow for opacity and for painting over, including on a range of surfaces, but require a level of mastery in conveying ideas in a fluid medium. Other paint media like watercolors are more demanding in that there are few opportunities to do over or erase perceived errors. Some media, such as wood or metal, require greater pressures and strength and might be especially suited for individuals with high energy or aggression to channel. Digital media allow for a range of expressions and modifications but are challenging for those who seek the tangible touch of materials (Kaimal et al., 2016c). Digital media like virtual reality (VR) are new enough that they are less imbued with expectations of skills the way that traditional art media tools are. Other media might require less strength and more sensitivity and might be better suited for mental states and moods that are low energy but attuned to the medium. The interaction of materials and media is something all art professionals are familiar with. Art therapists are especially trained in the attributes of art media and how they work with mental states to help express and communicate our inner stories.

Research on interactional, existential, developmental, neuroscientific, and creative processes remains limited. We continue to have a limited understanding of the processes involved and the complexity involved in measuring these attributes, but we do know some aspects that we can integrate into our life.

Key takeaways

In this chapter, I provided an overview of receptive and expressive experiences and how they relate to the physiological and psychosocial aspects of the brain and processing. Our sensory and embodied perceptions relate to our predictive processing capacities and work to help us form meaning, association, and narrative. These in turn help us make sense of the creative, imaginative, and expressive works—both our own and those of others. In the next two chapters, I provide more evidence on what we know about the neurobiological aspects of creative visual self-expression and findings from brain imaging studies.

5

Evoking the protector within

Neurobiological indicators and creative self-expression

There is no insurmountable solitude. All paths lead to the same goal: to convey to others what we are. And we must pass through solitude and difficulty, isolation and silence in order to reach forth to the enchanted place where we can dance our clumsy dance—but in this dance or in this song there are fulfilled the most ancient rites of our conscience in the awareness of being human and of believing in a common destiny.

Pablo Neruda

Everything that irritates us about others can lead to an understanding of ourselves.

Carl Jung

Terrain map: In the previous chapters we examined some of the evolutionary aspects of creative self-expression, especially how it relates to receptive and expressive experiences in the brain and body. Most research to date has focused mainly on receptive experiences, such as those that involve viewing or experiencing art and expressive experiences, and less on experiences related to creating or making an art product. Questions related to the impact on our psychological and physiological states when we create remain largely unanswered and continue to intrigue researchers. But the exciting developments of note are that we are increasingly seeing evidence of the interconnections between physical health and psychological well-being. In this chapter I focus mainly on neurobiological changes, such as those tracked in neurotransmitters, neuroinflammation (markers of infection in the body), and hormones, and how they are associated with different psychological and emotional experiences, especially those involving the creative expressive process.

The Expressive Instinct. Girija Kaimal, Oxford University Press. © Oxford University Press 2023.
DOI: 10.1093/oso/9780197646229.003.0006

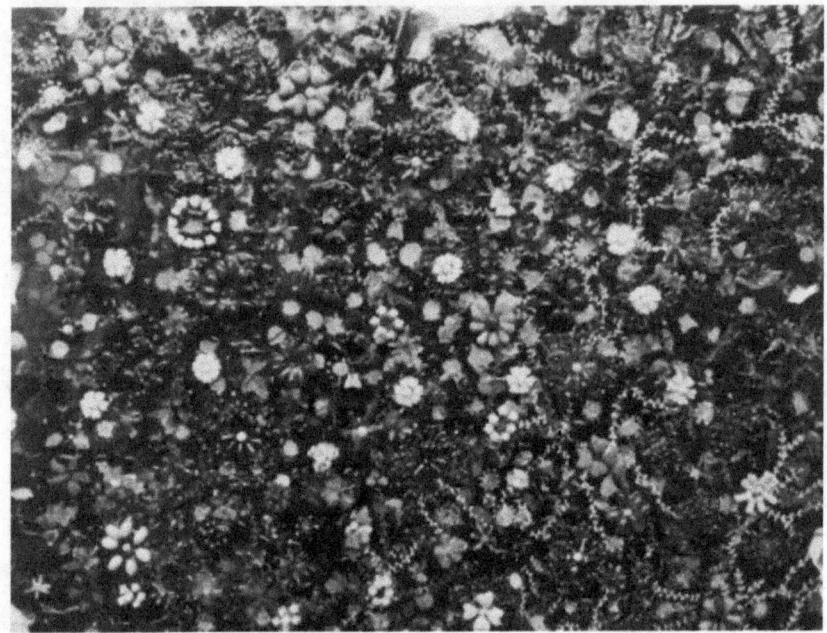

Figure 5.1. *The interconnectedness of all things* (Kaimal 2021). Mixed media: Birch bark, beads, wildflowers, ink, and resin. Dimensions: 2ft. × 3ft.

Coming to an interest in connecting physical health and self-expression

My interest in the value of examining the neurobiological aspects of art-making began in the late 1990s when I was in graduate school doing my master's degree in art therapy. I had heard of research by the psychologist Jamie Pennebaker. His research focused on self-expression, language, and its impact on health and well-being (Pennebaker, 1997a; 1997b). In a series of studies, participants were encouraged to write about any thoughts and experiences for 15 to 30 minutes a day over 3 to 5 consecutive days. The purpose was to examine whether the simple act of self-expression, especially of things we might otherwise not share due to feelings of shame, fear, embarrassment or guilt, was related to our health. The control group was asked to write about superficial topics such as how they use their time. All participants were free to retain or destroy their writing but were not required to share it with anyone. The topic of the writing was open-ended and could be about any aspect of life related to the participant's deepest emotions and thoughts. The participants' health was tracked 2 months and 6 months after the writing sessions, and it was found that those in the treatment group (those who engaged in the authentic expressive writing) were much less likely to go to the doctor compared to the control group (those who wrote about superficial topics) (Pennebaker, 1997). The act of expressing and sharing (even if only with oneself) that which was previously unsaid can literally help us feel physically healthier! Self-expression is not just something fun to do as a hobby but something that could transform our well-being in very concrete ways. This research really made an impression on me as an example of the physiological health benefits of creative self-expression. Beyond pedantic refrains of making a case for authentic self-expression, it was potent evidence that self-expression could significantly affect human health and well-being. Over the years, research on expressive writing expanded to show that levels of the stress hormone cortisol were reduced when participants engaged in authentic self-expression, namely writing about what they felt in the moment (Pennebaker & Smyth, 2016).

For almost 15 years, these studies stayed in my mind as a seed of inspiration. After completing my doctoral work on narratives of families with parental depression (Kaimal & Beardslee, 2010, 2015) and in my current role as research faculty, I finally had the chance to work on this question. With a small internal research grant, I examined this idea of the potential health benefits of visual self-expression (akin to the extensive studies on expressive writing). I was curious to see if we might get outcomes with visual expression similar to those found with writing.

For our pilot study, a colleague in the Nutrition Sciences Department and I developed a really simple quasi-experimental (pre–post) study that included a system to collect and analyze saliva samples. We asked people to engage in art therapy sessions. The sessions were facilitated by an art therapist, but because there are many preconceived notions in society about therapy, we called the sessions visual self-expression. We used an open studio format such that people came in, chose their preferred art media, and engaged in self-expression for about 45 minutes. To keep the study experience for participants from being overwhelming, we offered a limited set of art materials (in art therapy referred to as structured media). The participants could make collages, create drawings with markers and paper, or work with modeling clay. Some people just played with the art media, kinesthetically. Others drew a favorite memory, or they made something in memory of a loved one, or they made something to represent what they were experiencing in the moment. We collected saliva samples before and after to track levels of stress and also had them fill out questionnaires on mood and self-efficacy. I did the study with a doctoral student of mine and I still remember how we learned to collect the samples and rushed them to the laboratory for storage in the middle of winter. It was quite an adventure. We had no idea what we would find with this study because there was no precedent.

Once the data were collected and samples analyzed, we found that even in 45 minutes stress levels were significantly lowered as a result of our intervention (Kaimal et al., 2016d). I remember several participants saying that this was the first space in a really long time where they got to do something without a judgment or a grade associated with the experience. Interactions with participants in the study highlighted for me how few opportunities adults have for creative and playful self-expression. We treat these activities as children's activities, but we adults have as much need for authentic self-expression as anyone else. In subsequent studies, Beerse et al. (2019) further found that clay-based art-making reduced anxiety and stress levels, with the changes being more pronounced for the group that engaged in mindfulness-based art therapy rather than engaging in clay manipulation alone. The authors found that we really can manage our cortisol levels, and by proxy our stress levels, with opportunities for self-expression.

Why are these findings around stress relevant? I explain next how a psychological construct like stress relates to our bodies and physiological functioning.

Cortisol and our bodies

Cortisol is a stress hormone and a natural component associated with healthy functioning of our bodies. We need cortisol to survive: It is what wakes us up in the morning and essentially activates our bodies to get going for the day. In our circadian rhythms, cortisol levels are highest in the morning because cortisol gives us an energy boost to start our daily activities. As the day progresses, the levels steadily decrease, which helps us feel tired and go to sleep by the end of the day. In addition to the daily cycle, cortisol is also released in response to a perceived threat, which triggers a cascade of reactions in the brain. This perceived stress can be normal everyday life demands that motivate us to respond or it can be the perception of a threat to our physical or psychological well-being. Evolutionarily, a threat would be physical danger (like an animal attacking us) that puts us at risk of bodily harm. In response to perceiving this threat, cortisol levels would spike in our body, giving our muscles a boost to react appropriately: The cortisol would increase our heart rate and would make us sweat. All these physiological effects are to prepare us to, for example, fight or run to safety. Sweating in this context will presumably cool down our body whether we choose to fight or run to safety. Today, we are not often faced with physical threats. In the modern world, our threats tend to be more psychological (e.g., being treated poorly, discriminated against, bullied, insulted, or rejected).

To our brain, a threat is still a signal of danger to our well-being, regardless of the nature of the source. Sensory perceptions of danger or safety are interpreted by the hypothalamus, a structure nestled deep in the brain that serves to regulate a range of survival functions, including body temperature and hunger. When sensory experiences are perceived as a threat or as stressful, the hypothalamus releases the corticotropin-releasing hormone, which activates the pituitary gland. The pituitary gland then releases the adrenocorticotropin hormone to activate the adrenal glands, which in turn release cortisol. This cascade of neurological activities is referred to as the *hypothalamus–pituitary–adrenal axis*. Cortisol is released by the adrenal glands when the body perceives the need to respond to any kind of external stress. Cortisol activates us by pumping blood to our muscles, increasing our heart rate, and directing the body's resources away from activities that are not deemed essential for survival, including suppressing the immune response to focus on the active task response needed in the moment. Cortisol engages us to be alert and ready to respond to the perceived threat through commonly known responses like fight or flight and more recent additions like freeze or even faint.

Given that cortisol is an essential part of the healthy functioning and survival of the body, it is important to understand why high levels of cortisol can be a problem. Having elevated cortisol levels for extended periods of time can affect our bodies in several ways. Since cortisol essentially increases heart rate, promotes rapid breathing, activates the neurological threat response mechanism, and diverts resources from immune function and digestive systems, many bodily functions can get affected with chronic stress. Issues such as dysregulation of the dietary habits and gastrointestinal systems, sexual and reproductive malfunctions, cardiac impairment, musculoskeletal pain, as well as overall disturbances in the process of growth and aging can result from experiencing chronic stress.

Being able to manage the chronic stresses of everyday modern life is key to health and well-being. An expert on the stress responses in mammals, Robert Sapolsky (2003), argues that the stress response that helped us deal with threats also works against us due to our human predictive capacities. Because we can anticipate challenges, our stress response might be activated in maladaptive ways, leading to neuroses, anxiety, paranoia, and depression. This leads to a very real and unique challenge of being human: We are wired to anticipate stress and also debilitated by our capacity to anticipate it.

The stress-related psychological challenges manifest in our immune functioning as well. Cortisol is also associated with inflammatory responses. Inflammation is the human body's way of responding to infectious agents like viruses and bacteria. Inflammation is the natural fighter in the body. Interestingly, inflammation is also associated with psychological stressors, indicating that any threats perceived by the brain result in a physiological defense response in the body.

What exactly is inflammation and how can it be tracked?

Inflammation is the body's natural response to damage or injury caused to its tissues. Both physical and mental illnesses manifest as a result of or are exacerbated by inflammation, with stress being a leading cause (Smith et al., 2018). Reducing inflammation has been proven to provide a therapeutic effect in inflammatory diseases such as cardiovascular, neurological, and intestinal diseases (Mangin et al., 2014; O'Brien et al., 2017). The inflammatory response can be caused by environmental, lifestyle, or genetic factors (Shils et al., 2014). These factors include stress, excess weight, smoking, and vitamin deficiencies (National Institute of Health/National Cancer Institute, 2015; Startev et al., 2011). If the process does not resolve the damage and the inflammation persists, the body is then at risk for subsequent complications (Ehlers & Kaufmann, 2010).

A physical infection and depression stimulate similar levels of neuroinflammation in the body (Miller & Raison, 2016). Similarly, psychosocial challenges like loneliness have been found to affect physical health more often than chronic biological conditions like diabetes and hypertension (Petitte et al., 2015). Inflammation can also be triggered over generations with changes in the DNA of our mitochondria (which are carried through the mother's genes), which are particularly sensitive to psychological stressors and advance aging (Trumpff et al., 2019).

Diseases caused by chronic inflammation such as diabetes, cancer, and musculoskeletal and cardiovascular diseases have been regarded as the greatest risk to human health by the World Health Organization due to the life-threatening conditions associated with these types of illnesses. Inflammation has also been significantly associated with diminished mental health, resulting in conditions such as depression, meaning that inflammation may affect our body beyond physical illness (Smith et al., 2018). Research has shown an overwhelming association between inflammation and the many chronic diseases experienced by modern-day populations (Ehlers & Kaufmann, 2010).

Acute inflammation is a short-lived response to tissue injury that leads to healing by leukocyte activity. These white blood cells (WBCs) penetrate the affected site, remove the inflammatory stimulus, and repair the damaged tissue (Pahwa et al., 2018). Inflammation is a natural and essential process that is triggered as a response to tissue damage or pathogens detected by WBCs, which then causes the release of inflammatory mediators such as macrophages and neutrophils. Macrophages engulf and remove pathogens or particles and foreign debris remaining from damaged tissue (Askenase & Sansing, 2016). They are essential to the initiation, maintenance, and healing of inflammation (Fujiwara & Kobayashi, 2005).

Inflammation is tracked most often with cytokines, which are small proteins that have various functions related primarily to cell signaling. One of these is C-reactive protein (CRP) (Lackie, 2010); levels of this acute inflammatory protein increase with the presence of inflammation. It is estimated that areas in the body experiencing inflammation have a 1,000-fold increase in CRP concentrations. Macrophages, along with adipocytes, activate CRP that is synthesized in the liver. These proteins further enhance the phagocytosis that occurs during the inflammatory process; thus, CRP concentrations indicate the presence of inflammation in the body (Sproston & Ashworth, 2018). It also prompts the production of cytokines, especially interleukin (IL)-6 and tumor necrosis factor-alpha (Boras et al., 2014). ILs are a class of cytokines that facilitate signaling between cells to regulate immunity. They are mainly produced by WBCs, or leukocytes, but can be produced by other cells (Lackie, 2010; National Institute of Health/National Cancer Institute, 2020). An array of ILs has been identified and numbered by researchers; each IL carries out a specific function (Chen et al., 2020; National Institutes of Health/National Cancer Institute, 2020).

Although not all ILs are markers of inflammation, IL-6 and tumor necrosis factor-alpha are also proinflammatory cytokines. Levels increase as inflammation increases, and they play a critical role in the acute-phase response. There are also anti-inflammatory cytokines like IL-beta and IL-10, whose levels increase in the body as the immune response is enhanced. Tracking levels of these markers tells us how the body is responding to physiological and psychological threats.

Making intentional connections between the mind and the body

The incidence of chronic inflammatory diseases has risen continuously during the past decades and is expected to rise persistently during the next 30 years. The COVID-19 pandemic has added to this persistence of anxiety and distress (American Psychiatric Association, 2021). How does this increase manifest itself in everyday life in our efforts to manage ourselves and our stressors? Responding to stress first requires an awareness of its existence and an awareness of our own efforts to regulate it. When we are anxious or stressed about a task or interaction, our cortisol levels spike and our resources are diverted to the task at hand, which means that nonessential activities like digestion are not prioritized and stress responses like increased heart rate and sweating are. This situation is especially true for children, who are still in the process of understanding and processing their emotions and developing strategies for self-regulation. It would be extremely valuable if we could demonstrate a relatively inexpensive change or shift through an art intervention. These activities can take them out of a ruminative loop to a clear understanding of and perspective on what is going on and why. The expression thus helps us connect to the homeostasis of safety and belonging, away from the stress of the task that initially feels overwhelming.

The idea that the artistic process can offer a space for reducing our arousal and stress and calm us in moments of distress is something I have seen repeatedly in my own artistic practice (Figure 5.1), and most recently in the ways we responded to the lockdown and restrictions of COVID-19. During the initial weeks, as we struggled to find equilibrium and peace from the uncertainty and panic, I found myself pulling out old scraps of fabric from my time as a textile designer and creating a quilt (Figure 5.2).

Textile design was my first professional identity. Although I moved on to other work and professional degrees, through all my moves across countries and continents over the past 25 years, I had carried with me pieces of fabric I had designed. I also found that quilt-making was an activity that I could engage in with my children by using a simple stitch pattern. We worked together to piece together our new life. We all sewed as we could and adapted the pattern of hand quilting such that we could all work on different parts of the quilt simultaneously. My older daughter, who identifies more as a musician than as an artist, found herself enjoying the process and even sought to sit together under the quilt as we sewed different parts. We stayed connected through all the uncertainties, school closures, and termination of regular adolescent activities with this fully hand-constructed quilt-making process. We added layers and chose relevant pieces for the upper and lower layers; the shared process helped us respond with calmness

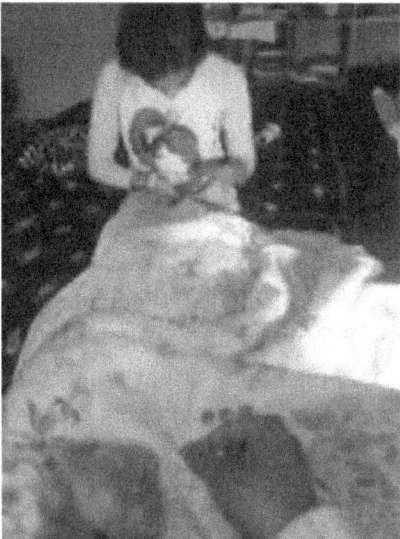

Figure 5.2. Stages of making a quilt together.

and community. The quilt is now a shared product. It also allowed me to reminisce and think of a time of great joy and comfort and share the story of the origin of the fabric scraps with my daughters.

This artistic process during the COVID lockdowns helped us be together in harmonious ways including doing activities that helped calm us. The resulting products of the activities gave us a sense of great accomplishment. Because it was hand-stitched, it took a long time to complete, which required some patience and delayed gratification but led to immense satisfaction in the final product. I do not know conclusively if it enhanced our immune function or reduced inflammation, but I imagine it did because of the choice of shared activity and the sense of comfort and belonging it engendered. I do believe the soft quality of the fabrics as well as the quilt product itself allowed for a shared connectedness that we do not usually have sitting separately at our desks and computers.

Creative self-expression to actively manage biological health

Several studies have shown that inflammatory markers in the body, the compounds that are released by the body's immune system, move toward healthier levels when we engage in creative works. Such works include textile arts and a range of writing activities. Collier (2011) repeatedly found that textile arts allow women to gather, share, or work individually. They first examined outcomes and responses from over 800 female textile handcrafters and found that those who engaged in these activities reported better mood, enjoyment of the beauty of their products, a feeling of being grounded, and the ability to cope with challenges. Active engagement with the textiles also gave women a sense of mastery and rejuvenation compared to those who did not engage in these activities (Collier et al., 2011).

Exploring these ideas with a group of 216 participants assigned to four experimental groups, Futterman-Collier and Wayment (2019) found that the aspect that was especially valuable in improving mood was not simply distraction alone but a growth orientation and contemplative approach to creating. Textile arts are literally about "making something new," a purpose often not seen in other arts practices. Priming and using the arts practice time for contemplation rather than as negative rumination was also highlighted as key to enjoying and promoting well-being. Furthermore, in examining the physiological changes that occur when one is engaging in textile arts, Futterman-Collier et al. (2016) found that textile arts and quiet contemplative practices were helpful in offsetting the impacts of negative moods as measured using salivary levels of IL-beta, a proinflammatory cytokine.

The creative process and active engagement in making bring us into the present moment and reinforce a feeling of safety and a sense of agency. Mirroring the immune response, creative expressive activities evoke responses in the body associated with positive emotions, including perception of rewards, pain relief, and joy.

Neurotransmitters of joy, contentment, pain relief, and reward perception

A consistent finding in research on therapeutic aspects of creative self-expression has been that it enables individuals to experience positive emotions, often in unexpected ways, including through possibly effort-based rewards pathways. There are indications that artistic practices evoke positive emotions and reward perception in the brain (more on this in Chapter 6). Four neurochemicals are widely associated with health and well-being, particularly as they relate to creative expression. Some of the hormones released by the neuroendocrine system that have been associated with positive emotions are serotonin, endorphin, oxytocin, and dopamine. Figure 5.3 shows the molecular structures of these microscopic hormones that influence our well-being.

The neurotransmitters affect many aspects of human work in complex ways, but their roles in health and well-being are of particular note.

Dopamine, for example, is a chemical messenger and neurotransmitter that has been associated with desire and reward perception. Dopamine stimulates us to feel joy when we anticipate a reward, even more than when we actually receive the reward. It is activated when we anticipate a potentially satisfying future event as well as when we have a sense of closure and of completing a task (Berridge & Kringelbach, 2013). Dopamine is involved in the anticipation of earning related rewards and the registration of surprising or salient events (Kandel, 2012, p. 425). Interestingly, dopamine is also implicated in dread because the anticipatory aspect of the neurochemical relates to both positive and negative aspects of expectation. The nucleus accumbens, a primitive part of the brain that exists in many mammals, has in particular been implicated as the brain center associated with activity related to reward perception as well as with feelings of dread (Berridge & Kringelbach, 2013). The nucleus accumbens functions as an on/off switch for dopamine. In studies in rats, depending on which part activates the release, the animals experienced either feelings of intense dread or intense desire. For example, we experience

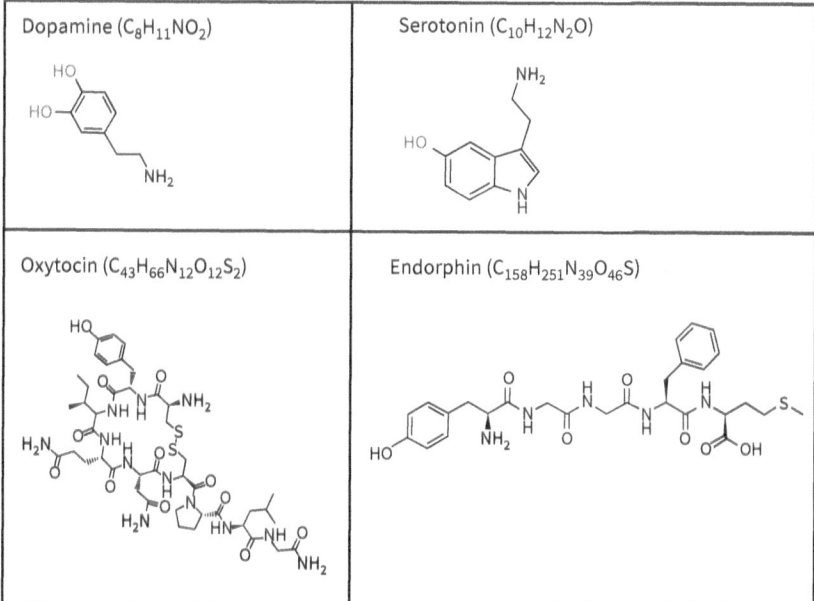

Figure 5.3. Molecular structures that shape our mental states: dopamine, serotonin, oxytocin, and endorphin

(*Source:* www.chemspider.com)

such feelings when we eat something we crave and then become sick of it or listen to a song repeatedly until we can no longer bear to hear it. Dopamine has been implicated in a range of functions, including movement coordination, reward perception, and, most recently (Vander Weele et al., 2018), responses to threatening stimuli. Together, these data highlight how dopamine in the medial prefrontal cortex can selectively route sensory information to specific downstream circuits, representing a potential circuit mechanism for valence processing.

Interestingly, dopamine has an important role in responding to predictions and uncertainty and is especially responsive to rare rewards, indicating a constant effort to gauge and respond to anticipation and rewards for different actions and responses (Rothenhoefer et al., 2021). Dopaminergic reward pathways are overridden by the release of dopamine related to a perceived threat, highlighting the brain's focus on survival and anticipation of potential threats. The findings highlight how pursuit of pleasure can also switch to distressing emotions like those experienced in the compulsive behaviors seen in addiction and paranoia (Baumgartner et al., 2020). This process also relates to the function of dopamine in anticipating rewards because anticipating danger is possibly a way to respond effectively to that threat. Psychotherapy sessions could help patients regulate this response by better understanding potential triggers in the modern social environment and offsetting the threat with appropriate health-promoting choices. Dysfunction in dopamine modulation is associated with a range of disorders, including schizophrenia and Parkinson's disease. Elkis-Abuhoff and Gaydos (2018) emphasized the role of the art media in helping address symptoms of Parkinson's disease in activating sensory pathways and coordinating movement.

Serotonin is associated with feeling valued and with self-esteem. It is a modulator of emotion rather than one that excites or activates intense feelings of reward or euphoria (Karayol et al., 2021). Serotonin is the basis of a class of antidepressants, and the serotonergic system is involved in a variety of emotional states, including a sense of safety, happiness, and sadness. Decreased activity of the serotoninergic system results in depression and mental dysfunction (Kandel, 2012, p. 425). Art therapists work to facilitate this sense of belonging and an inter- and intrapersonal sense of self. Kelly Lambert (2008) is a neuroscientist who examined the role of physical doing—or, as she calls it, effort-based rewards—in human health. She asserts that the human brain and body were made to be active, to be doing things, and not to be sitting around staring at screens. She suggests that we might be seeing higher rates of mental illness and depression because of our modern ways of sitting around and not actively creating.

Given that much of the brain's functional area is dedicated the somatosensory receptors particularly to the hands, we can assume that the expectation is that they are meant to be used in a range of ways during the human waking hours. Lambert (2008) spoke of serotonin as also being activated in repetitive physical activities such as knitting or drawing with recurring thematic styles. The effects are those of calming through safe, known activities. Doodling and doing Zentangle drawings are ways to engage in these comforting and simple repetitive-constructive activities that result in a product that is not only satisfying but also a reminder of the concrete outcomes from creative expressive activities.

Endorphins are the human body's natural painkillers. It is apt that the word "endorphin" comes from the terms "endogenous" and "morphine" (Chaudhry & Gossman, 2021). Endorphins are related to the activation of pleasure and the suppression of pain. Opioid medications mimic the endorphin receptors in the brain and are similar to the feelings of euphoria associated with endorphins.

Endorphins express functional duality because they fall into the category of either neurotransmitters or neuromodulators in the central nervous system and hormones in the pituitary gland (Chaudhry & Gossman, 2021). They are often released when an individual cries or after intense physical activity. Of the three types of endorphins, beta-endorphins are the most studied and prevalent, accounting for the majority of the functional properties of endorphins as generalized and understood as a whole. The pain relief experienced as a result of the release of endorphins has been determined to be greater than that of morphine. Patients who participated in art-making and therapy sessions, have reported feeling temporarily pain-free when they have been deeply engaged in a session. Stinley et al. (2015) found that art-making helped reduce the experience of pain in acute-care pediatric settings. Endorphins are also released when we laugh and enjoy humor, during sex, and when eating appetizing foods (Chaudhry & Gossman, 2021).

Oxytocin a hormone that encourages relational bonding, primarily in mothers and infants. It is released in large quantities during emotionally intense encounters, including during sexual activity and parenting babies, in turn deepening the sense of joy and pleasure with those we live with in close quarters (family, children). Interestingly, oxytocin can also work as a bonding hormone during adversarial experiences. De Dreu et al. (2011) found that oxytocin can promote bonding in adversarial contexts, including among warriors or tribal groups at war with an adversary. The relational bonding supports survival by making the individuals with heightened oxytocin levels care for and support each other (in-group love) even if possibly hating or wanting to kill an enemy (out-group aggression). Storytelling has also been found to release oxytocin as the narrator and listener (Zak 2015) engage in an empathic mutuality that engages several parts of the brain. Art therapists help patients and clients create narratives with and through the art-making process, often helping generate verbalizations that might previously have been absent or inaccessible due to histories of trauma and adversity, which are known to inhibit narrative production (Kearney, 2007; van der Kolk, 1996).

Oxytocin, unlike cortisol, is a difficult hormone to track and measure, so few studies have actually measured its levels in the body. It has been suggested theoretically that tracking oxytocin levels could help determine the quality and impact of creative self-expression, particularly in the presence of a facilitating art therapist (Springham et al., 2014). In a small preliminary study, Tanaka et al. (2020) found that participating in facilitated digital art-making helped increase oxytocin levels in both typically developing children and those on the autism spectrum. The study indicates the potential of participatory activities to enhance social connection. In a study with couples, increased oxytocin levels were seen in those who participated in art classes versus a comparison group that engaged in playing board games (Melton et al., 2019). Something about the sensory engagement and social connection through facilitated art activates these pathways.

If our body's response to a threat is clearly known through processes like inflammation and cortisol release, preliminary evidence indicates that art-making helps us manage this response. The response does, however, differ from person to person. For some, making art may distract them from whatever is worrying or threatening them. For others, making art may help them gain perspective. For yet others, the impact might come from being with the art therapist in the session and being able to share whatever is going on with them: positive, negative, or challenging experiences. My theory is that when you are working with someone who is a trained art therapist in an open studio format, that person helps you feel safe and validated. Feeling safe and validated fosters a sense of belonging. All of these activities help reduce the sense of threat and reduce the fear that you are alone and facing all these challenges by yourself. Using the arts to promote well-being is a nuanced process (more on this in Chapter 10).

In examining these neurobiological processes, it is clear that much remains to be understood about them. Gathering evidence about how and why these expressive experiences serve us has the potential to help us understand why art-making enables us to manage threats and feel safe enough to play. To be in the present moment is a big part of managing stress and perceived threats, and by default that is what art-making does. It forces us to be in the moment as we create something with our hands and look at it with our own eyes. To be fully present means being alert, learning, and being informed for the future. Expressive practices can be inherently powerful in keeping us in the present moment; they engage our senses and force us to actively engage with our physical environment.

Key takeaways

This chapter presented research on the neurobiological aspects of creative self-expression, especially as they relate to tracking hormones associated with reward perception, emotional connections, stress, and immune functioning. These creative acts of agency can also trick the brain out of distress and enable a reimagining of stressors and threats as well as our ability to respond to them. Much remains to be studied in this area, but there are indicators that our psychological self-regulation through creative expression can be associated with and mapped with physiological well-being.

6

Tracking creative self-expression through imaging tools

> How can a three-pound mass of jelly that you can hold in your palm imagine angels, contemplate the meaning of infinity, and even question its own place in the cosmos? Especially awe inspiring is the fact that any single brain, including yours, is made up of atoms that were forged in the hearts of countless, far-flung stars billions of years ago.
>
> **V. S. Ramachandran**

Terrain map: In the previous chapter, I shared the evidence we have so far on how art-making affects our hormones and neurotransmitters associated with creative self-expression, health, and well-being. Another way to track physiological changes is through brain imaging. There is some emerging evidence on how creative expression changes the structure and function of the brain by mapping its activation. Most imaging studies tend to focus on receptive experiences of viewing visual art. This chapter focuses on what we know from brain imaging studies about the impact of visual self-expression, including emerging evidence on how it promotes health and well-being.

Tracking creative expression through neuroimaging

One day when we were all sitting together reading and doing homework during the quarantine of COVID-19, I turned to check in on my 9-year-old's schoolwork. I saw that instead of doing her math problems, she was doodling on her math workbook. Above a page full of math sums, she was drawing a butterfly. "It helped me think," she explained. "The butterfly just had to come out." I laughed because I knew exactly what she meant. The essence of what she shared was that desire to get something out that is locked within us. Doodling has been stigmatized in the modern world, but it is in reality a powerful tool to combat a range of mental states, including boredom and

The Expressive Instinct. Girija Kaimal, Oxford University Press. © Oxford University Press 2023.
DOI: 10.1093/oso/9780197646229.003.0007

Figure 6.1. *Scribble-doodle* (Kaimal & Ahuja, 2016). Media: Photo paper and fine-tipped markers. Dimensions: 5" X 4"

distractedness (Figure 6.1). It has also been found to improve memory and recall (Andrade, 2010).

What does it mean when we say we want to get something out of our system, clear our brains, clear our minds? To each of us this might be something different. We might be moved to speak, write, paint, run, or walk, all of which are activities that require us to express and actualize our mental processes in some way in our world. What happens specifically when we express (and get out of ourselves) through visual art? What do we know about what goes on in the brain when we engage in creative activity?

It is increasingly evident that creativity occurs not in any one part of the brain but through a network. It is the interplay of multiple brain regions that come together to generate an innovative solution to a problem. Group musical forms of creative expression, for example, have been found to activate multiple brain regions, including empathy networks, oxytocin secretion through a sense of connectedness, dopamine release through reward perception, reduced cortisol (stress), and connection through group belonging (Greenberg et al., 2021). A recent functional magnetic resonance imaging (fMRI) study (Beaty et al., 2018) that scanned the brains of 163 individuals doing a divergent creative task theory concluded that creative activity emerges from the interplay of three brain networks: the salience network, the executive attention network, and the default mode network (DMN). The interplay between these networks is what helps us connect imaginal thoughts into concrete outcomes and actions.

While individual skill levels might vary, all of us have inherent potential to engage in creative expression. As seen in previous chapters, the capacity to be creative exists in our brain networks as part of our evolutionary strengths. As with any muscle or skill, as we engage in the activity we become more proficient in it. Spreng et al. (2020) found that social isolation in fact promotes connectivity in the DMN. Perhaps this is a unique aspect of the DMN that activates imaginative possibility that then is concretized and made real by the other networks. Perhaps the forcible experience of solitude engages the human imagination in ways that being around the stimulation of other humans makes harder to engage.

In an imaging study of how imagination works in the brain, Lee et al. (2021) found that much imaginative activity occurs in the DMN. As we saw earlier, it is the part of the brain that is active when we are not engaged in a specific goal-oriented task. Using fMRI technology, the researchers found that this imaginative task actually involves two distinct components: one was constructive and involved creating a vision of this imagined future, and the second involved evaluating whether this outcome was desirable. Participants were asked to imagine their responses to events like winning the lottery or sitting at a beautiful beach location. Sub-networks like the dorsal DMN were found to be related to the valence (perceived value) of the imagined future, while the ventral networks were activated for details in the events. This also explains why it is so hard to imagine the future because it often has very few details compared to our everyday lives and the realities where we see and experience physical and interpersonal details.

Could it be that our impulse to create can offer these concrete details that translate imagination to expression? Does active making help us visualize more and then express and communicate perhaps with an imaginary other? What we do know about imagination and creative visual self-expression is limited. Very few studies have examined brain activity during visual art-making tasks. Some of the ways in which brain activity has been tracked is via technologies such as fMRI, electroencephalography (EEG), and functional near-infrared spectroscopy (fNIRS). What we know so far from studies of brain imaging and making visual art is discussed next.

Findings from fMRI studies on visual art-making

Given that neuroimaging technologies are still being developed and require participants to be still or minimize their movement, most research has tended to be on receptive experiences: Brain activity is tracked while we sense something (seeing, hearing, smelling, etc.). This means that many studies have focused on viewing experiences rather than active creative experiences, and the studies I cite below clearly demonstrate the positive outcomes associated with creative self-expression that far outweigh viewing alone. The studies are few and include those that have examined structural (physical size or shape) and functional (brain activity) changes in the brain as a result of an arts intervention.

fMRI measures brain activity by detecting changes associated with blood flow. It relies on the fact that blood flow in the brain is associated with neural activity: When a specific area of the brain is in use, blood flow to that region also increases. fMRI technology measures differences in magnetic properties between oxygen-rich blood (arteries) and oxygen-poor blood (veins).

Chamberlain et al. (2014) used MRI scans to study the brain regions associated with drawing skills and artistic training. Their findings suggested that being able to draw from observation was associated with an increase in gray matter density in the left anterior cerebellum and the right medial frontal gyrus in the prefrontal cortex. Schlegel et al. (2015) showed that three months of art training resulted in changes in prefrontal white matter. In this study of youth who were art students, art-making was associated with increased plasticity in neural pathways, increases in creative cognition, and was found to mediate perceptuomotor integration. What these findings highlighted was the potential for the brain to be changeable like any other muscle in the body.

In a landmark study with older adults, Bolwerk et al. (2014) examined outcomes of art-making as part of art class among a group of older adults. They found that engaging in creative visual expression increases DMN activity, which is associated with cognitive processes such as comprehension of emotions, intentions of others, and introspection. Participants' brain activities were measured through fMRI technology. The researchers conducted the study with two groups of elderly participants who engaged in either a visual creative art-making group or a cognitive art-viewing group. A clear difference was found between producing art compared to viewing art. Visual art production was shown to improve the functional connectivity in several brain areas, particularly between the parietal and frontal cortices, as well as to cause psychological resistance to change (Bolwerk et al., 2014). Although these findings suggest that visual art production results in stronger brain connectivity than cognitive art evaluation or viewing art, evidence shows that even passive engagement in art affects the prefrontal cortex (Bolwerk et al., 2014). For example, when a person is viewing art, a reward circuitry is engaged that activates the ventral striatum, including the nucleus accumbens, along with the interconnected medial prefrontal cortex (mPFC) and the orbitofrontal cortex and amygdala (Lacey et al., 2011). Using fMRI technology, Lacey et al. (2011) found that art imagery alone activated the reward circuitry, whereas matched non-art images did not. Likewise, activation of the mPFC, along with the rest of the reward circuitry, was also reported in a study in which individuals viewed beautiful visual images of architectural spaces (Chatterjee & Vartanian, 2014; 2016).

The pathways and mechanisms of change vary by individual, their clinical needs, and the context of care. For example, in the case of an individual struggling with feelings of incompetence and inefficacy, the process of art-making involves problem-solving and serves as a "trial run" for gaining mastery. For example, there is evidence from brain imaging that for individuals who have experienced trauma, verbal expression is often not an option (van der Kolk et al., 1996; Walker et al., 2016) since the verbal expressive part of the brain tends to be impacted (Rauch et al., 1997). Thus, being able to "say the unsayable" becomes really critical in such situations. In other cases with elderly individuals, social isolation might be an issue; thus, the emphasis might be on social integration and expression through the art therapy process. Similarly, for an individual struggling with the ability to manage and contain emotional reactions, the process of effectively channeling these struggles through sublimating the emotions in the artwork (instead of harming self or others) in the art therapy session could be the therapeutic element. The therapeutic interaction and the opportunity to create also offer opportunities to imagine new possibilities, learn new things about oneself, and experience the rewards of effort-based behaviors (Lambert, 2008). Effort-based reward systems are dopaminergic pathways that connect reward centers with human actions and choices to "make" and "do" things in the environment. As seen previously, Lambert (2008) argues that humans evolved to be active and to make things, and just these acts can be ways to release dopamine in the brain and experience positive emotions.

In a correlational study of themes in artwork made by military service members diagnosed with traumatic brain injury and post-traumatic stress disorder (PTSD), Walker et al. (2018) assessed brain functioning using fMRI and found interesting associations. Visual themes in the artwork showing a sense of social connectedness were associated with improved thalamic functioning. Thalamic activity and DMN activity were explored in this study because both are impacted by traumatic brain injury and post-traumatic stress. The thalamus is implicated in sensory processing while the DMN is associated with relaxation and reflective activity. This study found that individuals who created certain types of imagery, such as patriotic symbolism, were more likely to have high thalamic connectivity and DMN activity and lower PTSD scores. The findings indicate that a sense of purpose and belonging underlying the depiction of patriotic symbols might have been protective factors for the service members.

Findings from EEG studies

EEG is a way to monitor electrical activity in the brain. It is typically non-invasive and uses electrodes placed on the scalp to measure activity. Due to the challenges in quantifying experiences in the creative process, it has been difficult to measure arts-based interventions to generate evidence on their effectiveness. Contemporary imaging technologies such as EEG and fNIRS have made it possible to measure brain functioning while the participant is engaged in naturalistic activities like art-making (Kaimal et al., 2017a; King & Kaimal, 2019). EEG and fNIRS are considered the two main mobile brain imaging technologies. Unlike fMRIs, which require participants to lie down and be still (not a natural state in which to capture active tasks such as art-making), EEG and fNIRS allow for naturalistic data collection because they are mobile tools that track brain activity in real time.

Belkofer et al. (2014) used quantitative EEG to observe brain functioning during a drawing task with oil pastels. Artists showed alpha frequency in the left posterior, parietal, and occupational regions, whereas non-artists had differences in alpha in the right parietal and prefrontal areas. This may suggest that non-artists had higher involvement of executive control over the drawing task, which was novel to them. A study by Kruk et al. (2014) used quantitative EEG to show increased gamma power in the right brain medial parietal lobe during clay sculpting and drawing. Both clay sculpting and drawing showed increased delta and theta activity in the frontal lobe and increased gamma activity in the right parietal lobe. Clay sculpting showed more activation in spatial-rotational processing areas than drawing, which may suggest that clay sculpting stimulates a meditative state and reduces anxiety.

In a unique comparative study, King et al. (2017) used EEG to investigate the differences in cortical activation patterns between art-making and non-creative motor tasks such as tossing a coin. Art-making showed a greater effect on cortical activation patterns as compared to baseline. Both art-making and the non-creative motor task resulted in increased cortical activation over both hemispheres, although art-making showed a greater increase in power than the motor task.

What about differences in brain activity between those who identify as artists and those who don't? Some findings to date with quantitative EEG indicate that different art media result in different levels of brain activity and that these differences are also associated with whether or not an individual is an artist. Belkofer et al. (2014) investigated the differences in patterns of brain activity among artists and non-artists during the process of drawing. Results indicated that there was more activity in the left hemisphere of the brains of artists, whereas more activity was reflected in the frontal lobe of non-artists. This result may have been based on the fact that drawing was a new task for them and that stimulation in this area of the brain is a sign of learning. There was an increased presence of alpha waves for both the artists and the non-artists, indicating potentially relaxed creative opportunities generated by drawing tasks. Similarly, in a quantitative EEG comparison of working with clay and drawing, activation was noted in regions of memory processes, meditative states, and spatiotemporal processing (Kruk et al., 2014).

Findings from fNIRS

Similar to EEG, fNIRS is a more recent mobile brain imaging technology. fNIRS was first performed on humans in 1992 and published in 1993 by a group of researchers in Hokkaido University, Japan, shortly followed by the University of Pennsylvania and the University of Munich (Ayaz et al., 2013; Ferrari & Quaresima, 2012). Since then, fNIRS has been used with adults, children, and infants to monitor underlying mechanisms in neural functioning (Pinti et al., 2019). fNIRS examines blood flow using infrared light and can detect blood flow as deep as 3 mm below the cortical surface. The fNIRS headband contains light-emitting diodes with electro-optical sensors that can be placed on the participant's forehead (Figure 6.2). The device uses near-infrared-range light to measure concentrations of oxygenated hemoglobin during neural activation. Hemoglobin, the oxygen-carrying protein in red blood cells, absorbs near-infrared light. When there is a neural activation in a brain area, there will be an increased metabolic demand for oxygenated hemoglobin. The increased blood flow and concentration of oxygenated hemoglobin in the local capillary network produces a change in the near-infrared wavelength, which is measured using fNIRS (Ayaz et al., 2013). Compared to other brain screening technologies, it is low in cost, portable,

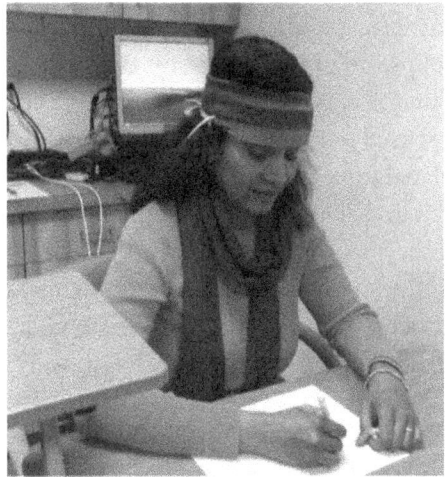

Figure 6.2. Setup of fNIRS headband for data collection

safe, noninvasive, and easy to use (Naseer & Hong, 2015; Pinti et al., 2019). fNIRS can be used during active engagement with cognitive and motor tasks because it can be attached to the head or worn on the body. It also provides better temporal resolution and access to subcortical brain signals than fMRI, making it appealing for use in neurofeedback studies (Naseer & Hong, 2015).

I am an avid doodler, as are many people I know, so I was struck by a study by Andrade (2010) that found that doodling helped participants recall information better than if they didn't doodle at all. Could doodling have inadvertent benefits, even though it is often considered a distraction? Could we quantify this using imaging technology? We wanted to explore this further in my lab and decided to use fNIRS technology. In our study (Kaimal et al., 2017a), we examined the outcomes of three different drawing tasks on reward perception as measured using fNIRS. Our underlying assumption was that blood in the mPFC would indicate activation of a reward pathway in the brain. We recruited 26 participants, 11 of whom identified themselves as artists. Participants were given three drawing tasks (coloring, doodling, and free drawing), lasting three minutes each, with intermittent two-minute rest periods.

The findings indicate that all of the drawing tasks activated the reward pathway of the brain compared with the no-activity rest conditions, with the doodling condition resulting in maximum activation. All three types of visual self-expression activated the mPFC, indicating that visual art-making stimulates reward perception. mPFC activity is also associated with emotion regulation and self-awareness. Findings also suggested that doodling and free drawing resulted in increased brain activation in the mPFC for both the artists and non-artists groups. Coloring activity, on the other hand, resulted in negative brain activation for artists. These findings are speculated to also mirror the theory of effort-based reward pathways (Lambert, 2008), wherein making and creating are related to feelings of reward.

Interestingly, even in the most structured and proscribed of activities, like a predrawn coloring sheet, participants choose different combinations of colors or in general color the sheet in different ways, highlighting the uniqueness of our expressive process despite common patterns of brain activation. In reflecting on the benefits of doodling, it clearly has a "feel good" aspect: We feel good when we doodle, perhaps because we all have a signature doodling style. In addition to keeping us focused and present in the moment, doodling helps remind us of our selves and what we like to do and see ourselves in our unique, authentic identity.

A few other studies have also examined creative activity (not necessarily creative self-expression) using fNIRS. Xue et al. (2018) used fNIRS to measure changes in performance when pairs of individuals cooperated to complete a creative task. They asked highly creative and less creative individuals to complete a task in a dyad. Results showed that people who are less creative showed increased creative performance when they worked together as a team of two. Lu et al. (2020) looked at gender differences in cognitive functioning when solving a creative task as a team. Teams were instructed to find as many creative ways as possible to use an everyday object (a book). They concluded that there are no significant differences in brain functioning between female/male, male/male, and female/female groups when solving a creative problem. However, they underlined increased cooperation between the female/female dyad (Lu et al., 2020). Mayseless et al. (2019) looked at inter-brain synchrony (IBS) when solving a creative task. Researchers formed 28 dyads of both male and female participants and asked them to work together to either (1) design a product that would encourage people to vote or (2) build a 3D model airplane. fNIRS showed increased IBS in the cognitive control system and activation in mirror neurons and mentalization areas (Mayseless et al., 2019).

In further examining the role of art-making and mood using fNIRS, Yan et al. (2021) found that drawing alleviates sadness more than anger. In this study participants were assigned to one of four conditions related to mood (anger or sadness) and tasks (drawing or calculating): drawing after triggering anger, drawing after triggering sadness, calculating after triggering anger, or calculating after triggering sadness. The participants' responses were tracked using fNIRS and the results indicated that drawing improved mood in the sadness condition and also reduced activation of the frontopolar and left dorsolateral prefrontal cortical areas. The authors concluded that drawing was helpful in reducing and regulating negative emotion. Drawing was also helpful in reducing anger but did not reduce the arousal associated with anger, implying that the self-regulatory aspect was not as evident for anger compared with sadness.

Taking the idea of art-making further into the digital realm, in a recent study we again used fNIRS to examine the effects of making art in virtual reality (VR). We invited 24 adults to participate in two sets of conditions: guided creative self-expression or a rote tracing task (Kaimal et al., 2020a). We also infused a calming fragrance in the room for half the session. We found that creative self-expression activated a greater relaxation response than the rote tracing task. Moreover, the fragrance in the room seemed to further improve these outcomes. Our sense of smell is a more primitive and crude sense compared with sight and sound and has the capacity to evoke emotion much faster than the other senses. There are many potential applications of such integrated sensory experiences, including managing stress and affect in subtle ways that complement the intense work of therapeutic engagement and practice.

This study used a within-subjects experimental design with order randomization to examine differences in fNIRS assessment of PFC activation with two VR drawing conditions (rote tracing and creative self-expression) with and without a fragrance stimulus. Participants were healthy adults and included 18 women and 6 men ranging in age from 18 to 54 years. Findings indicated significant differences such that rote tracing resulted in higher PFC activity than the creative self-expression task. Although there was no significant impact of fragrance on the overall sample, emergent differences in responsiveness to fragrance were seen by age and gender. The findings highlight that repetitive tasks like rote tracing can enhance focus and creative self-expressive tasks can reduce PFC load and induce relaxation and flow. The studies indicate many significant benefits to art-making and creative self-expression (Kaimal et al., 2020a; Kaimal et al., 2021).

A reference that is often made when talking about creative expression is the idea of flow states: the sense of losing space and time and becoming completely immersed in the task at hand. Some preliminary evidence from an EEG study indicates that flow activates several networks, including relaxed reflective state, focused attention to task, and sense of pleasure, as well as related motor networks. The EEG study indicates that flow is associated with theta waves and alpha waves, indicating high levels of cognitive control and low levels of working memory usage (Katahira et al., 2018). A lot of the research on flow is based on self-report from participants of having this experience of being fully lost and engrossed in an activity and feeling happy and satisfied. There is also some emerging evidence using fMRI and flow states (Ulrich et al., 2016) as well as fNIRS in the VR studies described above (Kaimal et al., 2020a; 2021). Some research on meditation (focused attention) can also overlaps with the concept of flow, but future research remains to be done to better connect the theory with actual tracking of brain functioning.

Other external and nonintrusive tools to track creative expression

The examples included above mainly included tools that track blood flow and electrical activity in the brain. They are focused on brain activity rather than tracking physiological functioning in other parts of the body. Similar to brain imaging that tracks internal activity by using external sensors, tools exist for tracking stress and bodily responses such as blood pressure, skin conductance, and heart rate.

Schrade et al. (2011) examined differences in blood pressure as a result of two art-making tasks (free drawing and mandala-making) and a neutral control condition in a small sample of individuals with intellectual disabilities. Of the two drawing tasks, mandala-making was found to lower blood pressure consistently compared with free drawing, possibly because of the cognitive aptness and stress-reducing aspects of the free drawing condition.

Measuring variations in heart rate is a nonintrusive way to track aspects of health and well-being related to arousal and relaxation. Heart rate variability (HRV) involves tracking the body's ability to respond effectively to stressors. People with high HRV can effectively increase and reduce their heart rate as needed; they have a higher level of self-regulation than someone whose heart rate is always elevated or always reduced (indicating an inability to modify responses as needed). The ability to up-regulate and down-regulate is essential to healthy and adaptive functioning.

Haiblum-Iskowitz et al. (2018) explored this idea using three different art media. One of the core principles of art therapy is that the use of art materials to express feelings and thoughts in a supportive environment is therapeutic. Art materials differ in their level of fluidity (also referred to as structured or unstructured art materials) and are thus postulated to differentially enhance emotional response: The more fluid the material, the more emotion is elicited. In this experiment, the authors used three media differing in fluidity: pencil (a relatively structured and monochromatic art medium), gouache paint (an unstructured and flowing art medium), and oil pastels (an intensely colorful art medium that offers a level of structure between that of pencil and paint). In this repeated-measures experiment, 50 adults were asked to draw with these three art materials (order randomized), with intermittent periods of music as the control condition. The emotional and physiological responses to art-making with these different materials were assessed using vagal activity, indexed to HRV, because of its association with numerous health-related outcomes. The authors calculated two indices of HRV, one indicative of parasympathetic nervous system (PNS) activity and the other indicative of sympathetic nervous system (SNS) activity. Art-making with paint and oil pastels resulted in improved positive mood, while pencil did not. Art-making explained approximately 35% of the variability in PNS reactivity, which may indicate changes in emotional regulation processes during the art-making task. Yet, fluidity was not sufficient to explain the reaction to art-making. Surprisingly, the largest suppression of PNS and augmentation of SNS occurred during art-making with oil pastels and not with paint. Moreover, PNS reactivity and SNS reactivity to oil pastels were related to emotional valance, which may point to emotional engagement. We can conclude that art-making with oil pastels (which were first created in Japan in 1924 to increase self-expression of students) results in unique emotional and physiological responses. These findings might be explained by the enhanced tactile experience of art-making with oil pastels along with their relative fluidity, triggering an arousal pattern.

How can we use these findings? What are the practical applications? King et al. (2019) summarized some of the practical applications of our learnings in neuroscience specifically for therapeutic aspects. They suggest that brain imaging research helps validate the very real emotional underpinnings of our functioning. Emotions serve as a thermostat indicating our inner states. To know our emotional states and to be able to express them is to better be able to manage them. Similarly, another takeaway is that creative self-expression is an integrative process that engages multiple brain systems and offers a workout and a form of integration connecting physical movement, emotional activation, and personal meaning-making. Lastly and most importantly, that fact that the our brain is essentially open to change and adaptable is fundamental to survival. This ability of the brain to change, referred to as neuroplasticity, accompanies us throughout life. What the brain imaging studies highlight for us is that hope of change and transformation.

Key takeaways

In this chapter I shared the many different ways in which visual self-expression has been tracked and some findings on what it means for health and well-being. As seen in the studies cited, visual self-expression seems to help with structural as well as functional outcomes associated with the brain. Most studies, however, have been conducted with relatively healthy adult populations and have mostly involved self-led art-making. More research is needed on the role of therapists and facilitators as well as from those who live with clinical conditions. Technology is still very simplistic and crude and really cannot capture the complexity and nuance of the many different ways in which self-expression engages all parts of the brain. At present, most of what we can track is simple aspects such as arousal, activation, and relaxation responses. The self-report and narrative responses complement these imaging outcomes. As technological and imaging tools advance, we will be better able to capture the impacts in real time as well as in the long term of how self-expression impacts human functioning.

PART III

WEATHERING STORMS

Facilitating creative self-expression to cope with stress, adversity, and trauma

In Chapters 1 through 6, I shared historical and theoretical perspectives as well as evidence in neuroscience and neurobiological approaches around how visual self-expression and related narratives emerge and impact human functioning. Most of the studies cited so far have been on normative development and how art-making, and creative self-expression broadly, is a natural and relevant part of being human and enhances our functioning and ability to survive and thrive.

An important aspect of creative self-expression is its value and protective role when we face adversity and trauma. In such circumstances, and when our own capacity for functioning is threatened, working with a professional who can serve a facilitative role as a form of scaffolding can help us become whole and reconnected with our tribe of fellow human beings. Creative expression can span a range of ways in how it helps us, from distracting us in the moment all the way to processing, learning, and making meaning of the experience to effectively integrate it into our ongoing life story narratives.

I begin this section by describing the ways in which art-making by ourselves differs from art-making with others. In Chapter 7, I describe the differences between the many professionals who facilitate and scaffold creative expression and engagement, such as art educators, arts-in-health professionals, and art therapists, as well as how they work with aspects of our functioning to promote human development. This chapter is primarily about the ways in which creative self-expression can be facilitated by professionals. In Chapter 8, I share how creative expression promotes and supports children's coping responses. I include the developmental aspects of self-expression and how this plays into later coping strategies. In Chapter 9, I share examples of how arts engagement and facilitated self-expression can help us across the lifespan to cope with trauma and adversity. In particular, this chapter includes research studies related to the clinical profession of art therapy.

7

Creative self-expression by ourselves and with others

What if everything you are going through is preparing you for what you wished for?

Author unknown

If you want to travel fast, go alone. If you want to travel far, go together.

African proverb

Terrain map: The experiences of traveling alone are different from those of journeying with others. Bringing this analogy to art-making, there are differences between making art by ourselves and creating with or in the presence of others. When we are challenged or unable to express ourselves, trained professionals such as art educators, arts-in-health workers, and art therapists can serve a facilitative role in externalizing, experiencing, and processing our creative instincts. I address these aspects of creative work in this chapter and offer how these varied contexts of self-expression contribute to our development and well-being in life. I conclude with a theory that explains how self-expression is an adaptive response that offers different outcomes and benefits based on the level of adversity and our ability to cope.

The value of perspective-taking and a home improvement analogy

A few years ago, three colleagues and I gathered regularly for an hour during the work week to create something together. We referred to it as Wellness Wednesdays. We would get together with no preset agenda; rather, the purpose was only to dance or make art that felt right in the moment. We would create group pieces or work individually, led by the mood of the moment on that given day. As we created in these sessions, I was struck by how different my resulting artwork would be when working in this group context compared

The Expressive Instinct. Girija Kaimal, Oxford University Press. © Oxford University Press 2023.
DOI: 10.1093/oso/9780197646229.003.0008

Figure 7.1. *Prismatic PoV* (Kaimal, 2016). Media: Canvas sheet and Cray-Pas. Dimensions: 11" X 15"

with when I worked by myself. My work in the group was exploratory, and I tended to create new pieces in styles quite different from those of the usual projects I worked on when I was by myself. Visually, my work created in solitude included explorations that were more detailed, whereas my work with others was somehow bolder, but less nuanced. I liked both of these experiences because they allowed me to work in many different ways. The group work also offered me something that working by myself did not: new perspectives and points of view. The painting in Figure 7.1 is an example of that. I worked with my colleagues to draw and color in images on the right with no end product or image in mind. And yet, when our time was up, my colleague looked at the painting, turned it around, and helped me see the goblet with sparkling colors that I had not seen myself from my vantage point. Without their witnessing and offering different perspectives, I might never have seen what was in plain sight before me in my work.

When we talk about the benefits of art-making, a question that I am often asked is whether it matters if we work by ourselves or with others, including professionals trained in art-making, art education, and art psychotherapy. In response to this question, I offer an analogy from home improvement. When we live in a home, things are bound to break down, undergo wear and tear, and need repairs. Some repairs might be simple, such as painting a wall where the paint might be old or peeling. Many such things in the home can be fixed by the residents of that home: for example, changing a lightbulb, cleaning and scrubbing dirty floors, drilling nails into walls. We might also be proficient in fixing minor cracks and breaks using glue or duct tape. These are expected and doable if one is able and mobile. Some people might also be skilled in doing things like replacing floors and repairing appliances. What would you do if bigger problems arose, such as problems with the plumbing or electrical system? If you have the skills and expertise, you could repair the problem yourself. However, if you are not skilled in the systems that underlie a home, you are actually safest hiring a certified professional who can do these things for you. In fact, if you do not use a professional, you might actually be putting your home and your own health in jeopardy.

Applying this analogy to the arts and health, I argue that most of us can respond effectively to the everyday challenges and adversities of living. As human beings we are resourceful, resilient, and capable of taking care of aspects of ourselves that need healing and restoration. Some forms of artistic practice are suitable to promote health and well-being: for instance, you might teach yourself particular skills or refine your existing skills. These acts of creative expression help you feel better; they might enhance aesthetic, meditative, contemplative, and mindful experiences. There are tremendous benefits to self-led arts practices as a means to support health. The idea of social prescriptions (Husk et al., 2019) emerged from the recognition of the preventive and health-enhancing potential of arts participation. Social prescriptions are the concept that, akin to prescriptions for medicines, health care providers could be encouraged to recommend participation in arts and culture events. There is emerging research (Fancourt & Finn, 2019) on the health-promoting aspects of attending arts and culture experiences (both receptive and expressive), including prosocial behaviors, positive emotions, and feeling validated and connected to human experiences that might otherwise seem isolating.

However, when the challenges are overwhelming, a trained expert, a clinician, can help us address the challenges and problems more effectively than we could ourselves. Beyond a certain point, akin to the home improvement analogy, you might be doing more harm than good if you do not get a professional's perspective on your health and well-being. Even for things that we might be able to do adequately, working with an expert exposes us to the ways in which even simple tasks can be accomplished with beauty, meaning, proficiency, and effectiveness. Note that the "others" (other human beings we make/create with) might be peers and professionals such as art therapists, art educators, teaching artists, and other arts-in-health professionals. These settings and contexts of art-making differ in terms of the skills and preparation of the facilitator and the resulting experiences and outcomes.

One way to conceptualize this is by means of a continuum. On one end of the spectrum, if you have an artistic practice in your wellness toolkit, practice it by all means. Most days, most of us are able to manage ourselves and meet our basic health and wellness (physical and emotional) needs. On the other end of the spectrum, if you are struggling to function, a facilitating professional can offer perspective and support your functioning in ways that cannot be accomplished without their expertise. When we have a hard time with self-regulation, mental health, or physical health, we are more likely to feel better if we go to a professional mental health care provider. Such individuals know the ways in which human functioning can be impaired and can work with us to learn more about our specific challenges and work to support our recovery. As we saw in previous chapters on the descriptions of brain processes in self-expression, our emotional centers are incredibly powerful. If we think of our artistic and expressive drives as fuel that inspires our emotions, and if we are not able to regulate the flow of this fuel, it can very likely burn the house down. In such situations, an external perspective can help us better understand our distress and consider ways to re-channel our energies.

To make art by ourselves or with peers and facilitators?

Is there evidence for differences between art-making by ourselves and art-making with a facilitating professional? Studies indicate that even participating in art, such as singing in a choir, attending arts events, and taking dance classes, promotes health (Fancourt & Finn, 2019). In my Health, Arts, Learning, and Evaluation (HALE) lab, we have examined this question with a series of studies. We found that art-making can help reduce cortisol levels in the body (Kaimal et al., 2016d) and improve mood and self-efficacy while reducing perceived stress (Kaimal & Ray, 2016), including in the context of new media like virtual reality (VR) drawing tools (Kaimal et al., 2019). We also found that among healthy adults, some solitary activities like coloring can help reduce stress but might not necessarily shift other aspects of well-being, such as self-efficacy and feelings of joy. These findings relate not only to traditional art media but also to digital and virtual artistic expression as well. Doodling and free art-making, even in digital media like VR, enhance our sense of self and help remind us of our capacity to create from a completely blank slate. From participant responses, we found that solitary activities like coloring might help with focus and act as an easy distraction. Babouchkina and Robbins (2015) designed a randomized control trial to test whether creating mandalas reduced negative mood. Their results showed that coloring circular shapes resulted in significantly higher mood enhancement compared to coloring squares or free drawings. Even the choice of medium matters and evokes different responses. In a study examining variations in heart rate based on the art medium selected, Haiblum-Itskovich et al. (2018) found that using oil pastels resulted in a positive mood and a relaxation response, more so than paint or pencils, perhaps because of the physical proximity and specific pressure and effort needed to express with this medium. The results of these studies show that many aspects of our expression are deeply intertwined with our choice of expressive tools.

Ideally, when we make art or engage in any creative activity by ourselves, we recognize its value and make time and space for it in our lives. The boom in coloring books and coloring pages in the past few years is one such example. It takes away the challenging part of visual art-making and skills and provides us with a level of challenge that is relatively easy and manageable. Our studies with cancer patients and caregivers showed that solitary activities like coloring helped in meditative and reflective ways by taking us to a space of distraction away from everyday concerns (Kaimal, Carroll-Haskins, Dieterich-Hartwell, et al., 2020d). Such activities do not necessarily help us resolve our problems; rather, they provide respite and a way to focus our attention elsewhere until such time as we can address them directly. When we make art by ourselves, it can help us self-regulate; feel a sense of mastery, control, and agency over our lives; and engage in reflective, validating, contemplative, or meditative practices.

In turn, our expressive experiences help us recognize the need for caring and making room in our lives to create, to play, and to invest in ourselves. Not all creative activity or works, however, help us feel good. The self-regulation that we hope to achieve every day can be hindered or helped with creative self-expression. We experience flow (that sense of losing ourselves in our work) when we achieve an optimal balance between challenge and skill (Csikszentmihalyi, 1990). According to Csikszentmihalyi (1996), if the task is too difficult, we are not likely to enjoy it. Similarly, if we do not like our end product, have struggled with implementing our ideas, or felt incompetent when working with the medium, we are not likely to feel a sense of accomplishment and satisfaction. This need not be a negative, however: The frustration may lead to awareness, insight, and the willingness to work with others to facilitate this learning. Self-expression also promotes well-being when we allow it to be a source of release, learning, and gaining perspective.

How is it different to make art with others?

Working with facilitators of art forms can be conceived of as a continuum, depending on the patient/client's mental and physical health needs. Working with a group of peers has benefits, including experiencing feelings of community, belonging, and shared experiences. The interactive connection with peers that I shared at the beginning of this chapter is relevant to the idea

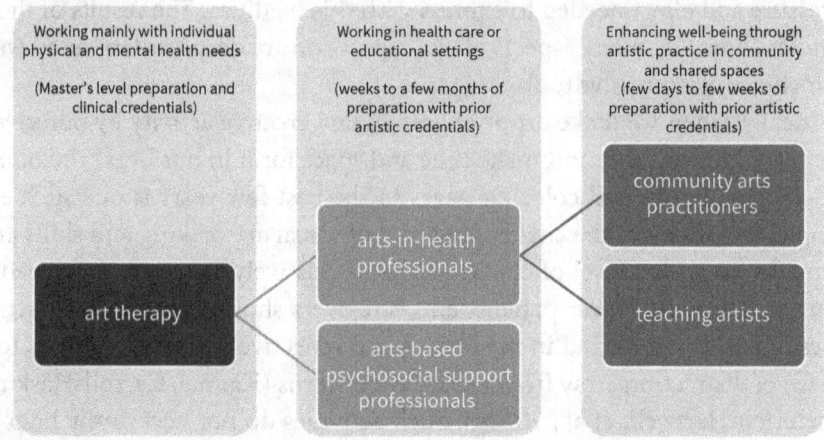

Working mainly with individual physical and mental health needs

(Master's level preparation and clinical credentials)

Working in health care or educational settings

(weeks to a few months of preparation with prior artistic credentials)

Enhancing well-being through artistic practice in community and shared spaces (few days to few weeks of preparation with prior artistic credentials)

art therapy

arts-in-health professionals

arts-based psychosocial support professionals

community arts practitioners

teaching artists

Figure 7.2. Different arts and health professions and areas of impact

that art-making with others reinforces our need for social connectedness and belonging. This outcome is different from the facilitation provided by a trained therapist or therapeutic arts practitioner.

In a recent white paper, Lambert et al. (2017) delineated the differences among professionals working at the intersection of arts and health care settings. They identified the following roles of different arts and health professionals: creative arts therapists, expressive arts therapists, and arts-in-health practitioners. Depending on the professional's area of expertise, they might contribute to the physical environment (creating artistic pieces or designing for the setting to promote health), support patient care and well-being, care for the caregiver (families of patients as well as professional health care providers), care for the community of people (through interactive programming), or promote education (using the arts to enhance observation or cognitive or motor skills). In addition, art educators and teaching artists also contribute to psychosocial health, but in different ways. Brief descriptions of these professions are given below (Figure 7.2).

Creative arts therapists

Creative arts therapies include the regulated health professions of art therapy, dance/movement therapy, drama therapy, music therapy, poetry therapy, and psychodrama therapy. These board-certified professionals use their particular art form to achieve clinical and therapeutic outcomes. Each of the professional disciplines possesses a definition of the profession, a legally defensible scope of practice, educational competencies, standards of practice, a code of ethics, and evidence-based research. Creative arts therapists encourage creative expression through a specific art form, but each profession is distinct. In the United States, there are five recognized creative arts therapies: art therapy, dance movement therapy, drama therapy and psychodrama, music therapy, and poetry/biblio therapy. The definitions of these professions are provided below (deWitte et al., 2021).

- *Art therapy*: Using a spectrum of two- and three-dimensional structured and unstructured art media within a psychotherapeutic relationship with an art therapist, the art therapist facilitates nonverbal and verbal self-expression and reflection through the process of art-making.
- *Dance movement therapy*: Employs dance and movement as a way into and means of therapy within a psychotherapeutic relationship and with the goal of promoting physical, emotional, cognitive, social, and spiritual integration of individuals. It is based on the premise of the interconnection of the body and mind.
- *Drama therapy and psychodrama*: Drama therapy involves the intentional use of drama and theater processes such as embodiment, dramatic projection, improvisation, role-play, and performance to facilitate physiological, psychological, and social change. Psychodrama uses guided role-play and specific techniques to explore the client's personal and interpersonal problems and possible solutions. While both operate in a dramatic reality, in drama therapy the story and characters are mostly imaginary, symbolic, and fantasy-based, while in psychodrama these are mostly reality-based.
- *Music therapy*: Uses music and its properties as well as songwriting, improvisation, and singing within a therapeutic relationship to optimize the client's quality of life and improve their physical, social, communicative, emotional, intellectual, and spiritual health and well-being. Music therapy can involve active music-making and/or receptive music listening according to the client's needs.
- *Poetry/biblio therapy*: Uses written language, poetry, reading, expressive writing, journal writing, and story writing and reading within a therapeutic relationship.

Expressive arts therapists

Expressive arts therapies, by contrast, are defined as the integration or use of all the arts in therapeutic practice, "at times working with the arts in sequence, at other times using the arts simultaneously, and at still other times carefully transitioning from one art form to another within the therapeutic encounter" (Estrella, 2005, p. 183). Many factors are often considered, such as principles of play, creativity, improvisation, aesthetics, space, time, rhythm, resonance, and mind/body connections (Kossak, 2021). The primary purpose is the promotion of expression and imagination. What distinguishes expressive arts therapists from creative arts therapists is that expressive arts practitioners are trained to combine two or more art forms in clinical practice. They also need to be conversant and proficient in multiple arts modalities.

Arts-in-health and arts-in-medicine practitioners

A growing number of medical centers have an arts coordinator or director who manages a variety of arts experiences, such as visiting artists, artists in residence, arts programming developed in partnership with community arts agencies, art collections, and rotating art exhibits. A major focus of their work is using the arts to enhance the working environment and reduce the impact of stress on professional caregivers. "Arts in health" is the term used for these other arts programs and initiatives, both in health care settings (referred to as "arts in health care") and in public health ("arts in community health"). According to Van Lith and Spooner (2018), practitioners of arts in health care tend to be artists who are drawn to serve in the medical setting, usually through personal health experiences. Their work is led by the positive aspects of arts experiences and tends to be geared toward providing comfort, recreation, and enjoyment rather than deep emotional processing work.

Art educators and teaching artists

Art educators focus mainly on the development of artistic skills and excellence in the artistic product. Even though much psychosocial learning occurs in art classes, the aim is primarily to develop artistic skills. Art educators are required to have extensive training and student teaching experiences (akin to the internships and supervised training of art therapists), but these are directed toward educational standards rather than psychosocial development.

Art educators and art therapists might work together effectively to address the learning needs and developmental needs of students. Both roles can promote human development and are facilitative, albeit in different aspects of human functioning. In addition, there might be times when art therapists teach patients/clients how to use some specific medium, and there are definitely aspects of personal development and insight in working through and learning in art education.

Teaching artists work in a range of school and college settings as well as in professional development environments. Teaching artists are professional artists with advanced expertise in a specific art form as well as training to teach aspects of the art form to a lay audience. Teaching artists link aspects of learning and development through the arts. Having worked with teaching artists in some of our research on arts and leadership, I will say that although the work can seem similar to that of art therapists, there are subtle differences. In one study (Kaimal et al., 2014) we evaluated the outcomes of professional development with school principals in a museum setting. The act of viewing art and making responses to art in this setting highlighted to all participants the importance and value of seeing a situation from different perspectives. Teaching artists in this context encouraged learning through awareness of self and others and but not psychotherapy.

Interestingly, in research studies, workshops, or clinical intervention, I often hear participants, patients and clients, refer to me as an "art teacher" or the art therapy session as an "art class." Even when I introduce myself as an art therapist, I am often referred to as "the art teacher." My assumption is that this occurs potentially because it is more socially acceptable to acknowledge learning than referring to an experience as therapy. Each of these professions offers a much-needed aspect of human experience: the experience of being "seen" through our words and works.

Each of the professions described above promotes a range of beneficial skills, but the intentional practice of therapy requires a credentialed professional (American Art Therapy Association, 2018). I will share next what this means in terms of the specific mental health and human service profession of art therapy and how facilitated art-making is therapeutic.

Self-expression through a facilitated process with an art therapist

Art therapists are often asked how they differ from artists in residence, art educators, or arts facilitators. Art therapy is also different from therapeutic art-making, which can be facilitated by non-clinicians to promote overall health and well-being. A core difference lies in the focus on the expressive process and facilitation of the session in a way that supports the development of the individual. This includes promoting emotional processing, cognitive shifts, developmental insights, and psychosocial learning while being attuned to the psychosocial needs and strengths of patients and clients. Note that a core assumption in art therapy is that everyone is an artist, if art is defined as the capacity for visual self-expression. Art-making in the context of art therapy does not involve judging the aesthetic qualities in the traditional sense; rather, art-making is treated as a form of self-expression that allows for communication, learning, and awareness. Although patients/clients are not expected to have artistic skills, the artistic/expressive knowledge of the art therapist facilitates the clinical session. This outcome is one of the key differences between art therapists and artists/art educators, who might be more focused on the artistry or quality of the artistic product. Art therapists typically are less concerned with the aesthetic merits of the product and more with the process and reflections on the process.

Art therapists serve a range of populations, including those with mental and physical illnesses, developmental challenges, and differential abilities and those who have experienced adversity and trauma. Art therapists bring to their practice skills in human behavior and psychological needs as well as the knowledge of artistic methods and the unique qualities of different artistic media. Art therapists are master's-level-trained psychotherapists with expertise in human development and the needs of diverse clinical populations as well as artistic skills to facilitate a nonjudgmental space for creative self-expression in order to meet psychosocial health goals.

Art therapy is the interplay of four components: the patient, the therapist, the art-making process, and the artistic product. Art media play a key role in art therapy practice, and art therapists are skilled in the role of art media in capturing, supporting, and empowering patients and clients. The art therapy session is set up as a space that is nonjudgmental about the artistic process and product; it is a place to express oneself visually in order to learn about oneself and move toward adaptive choices and behaviors and reduced psychopathology in a safe space. A typical art therapy session involves art-making, review of the art product, and verbal processing (as applicable and as the patient/client is able) with a master's-level-trained art therapy clinician. Art therapy can be short term (on average one or two sessions) or longer term (spanning a few weeks to several years). In group sessions, peers become a part of the therapeutic process by providing community and belonging, beyond that of the individual therapist alone. Art therapy sessions (which can be in groups or individual, based on client needs) provide time for engagement of all the senses (sight, sound, touch, smells) and for integrating these sensory and aesthetic experiences to re-imagine and rework established neural pathways to new ways of seeing, thinking, and experiencing (Figure 7.3).

Several art therapists have developed explanatory frameworks for practice and research in neurobiological approaches to art therapy. The best known of these is the expressive therapies continuum (ETC), which comprises three stepwise levels—kinesthetic/sensory, perceptual/affective, and cognitive/symbolic—interconnected by the creative level (Lusebrink et al., 2013). Lusebrink (2004) linked three levels of processing, sensory perception, emotional engagement, and cognitive understanding and meaning-making, as components of self-expression. This framework is widely used in art therapy as a means to explain the many ways in which different brain systems work together to enable human visual self-expression. Research on this theoretical framework is limited. Beyond its implicit relevance to clinical practice, the CREATE framework (Creative Embodiment, Relational Resonating, Expressive Communicating, Adaptive Responding, Transformative Integrating, and Empathizing and Compassion) proposes that the art therapy–relational neuroscience (ATR-N) approach can support resilience in human beings (Hass-Cohen et al., 2014). Czamanski-Cohen and Weihs (2016) further developed a theoretical body/mind model that captures the psychological and physiological outcomes of art therapy with therapeutic mechanisms of change that could be tested empirically.

Figure 7.3. An open studio table where a study participant works on a mixed media collage

How art therapy builds on the brain's predictive capacity primed for imagination

Visual self-expression and art-making helps promotes safety (reduces stress) and encourages creative agency. Artistic expression is in this context a way to channel maladaptive or dangerous instincts into creative products that promote prosocial behaviors while allowing for relational development through communication of difficult thoughts and complex emotions.

As we saw in Chapter 1, the human brain is analogous to a prediction machine rather than to a computer. To maximize survival options, the brain is inherently wired to imagine possibilities for the future that enhance safety and access to survival resources while minimizing risk and danger. A threat can pertain to physiological safety (e.g., injury, violence) as well as psychological safety, affecting identity, and belonging (e.g., abuse, bullying, isolation, rejection). In addition, if individuals have been through disruptive, abusive, or traumatic experiences in their developmental years, the accurate perceptions of threat and safety can be significantly affected throughout life. De Witte et al. (2021), in the largest scoping review to date, found that the unique mechanisms of therapeutic change through the creative arts therapies were the use of symbolism and metaphors, concretization, and embodiment.

Art therapy, specifically if seen from the intersection of biopsychosocial-spiritual aspects of human development, takes into account the human instinct for survival and the capacity to develop life story narratives. I refer to this framework as Adaptive Response Theory (ART). ART is a framework based on evolutionary biology (survival, imaginative capacity, narrative) and the interrelated components of client, therapist, art product, and art-making in influencing adaptive choices. The proposed framework integrates biophysiological aspects of surviving and psychosocial and spiritual constructs of thriving that could be used to track clinical goals, processes, mechanisms, and outcomes for research in art therapy.

Figure 7.4 presents a schematic diagram of art therapy within the ART framework as a process of promoting adaptive and creative responses to perceived stressors and threats by supporting clients to survive and thrive. The horizontal axis represents the continuum of surviving from threat to safety through accurately assessing the environment for real and perceived threats to survival. The vertical axis represents a continuum of thriving from being unable to express oneself (unsayable/constricted) to imagination and creative/expressive agency. Constructs like safety and threat can have positive and negative associations. As we saw previously, neurotransmitters like dopamine are associated with reward pathways in the brain that respond to pleasurable

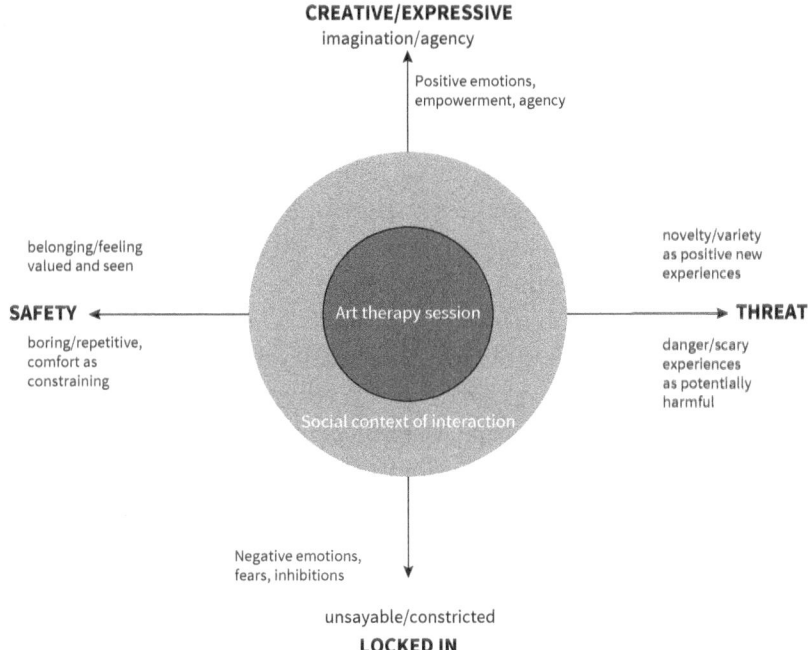

Figure 7.4. Adaptive Response Theory (ART) framework in art therapy

experiences (Taber et al., 2012), including those associated with novelty (Costa et al., 2014). Safety can, therefore, imply belonging and feeling valued but can also feel limiting, redundant, and boring. Similarly, threat can be perceived as dangerous, risky, and scary or as new and invigorating.

As such, we know that creative self-expression taps into the brain's innate predictive and narrative capabilities by enabling individuals to imagine alternative and potentially adaptive and healthy personal narratives. In times of distress, having a way to respond provides mammals with a sense of agency and a safety valve of sorts so they do not become completely overwhelmed/incapacitated by the external threat/stressor. In animals, the response might be doing things like gnawing on an object or accepting the stress if it means moving up in the tribe's hierarchy, as is the case with baboons (Sapolsky, 2003). It is no different for humans: Our creative expressive outlets provide us just that sense of agency and control over our lives. These stressors, when chronic, acute, or unmitigated, can lead to dysregulation in our limbic systems, such that fears and responses become hyperconnected in the brain, which responds in a hyperreactive way. These are the triggers and misplaced responses in reaction to trauma whereby the heightened connections make us respond with fear or vigilance or cause us to become completely numb. All of these responses might ostensibly seem maladaptive, but they are still a survival response. It becomes imperative to get help once we reach these points that are beyond our own abilities to cope and manage. When individuals go through disruptive, abusive, or traumatic experiences, their ability to process sensory information effectively is hampered. We know that the arts can evoke intense emotion and self-expression for highly stressed or psychologically vulnerable individuals, and a lack of adequate support and facilitation can lead to harmful outcomes. Art therapists therefore work with individuals struggling with physical and psychological difficulties to imagine, explore, try out, and finally live out healthier and more adaptive lives.

When individuals struggle to adapt effectively to stressful or traumatic experiences, an art therapist can help redirect them to an adaptive choice that supports self-awareness and development. This approach, in turn, can lead them toward achieving therapeutic goals and improved health outcomes. The power of the arts lies in their multidimensionality, nonlinearity, and timelessness, which allows the process to hold metaphors and meaning concurrently. Art media and facilitated art-making are unique strengths of art therapy and encourage active engagement and self-efficacy by leveraging the unique response characteristics of expressive media that allow for more or less control (Moon, 2011a, 2011b). The opportunity for creative expression and unlocking the imagination leads to a sense of agency and possibility that might previously not have been available to a patient/client (Kaimal & Ray, 2016; Kaimal et al., 2016d, 2017b). The process of art-making, including media choice and creative expression, can result in gaining mastery and confidence, which can promote learning transfer into life outside of the therapy session.

There are four main components that enable art therapy to facilitate adaptive responses: (1) the art-making process, (2) the art therapist, (3) the patient/client, and (4) the artwork or product created in the session. These four components intersect to address biological, psychological, social, and spiritual needs. Figure 7.5 shows the interaction between the four components in an art therapy session and how they work together to facilitate adaptive responses and mechanisms of change. The components are intentionally shown as intersecting and bidirectional to highlight the interlinking of all four aspects in a session.

These components in turn lead to clinical outcomes such as the following:

- *Biological-physiological:* reduced stress, fear, pain, and fatigue and increased safety, belonging, and reward perception
- *Psychological:* externalization, perspective-taking, re-storying the personal narrative, hedonic joy, flow, concentration, distraction, emotional regulation, distraction, self-awareness, self-efficacy, and creativity

Figure 7.5. Adaptive Response Theory (ART) processes, mechanisms, and outcomes (*Source*: Kaimal, 2019)

- *Social:* empathy, mutuality, secure attachment, interpersonal learning, expressing the unsayable, communication (including with metaphor), reduced loneliness, social integration, and belonging
- *Spiritual:* eudaimonia, purpose, meaning, and integrated identity

When art therapy initiates clients' adaptive responses, the components combine in dynamic and interconnected ways to result in successful outcomes such as sublimation (effective artistic channeling of negative or difficult emotions or urges), social integration, longer-term purpose and meaning, and reduced psychopathology or symptoms. Artistic expression, to be truly meaningful, goes beyond pure venting and self-expression in that it helps us re-imagine and re-view, with new perspectives, our challenges and circumstances.

It can be argued that ART places importance on neuroception, the sense associated with responding to threats. Much of the framing of ART begins with reducing perceived threats and establishing safety (horizontal axis) and then modeling effective ways to channel authentic self-expression (vertical axis). Beginning with the establishment of safety and unconditional positive regard, which is essential for any therapeutic interaction, ART then goes on to help engage all the senses and connect to sensory as well as symbolic and engaging-making activities. It thus has implications for clinical practice and research. For example, with older individuals, challenges might include loss of physical and cognitive capacities and social isolation. The adaptive response goals could be offering group art therapy to promote safety through social integration, careful choice of art materials, meaning, and purpose through the act of making. For individuals struggling with chronic stress and feeling disempowered by relentless adversity, art therapy might help by providing a space for relaxation and experiencing positive emotions as well as thriving through active problem-solving. The session then becomes a place to practice challenges and responses that can be taken out to the real world. In response to trauma, the adaptive responses in art therapy would be to establish safety and later to encourage self-expression and self-management of symptoms in order to better manage triggers. Lastly, a patient trying to manage overwhelming emotional reactivity (internal threat) can learn to channel reactions through sublimation in the artwork (instead of harming self or others). These examples will be explicated further in the chapters on creativity in adversity. In particular, in the next two chapters, I will share examples of how self-expression can promote awareness, insight, and post-traumatic growth.

That said, it is also possible for each of these components to be weak links. For example, if the therapist is not attuned to the culture and history of the patient/client, their relationship will remain superficial or at worst will disintegrate. Similarly, if the art media and materials are not relevant and meaningful, and the art product is not contextualized, the experience may remain unimpacted or even harmed. Therapists who do not seek supervision and reflect deeply on the practice might bring their own baggage and trauma and be unable to truly be present for the patient/client. Staying mindful and engaging in lifelong learning about one's practice and the interpersonal and intercultural aspects of practice are essential for the adaptive dynamics to work toward the biopsychosocial and physical aspects. The dynamic aspects of the framework require both the therapist and the patient to be learning together. In particular, therapists need to be especially sensitive to and aware of ways in which they might inadvertently be perpetuating colonizing values, since the profession of art therapy evolved from Eurocentric and Western belief systems.

The role of the viewing/witnessing when creating by ourselves or with others

Attention is the rarest and purest form of generosity (Weil, 1970). When we, pay attention to each other and perhaps more so when the expression is authentically one's own, we engage in this very generosity. To create is to see our inner state reflected back to us, the outside offering us literal and metaphorical perspective. Each of the professions in arts, health, and human development contributes to being a witness in different ways. Moreover, the context of creating, group or individual, adds additional perspectives on the process and product. To create is to have an audience (real or imagined). The audience (beginning with ourselves) is the observer who helps us see what we have created in new and possibly different ways. Many scholars talk about the idea of voice (Gilligan, 1982). To have a voice is to be able to express who we are. To have a voice is to have agency, presence, and the ability to challenge, shape, and create discourses that feel authentic and embedded in the truth and reality of one's subjective experience. Akin to voice is the feeling of being "seen." As discussed earlier in this chapter, working alone has its value but also limits the number of perspectives on the creative experience. Our creative works are an offering of vulnerability: They invite being seen for who we are. The greater our vulnerabilities, the more sensitive the need to be seen with care and compassion.

I wrote this section in the midst of the coronavirus stay-at-home orders. Being at home during the enforced lockdown meant fewer and more intimate witnesses to our lives, if any at all. We were quarantined and locked down, and in this context, home was both a sanctuary and a jail. It went from being a source of nourishment and rest to being a place of uneasy amalgamation of work, school, and residence. Underlying all the responses to the coronavirus pandemic, including medical, public health, and social interaction issues, mental health issues were sorely neglected. However, there is increased recognition of post-traumatic stress disorder for essential workers, domestic violence, abuse, and burnout, which are expected to impact vast swaths of society. The quarantine is harder for those in homes with abusive family members and limited space. It is difficult to coexist in this prison cell without being abusive to ourselves or others.

To an extent, humanity came together briefly on a global scale as we learned to be creative and adaptive in this confinement. We became better cooks. We became creators of scenes and views as we looked out our windows and shared as best we could within our pods and using digital tools. We noticed and appreciated things around the home; we remembered and recreated famous artworks or our own memories. Home is where we are ideally most ourselves, least defensive, and most protected to fully be ourselves. We might have coped, but we might not have processed the experience fully. Members of the arts and health workforce were recognized as essential workers through the pandemic and will likely continue to be needed as we emerge from its devastation. In subsequent chapters in this section I will share more on role of facilitated self-expression through adversity among adults and children.

Key takeaways

Each of the disciplines that connects to the arts and human development serves us in different and valuable ways. They help us engage with our naturally creative imaginative and expressive selves. Art educators provide us with tools and skills and help us experience the joy of mastery and aesthetic development. Arts-in-health and therapeutic arts professionals help us experience joy in artistic experiences in receptive and expressive ways. Art therapists typically work closely with patients and clients who have endured adversities and challenges to process and express their inner experiences in ways that might be difficult in traditional verbal psychotherapy settings. Compared with other arts professionals, art therapists are trained educationally and clinically to be attuned to and to help patients with social and emotional challenges and needs by building on their inherent creative strengths. In particular, art therapy builds on the foundations of the brain's predictive capacity and the natural human instincts to be imaginative and expressive.

8

When words are not enough

Creative self-expression and adversity in the developing years of childhood and youth

> We make art with everything we are, the doom and the glory of it. We make art to know ourselves, to locate ourselves in the web of being, to make ourselves more alive. We make art that, at its best, helps other people locate themselves and live.
>
> **Maria Popova**

Terrain map: My purpose in writing this book was to make the idea of creative self-expression democratic and accessible: to recognize and accept this superpower that is innate in us all as an attribute of being human. Our adult selves are founded on our developmental experiences. Although we have the capacity to change our lives, in many ways the developmental years of childhood and youth form the structure of our lives, including our worldview, self-perceptions, and approaches to challenges and ongoing stressors in life. No child is without stressors, and stressors are the essential source of resistance that we need to grow our muscles of resilience and strength. That said, there is "eustress" (which strengthens us) and distress (which can be developmentally hurtful and unhelpful). When they occur during the developmental years, adversities like illness (Figure 8.1), death, injury, violence, abuse, and trauma can fundamentally alter perceptions of self and complicate perceptions of danger and safety in self and others. Perceptions of adaptive and maladaptive responses are often complex and complicated especially in non-normative development contexts of adversity. In the developmental years, children and youth are still growing, and the brain is not fully matured until the mid-20s. This period therefore offers opportunities to embed resilience and help children and youth learn tools and strategies to manage and process experiences as they approach emerging adulthood.

The Expressive Instinct. Girija Kaimal, Oxford University Press. © Oxford University Press 2023.
DOI: 10.1093/oso/9780197646229.003.0009

Figure 8.1. Artwork by a pediatric oncology patient Lauren (age eight), *Team Ohana*, in which she expresses the idea that "Nobody suffers alone because we are all family." Media: Acrylic paint and markers.

Creative self-expression and childhood

How are self-expression and creative expression different in children than in adults? Children are not necessarily mini-adults. Although basic emotional experiences remain unchanged throughout life, there are significant differences in how children process life experiences. Our thought processes, our ability to deal with complexity and ambiguity, as well as our instincts and emotions gain nuance and depth as we grow older. As they grow children and youth are better able to distinguish and differentiate experiences and emotional responses and position themselves from focusing on self to being increasingly aware of the world around them.

In many ways children are less self-conscious than adults and less premeditated/aware of their creative processes. As seen in Chapter 2, an accepted definition of creativity is that it has two aspects: novelty and usefulness. It is argued that children can only address novelty, not usefulness, because their creative explorations are part of play and learning (Russ, 2016). It is only later in adulthood that we have the mental capacity to focus on purposeful products. This focus on a creative end product is not necessarily or typically an expectation for children, even though they are able to problem-solve with purpose in their own ways.

Vygotsky (1978), one of the foundational theorists in childhood development and education, suggested that creativity and imagination are essential to children's development and that their development in fact includes three stages: creative imagination in childhood, connection to creative thinking in adolescence, and finally implementing useful outcomes in adulthood. Children practice imagination through play, and there is significant evidence that pretend play, which is a part of normative childhood development, is positively associated with emotional self-regulation, storytelling, and divergent thinking (Hoffman & Russ, 2016). Furthermore. Beghetto and Kaufman (2007) suggest that the arts for children and adolescents can help with "mini-c" (intrapersonal learning from engaging in the creative process) and "small c" creativity that result in everyday innovation. Mini-c is particularly relevant to children as they are learning the arts practices while also going through natural developmental stages where play is key.

Play implies safety and opportunity for exploration and joy. To be able to play means that there are no threats to worry about or burdens to bear. To play is to feel free and safe: to experience joy and pleasure in exploration without an expectation of rewards, products, or destinations. Play thus for children is a practice of imagination and possibility. Through play and exploration, children gain insights and solutions that are meaningful to them at their developmental level and the milestones they need to reach (Russ, 2016; Singha et al., 2020). Singha et al. (2020) recognized the value of play that begins in childhood as a way to practice skills and strategies and strengthen the creative learning muscle. Seeing the lightness and humor in life, its manifestations and experiences, is a skill that serves us well throughout our lives. Play is a way for children and youth to pretend and to try out various creative solutions and options, including those for everyday life contexts (e.g., relationships, skills) without the pressure of having to produce any meaningful or tangible final product. Unstructured games and play allow the child to explore; this freedom to explore is essential to allow for new ideas and possibilities to enter our consciousness.

In terms of physical health, there is emerging evidence on the biological benefits of playing outside in nature. Bacteria in the soil help build immunity in childhood and serve to release "feel good" hormones in our bodies (Gilbert et al., 2017). Moreover, soil and dirt have microbes that prevent our immune system from attacking itself.

Play allows us to process difficult emotions and social interactions, including those seen during the 2020 COVID pandemic, which activated fears and anxieties among children. Creative explorative play (Russ, 2016) allows us to make sense of the uncertainties during situations like this. Taleb (2014) in fact argued that overly scheduled and helicopter-parented children end up being vulnerable and fragile as adults because they have not been able to gain the life-transforming skills of self-directed learning through creative problem-solving and joyous play.

Ideally, play is a natural process and skill, but unfortunately this is not case for many children who face life challenges and adversities (e.g., abuse, illness, violence) or even developmental delays that affect the freedom to play (Russ, 2016). The natural developmental processes of imagination, innovation, and expression essential to survival are disrupted. Artistic practice in these contexts helps with reimagining the past as well as the future. Some children are able to do this on their own with initiative and an instinctive understanding of the ability of self-expression to help us manage ourselves. But many can benefit from facilitated options (discussed later in the chapter), which represent ways in which we can teach and help children to have a range of tools to understand, manage, and self-regulate their inner and outer lives. Let us first review the normative stages of artistic development and then dive into how this can be helpful to support children through adversity.

Stages of artistic development in childhood

If you have observed young children, you will have seen that they freely dance, move, sing, and scribble without fear or artifice. Just like there are stages of cognitive and emotional development, there are stages of artistic development (Figure 8.2). Viktor Lowenfeld was an art educator who suggested that creative and mental growth was a means for self-actualization and that it could be seen distinctly in children's drawing styles (McWhinnie, 1991).

| Scribbling | Pre-schematic | Schematic | Dawning realism | Pseudorealistic |

Figure 8.2. Developmental stages of drawing

In examining hundreds of thousands of artworks (limited to population samples from Europe), he developed an initial developmental theory on children's visual expressive styles (Lowenfeld & Brittain, 1987). The theory has since been critiqued for not being adequately transparent in methodology (Michael, 1986) and not being representative of children all over the world (Alter-Muri & Vazzano, 2014). In addition, anyone working with children will see that these stages vary by child (Levick, 2003). It does, however, offer a sequential presentation of how visual expression develops over time in childhood and early adolescence (Deaver, 2009) and mirrors concurrent cognitive and socioemotional development.

1. Scribble stage (2 to 4 years): In this stage children go from making random disordered marks on a surface to slowly making lines and circular motions. Toward the end of this stage, children can make a scribble and name it in some way as part of their imagination and a storyline. Usually the scribble is still very much a full-body activity.

2. Pre-schematic stage (4 to 6 years): At this stage the child is able to make a simple circle and lines radiating out of it, typically representing a human being. This is the beginning of their ability to represent the human form and also to draw it in relative importance to themselves rather than as a depiction of actual proportions in the world. For example, the child will typically draw the people they love (including themselves often as the largest). The use of forms and figures is more idiosyncratic and playful than realistic.

3. Schematic stage (7 to 9 years): During this stage, akin to the expansion of the social life and learning in school and their communities, children become more realistic in their representations, including creating baselines, skies, realistic colors and shapes, and representations of people in groups. Exaggerations and effects are still used to depict an emotional idea rather than obsessing on accurate visual representation.

4. Dawning realism stage (9 to 11 years): At this stage children are increasingly self-conscious of their drawing abilities, styles, and depictions. Efforts tend toward realistic depictions, and being self-critical comes with the self-awareness of this age. Spontaneity and playfulness lessen, possibly as they hear feedback about their works from teachers and peers.

5. Pseudorealistic stage (11 to 13 years): At this stage the product becomes more important to the child than the process, and there is increasing focus on depictions and comparisons with reality.

6. Period of decision: Children and youth often stop drawing altogether at this stage if they perceive themselves as not being skilled. Unfortunately, in our modern competitive education system, this is often the last time youth engage in drawing. Unless engaged, interested, or skilled in drawing, they rarely engage in it as adults.

Although these stages and ages vary in terms of when and how children draw, the progression from scribbling to representation is seen in almost all children. The theory offers a broad framework for children's art and helps us see when they might be developmentally different from peers. It emphasizes the natural expressive tendencies in artistic styles. The theory has been criticized for de-emphasizing content and skillful expression, but the value of the theory lies, I believe, in a humanistic and compassionate approach to children's natural instincts and developmental aspirations. Interestingly, in some of our studies, we have found that when adults learn a new art form, they recapitulate the stages of artistic development. Even though they do so quickly, often within minutes, they still start with scribble-like features before moving into representation (Kaimal et al., 2019).

I once worked with a young man in the foster care system as part of a study looking at the behavioral outcomes of a 10-week art therapy intervention (Kaimal, 2001). This teenager had a long history of abuse as well as his own history of being a sexual predator on younger children. He had behavioral challenges and was consistently doing poorly in school. He had many encounters with the juvenile justice system. Although he was never officially diagnosed with any developmental delays, his drawing levels, thinking, and functioning were that of a much younger child at a different developmental stage (Figure 8.3). That did not absolve him of his misbehaviors, but the artistic representations and my interactions with him helped me see him in a new light. It helped me see his needs and in turn communicate them to his

Figure 8.3. Artwork by an adjudicated youth indicating undetected developmental delays

teachers and caregivers in the foster home. In Figure 8.3, the image on the left is his drawing of his family. He refers to them as "doing nothing together" and yet imagines that they are "at a fair eating candy together." The second image is a drawing of a boy who, in his words, "is a teenager who is always getting into trouble."

Appropriately, a child's drawing goes from scribbles to the attempt to draw a basic human figure and then the addition of the environment and other people. Concurrent with artistic development, as seen above, is the emerging construction of the personal narrative. As we saw earlier, children's natural preference is representational, and this develops further as they see the inherent meanings and metaphors in more abstract imagery (Lilly & Venukapalli, 2021). This parallels the development of autobiographical narratives as delineated by theorists of the human life story (Habermas & Bluck, 2003; McAdams, 2001).

Uncertainty in childhood is managed through play. Children can express all sorts of scenarios, "playing out" their ability to foresee and anticipate and therefore prepare. Playing, making, creating, and storytelling are all intertwined for children. Fantastical tales and storylines with real and imagined characters are part of the developmental trajectory and indicators of normative explorative processes. Stories can help children name and manage their anxieties. Watch children play and you will see that the tales are intense and full of loss and attempts at survival. In reality, these are aspects that they worry about. Through imagined tales like these, they process their worries and uncertainties. By expressing emotions associated with possible loss, they implicitly reinforce the idea that they will survive.

Things can be said using the metaphor of a story (embedded in any art form) that might not otherwise be possible to say and process in real life because of the pain inherent in such a reality. These tales might not have the coherence, sequential logic, and complexity of adulthood, but we see the beginnings of it in childhood. Similar to artistic development, narrative constructions mature in capacity in adolescence. Iacoboni (2009) further suggested that stories help us see each other in empathic ways and attributes this at a very fundamental level to mechanisms of mirror neuron activation. Mirror neurons are a mechanism that allows us to be socially attuned beings, constantly defined and shaped by each other. Through stories in pictures, books, or interactions, we learn to pay attention to similarities in our experience as human beings. It helps to build secure attachment as well as to recognize both the safety of relationships and the letting go without clinging that is essential to our sense of self.

In a recent study, Brockington et al. (2021) found that the act of listening to a story had physiological benefits. The authors had children in intensive care units listen to a story narrated by a storyteller (treatment group); results were compared with those from a group of children who were solving riddles that also involved social interaction but lacked the immersive narrative aspect (control group). Compared with the control group, children in the storytelling group showed a marked increase in oxytocin combined with a decrease in cortisol in saliva after the 30-minute intervention. They also reported less pain and used more positive lexical markers when describing their time in the hospital. The findings highlight the natural aspect of storytelling that connects with our instinct to respond to narratives as a familiar evolutionary structure providing safety and metaphorical reassurance. The authors provide a psychophysiological basis for the short-term benefits of storytelling and suggest that a simple and inexpensive intervention may help alleviate the physical and psychological pain of hospitalized children on the day of the intervention.

Adversity in childhood and youth

When I was about 11 years old, for the first time in my life we moved to a new city and school. I was excited about the move since we were going from New Delhi, India, to Kathmandu, Nepal. The idea of the new experience was compelling from a distance since it meant better times for my family, as the job paid a higher salary and in many ways we would be better off and comfortable in ways that we had not been previously. My father moved first and my mother and we children joined him a few months later. My brothers, who were much older than I was, were already in college, which meant that the family unit was also going to change. Everything about this move promised new beginnings and experiences, including my first time being on an airplane. Although the flight itself was only a half-hour long, when we landed in Kathmandu airport nestled in a valley amidst the mighty Himalayan mountains, it was all very magical. As I mentioned previously, I am named for the Goddess Parvati, and my name means "daughter of the mountains." My mythical father is Himavan, the king of the Himalayas. Thus, seeing and living in the Himalayas was for me a sort of homecoming. We reached our new home and I settled into my own room for the first time; previously I had shared a room with my brother.

The newness and novelty soon wore off, though, as I started my new school. Everything about it was unfamiliar. It was smaller than my old school, which meant everyone already had their little impermeable social groups. I knew nobody and nobody knew me. I still remember the first lunchtime and waiting for someone to sit with me or tell me where to go—but nobody did. I choked back my tears and sat by myself in a stairwell and ate my lunch. That crushing sense of loneliness and isolation in a teeming social setting was devastating to my child self. How did nobody see me sitting by myself and tearfully choking on my lunch? Even though my lunches were packed by my mother with great care, including a chocolate treat she would include, I remember being unable to enjoy the meal itself. Its taste was imperceptible and meaningless when there was nobody to share it with. After a few days, I eventually found my identity (nerdy-social), made friends, and found my place in the landscape of the new school. I went from the survival mode of seeking a sense of belonging to thriving in that school over the next few years (until we moved again).

This ostensibly minor adjustment challenge was one of my first emotionally trying experiences, and it is seared in my memory and my identity in many ways that play out repeatedly in life. I remember this isolation and aloneness as an existential threat every time I am in a new, unfamiliar place. That memory of being an isolated 11-year-old is my template for negotiating challenging new settings. Be it an unfriendly city or indifferent people at a meeting, my reaction is that of the child feeling rejected and unwanted in a new place. I also remember in those moments that the experience will not last, that someone will eventually ask me to join them for lunch or smile and include me in their social group. The adversity of a childhood move was my reminder that uncertainty lies ahead and I will temporarily be in that isolated survival mode looking for a tribe to protect me, but eventually I have hope that some community of individuals will give me safety and protection and allow me to be. All I have to do as an adult is remember that pain and know that it can be overcome.

I was fortunate in many ways that the adversities I faced as a child were manageable and allowed me to fortify myself with strategies and approaches for the future. Adverse childhood experiences (ACEs) can, however, have devastating impacts: They have been found to impact physiological and psychological health. ACEs in the physical and psychosocial realm significantly impact children's development (Luby et al., 2013) and have been found to significantly impact development across the lifespan (Anda et al., 2010). Harsh parenting, for example, has been found to have lifelong effects on brain volume, fear response, and connectivity in the brain (Suffren et al., 2021). ACEs such as abuse, deprivation, neglect, caregiver losses, and violence have been related to risky behaviors, chronic health conditions, and early death (Anda et al., 2010). In terms of physiological impacts, poverty and deprivation in childhood have been found to impact brain development, including reduction in gray matter and reduced volume in the frontal and temporal lobes and the hippocampus (Hair et al., 2015), in irreversible ways, including lifelong reduced brain volume and maladaptive response pathways (Hackman & Farah, 2009; Hair et al., 2015; Luby et al., 2013; Noble et al., 2015).

Growing up in adversity also affects a child's capacity to process difficult emotions. The stress of living in conditions of violence and trauma can have cumulative effects. Children in poverty and high-stress contexts have more difficulty understanding and coping with emotions, which in turn can affect later social and academic milestones (Hackman & Farrah, 2009; Izard et al., 2008). Dubow et al. (2012) found that children aged eight and over facing multiple stressors had significantly more symptoms of post-traumatic stress compared with those who had faced fewer stressors. Heckman (2006) demonstrated that emotional support interventions in the form of enhanced stimulation, support, and nurturance applied during the preschool period of development have very powerful positive effects on adult outcomes. Heckman's (2006) analyses also provided evidence that environmental enhancements applied during the preschool period have a far more robust effect compared with similar interventions applied in later childhood, adolescence, and early adulthood. Mental ill health and poverty are found to interact in a negative cycle worldwide, yet there are few interventions that address this issue (Lund et al., 2011). There is a recognized need for further research and study to develop interventions, scale up existing approaches, and invest in mental health and psychosocial support programs.

In particular, it is worth noting that as children develop, they gain a refined and nuanced understanding of emotions. As seen in previous chapters, our primal instincts are approach and avoidance (Kandel, 2012). As our brain matures, we develop words and meanings associated with these two instincts and identify the specific feelings and emotions associated with different experiences and people. To know and to be able to name these accurately (or at least the best we can) then become essential to better integrate them into our life stories and the ongoing narrative of our life.

Protective and benevolent childhood experiences

To counter ACEs, there are also protective factors: experiences that shield the challenge of the adversities and make them manageable or help reduce the damaging impact. These are referred to as protective and compensatory experiences (PACEs) or benevolent childhood experiences (Narayan et al., 2018). If ACEs are related to losses and aggression, PACEs (Hays-Grudo & Morris, 2020) are associated with gains related to relationships, activities, and attitudes that can offset the destructive impact of ACEs. PACEs include having unconditional love from a parent/caregiver; having a best friend; volunteering in the community; being part of a social group; having support from an adult outside of the family; living in a clean, safe home with enough food; having resources and opportunities to learn; engaging in a hobby; getting regular physical activity; and having daily routines and fair rules. The Benevolent Childhood Experiences Scale measures attributes that are considered protective, including having caring adults, such as teachers and neighbors, supportive close friends, predictable home routines, opportunities to have a positive self-concept, feelings, and beliefs. These benevolent experiences were found to offset the effects of difficult times (Narayan et al., 2018), including those engendered by the COVID-19 pandemic. Having benevolent experiences like these resulted in lowered stress, depression, and loneliness among children who were otherwise considered to be living in adversity (Doom et al., 2021).

Masten (2014) refers to these as "ordinary magic": the simple everyday things, like the love and support of a caring adult, that help children and youth find strength within. These factors can help children regulate themselves, understand their experiences, and gain a sense of agency and safety in the face of overwhelming external threats to well-being.

We know that creativity is inherent to humans and that nurturing that capacity in children provides them with inner resources throughout life. The arts and engaging in art therapy or art activities with a facilitating adult can thus serve many therapeutic purposes, including expressing difficult or wordless emotions as well as gaining self-efficacy through the trials, errors, and successes of artistic and/or creative practice. Levick (1983) was one of the first art therapists to document and demonstrate how drawing was a way for children to communicate, especially when they didn't have words. Rubin (2005) further articulated the many ways in which we can support children who have faced adversities using a variety of art media and creating the safe and normalizing environment of a facilitating adult and peers in the art therapy studio.

Research indicates that opportunities for arts engagement have profoundly positive impacts on verbal expression, reduce disruptive behaviors (Klorer & Robb, 2012), enhance academic achievement (Hardiman et al., 2014; Izard et al., 2008; Ruppert, 2006), and reduce stress (Brown et al., 2017), especially in students from socially and economically disadvantaged backgrounds. In a study of recreational arts engagement and mental well-being among youth in Australia, Davies et al. (2015) found that 100 hours or more of arts engagement in a year was associated with significantly higher levels of mental health and well-being compared with fewer hours of arts engagement. Dance- and music-based interventions for preschool-age children living in poverty also showed that children in arts-enriched environments (music and dance) demonstrated improved social skills, positive emotions, and fewer disruptive behaviors compared to children who did not receive these programs (Brown & Sax, 2013; Lobo & Winsler, 2006).

The arts are a means to encourage adaptive emotional expression, especially for children and adults living in conditions of adversity and trauma (Malchiodi & Perry, 2008). The arts provide a means for sensory integration of emotionally challenging experiences and enable a pathway to self-expression, verbalization, and socialization (Levick, 1983). In particular, the arts can be a form of self-expression and communication for children who are unable to speak due to experiences of trauma and disability (Levick, 1983). This is a fundamental principle of the creative and expressive arts therapies (e.g., art therapy, dance movement therapy, music therapy, drama therapy). The idea underlying these therapeutic approaches is that the creative self-expression taps into the resilient part of individuals and enables humans in distress to communicate and connect with others.

A study from the late 1990s referred to as the "Champions of Change" report (Fiske, 1999) found that the children who benefited the most from past participation were those living in conditions of socioeconomic disadvantage. Space, resources, and time for creative self-expression have been found to be a sanctuary in times of adversity. Brown et al. (2017) examined the impact of arts participation among children in economically disadvantaged settings. They tracked cortisol levels among children aged 3 to 5 years who were identified as being from economically disadvantaged backgrounds. A total of 310 children who attended a Head Start preschool were randomly assigned to participate in different schedules of arts and homeroom classes on different days of the week. Baseline cortisol levels were obtained in the morning; subsequent levels were obtained after arts and homeroom classes on two different days at the beginning, middle, and end of the year. Over the course of the year, it was found that cortisol levels were lower after an arts class versus after a homeroom class at the middle and the end of the year but not at the start of the year. This finding indicated that something uniquely stress-reducing was occurring as a result of the arts classes. The study implications are compelling on the health-promoting, "safety valve" potential impact of arts in children facing poverty risks.

A study inspired by art therapy practices examined outcomes for a group of preschool children in Malawi, Africa (Kaimal et al., 2022). HEART, which stands for Healing and Education Through the Arts, is an arts-based approach to providing psychosocial support for children. It uses the arts to help children process stress and express feelings, experiences, or ideas in an emotionally supportive environment where they can connect with peers and caring adult facilitators. This was an outcome study of a 9-month program intervention of HEART in rural preschools in Malawi (203 children). The quasi-experimental study compared group outcomes on emergent literacy, emergent numeracy, motor development, and social-emotional development between preschools with (n = 10) and without (n = 10) an integrated HEART intervention. Findings indicated that children in HEART-integrated schools experienced significant gains in the four assessed domains of early learning and development compared to those in schools without a HEART integration model. Implications and limitations of the study are discussed in Phiri et al. (2016). The arts-based psychosocial support promoted academic outcomes for kindergarten-aged children, with significant gains made by children in the HEART program versus children in comparison schools (Kaimal et al., 2022). Although there are always natural developmental gains as children grow throughout the year, the improvements were significantly greater in the children who had creative and expressive options. See figure 8.4

In addition to improved school outcomes for children, further studies at other sites such as in Mexico found that teachers and parents also found

Figure 8.4. Children in Malawi painting using bird feathers
(*Source*: Save the Children)

outlets and calmness by seeing their children manage their emotional lives better. Communicating, connecting, and sharing in the expressive activities helped families strengthen their understanding and compassion for each other and helped teachers connect better with their students and parents (Kaimal et al., 2021). An aspect of working with children is recognizing that they are inevitably connected to family and caregiver units as well. Family-based interventions can help address the dynamics that affect the well-being of the child by bringing in the whole unit. When arts-based psychosocial support such as the HEART intervention is offered to children, they invariably bring in family by sharing their work and translating lessons learned into improved communication and attunement with family members and caregivers.

Another area relevant to children is medical care. In pediatric settings, physical distress and psychological stress become intertwined in complicated ways, especially for developing children. In a recent study (Snyder et al., 2021), we asked health care providers what they thought interventions like art therapy offer to pediatric cancer patients, their families, and the setting itself. We found that they deeply valued the services because they offered verbal and nonverbal ways for children to communicate their distress. In particular, art and the art-making process, when decoupled from critical appraisal of artistic merit, allow for expression of socially taboo emotions such as shame, guilt, anger, and fear in visual metaphors. In the visual representation, the experience of the moment gets captured as a snapshot, with all the ambivalence and positive and negative emotions, and remains as a reinforced reminder of the voice of the person who created it. In this visual voice, others might find solace, connection, and a sense of belonging when they go through the vicissitudes of trauma related to medical care for a life-threatening illness. Figure 8.5 is an artwork created by a patient recovering from oncology treatment who experienced both isolation and support of caring friends and family.

Art therapists who have worked with pediatric cancer patients and families also recognize the value of art as a legacy and a means to help the children experience "normal" experiences like explorative play and creative expression that are absent in their "abnormal" experience of being hospitalized (Councill & Ramsey, 2019). Moreover, the art space becomes a welcoming environment for family members and siblings who might be feeling overwhelmed and neglected in a situation when one family member requires extensive care. The art space becomes a metaphorical equalizer where everyone's experiences are relevant whether or not they are the identified patient.

Figure 8.5. Artwork by a teenage pediatric oncology patient, reflecting on her recovery (feeling both shaken up and also sheltered by family and friends). Media: Watercolor and markers.

(*Source*: Kaimal, Councill, et al., 2018)

New digital media, telehealth-based creative expression, health, and well-being

Children in the 21st century are digital natives, and online options is ubiquitous. Even in low-income countries, cellphones have bypassed the need for telephonic infrastructure and are a means for education and communication. We are only beginning to understand the value of digital tools: what they provide as well as the limits of how they serve our needs. In examining the unique attributes of online therapeutic interactions (Kaimal et al., 2016c), we found that digital tools make it easier to both make and fix mistakes than traditional physical art media. With digital tools, things can be "undone" and "redone." Although there is not the satisfaction of having a tangible work (unless printed out in two or three dimensions), there is the experience of creating without limitations of space and flexibility in the product.

The COVID-19 pandemic also highlighted the need for options that are not sources of contagion. For example, art therapists had to consistently sanitize supplies, especially when working with vulnerable and immunocompromised patients. In the context of disease and infection risk, digital media are particularly valuable. The digital options are leading to innovations in art therapy practice, including new online-only interactive options and methods that will continue to provide media choices to satisfy our basic needs for self-expression.

My own children tried new tools and ways to manage the loneliness and isolation as well as the disembodied experiences of online education. My 10-year-old began writing a series of short novels and making YouTube video tutorials, all efforts to connect and create through baffling times. For many of the story series, she would write a chapter and then drop it to start another. Part of me wished she would persist and finish any one of them, but I backed off when I realized that her goal was not completion; rather, it was to relentlessly explore self-expression as a way perhaps to manage the unknown. These websites became her creative community. We all got creative with Zoom and Instagram filters as we began to get used to seeing ourselves on the screen all the time. It was a year of seeing ourselves in ways we never imagined possible. There was not necessarily a resolution of the expressive quest: It was one continuous creative search and a way to connect digitally and metaphorically with family and friends around mental process and anxieties.

We do need to keep learning what the digital tools provide and where they are limited. As children develop, there is no replacement for fully embodied multisensory in-person learning and experiences. Our challenge is to recognize the therapeutic and creative value of digital tools and programs and how they can best support our functioning in the real world as we have evolved to be.

Key takeaways

Children are natural artists and creators. Working with art is a natural developmental process that helps them make sense of the world, build skills, and develop a personal narrative and ability to imagine and problem-solve. Although some stress is essential to building resilience and strength, extremely adverse childhood experiences and trauma can challenge children's natural abilities to cope, including across their lifespan. Opportunities to express and integrate these experiences, including with a trained facilitating adult, can help children cope with the experiences. This experience helps them as adults as well, along with the families and peers in their lives. Verbal and nonverbal expression and visual and verbal metaphors help shed light on the unique inner lives of children, including feelings that they might be embarrassed and ashamed to share. Inability to express themselves leads to a risk that they will make maladaptive choices and will not feel as if they belong in their communities.

9

Navigating adversity in adulthood through creative self-expression

Go to the limits of your longing . . . let everything happen to you: beauty and terror. Just keep going. No feeling is final.

Rainer Maria Rilke

Science will get us out but art with get us through.

Mo Willems

Underneath the trauma is a healthy person who hasn't found expression in life.

Gabor Maté

Terrain map: In the last two chapters, I focused on human responses and experiences of art-making, including throughout childhood. Creative self-expression has a unique role in the times of adversity and challenges that we all inevitably face in life. The relationship between trauma and adversity across the lifespan can be mitigated with artistic practices. These might help distract us in the moment or help us make sense of the experiences over time. Stress and trauma might devastate us but can also transform us, as seen in recent research on creative and post-traumatic growth. Our creative capacity as humans has helped us cope, innovate, adapt, and even learn, especially on art, in times of difficulty and adversity. Although adulthood is less associated with neuroplasticity and ability to adapt, the potential for change is lifelong. In this chapter, I share specific examples, including from studies on the outcomes of visual self-expression among cancer patients and caregivers, as well as with military service members with post-traumatic stress disorder (PTSD).

Uncertainty, adversity, and creative expression

In Chapter 1, I introduced the idea of uncertainty and how our imagination helps us prepare for an unknown future. Manson (2013) refers to uncertainty

The Expressive Instinct. Girija Kaimal, Oxford University Press. © Oxford University Press 2023.
DOI: 10.1093/oso/9780197646229.003.0010

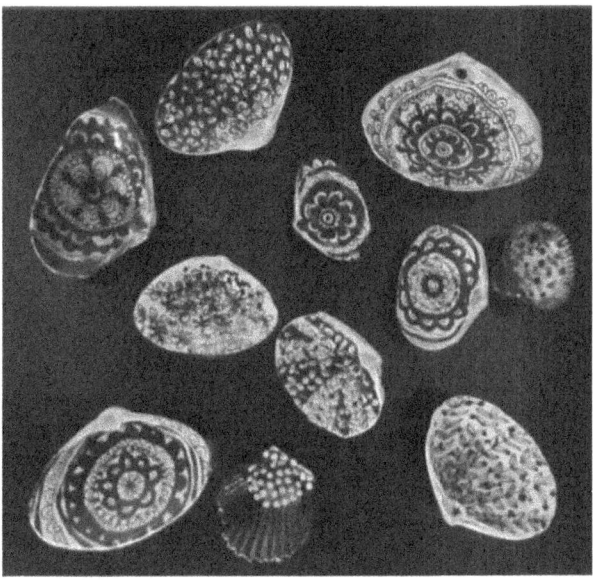

Figure 9.1. A shell's journey (Kaimal, 2021). Media: Atlantic Ocean clamshells, paint pens, and magnets.

as a positive aspect of human existence since it keeps us curious and eager to learn.

In the context of adversity, it is of note that we are wired biologically to experience, expect, and respond more to negative emotions than to positive ones. This is because evolutionarily, we were more likely to survive if we stayed alert and on the lookout for dangers and threats. Psychologists Rozin and Royzman (2001) refer to this as "'negativity bias" to reflect their finding that negative events are especially contagious and memorable. These biases toward negativity have served us well and helped us to survive by keeping us away from dangerous places, toxic individuals, poisonous foods, and so forth. In a twisted way, this is the power of negative thinking: If you imagine the worst outcome, you will eventually be happy because rarely do things turn out as badly as you imagined them to be. In fact, this is one application of imagination that has served over the millennia by keeping us alert to potential imagined dangers in our uncertain futures. Our responses to any threats are designed to optimize survival.

A recent study examined how we can change and respond to the existential uncertainty of an unknown future and how it can be better managed using improvisation techniques. Improvisation involves responding to events in the moment with an underlying evolving storyline. In this study, Felsman et al. (2020) found that training in improvisational theater improved divergent thinking and can boost positive affect and increase uncertainty tolerance relative to other social interactions. In two experiments ($n = 74$, $n = 131$), participants completed measures of divergent thinking, uncertainty tolerance, and affective well-being before and after engaging in 20 minutes of improvisation exercises or a matched control condition including social interactions. To enhance psychological health, improvisational theater training offers benefits without the negative stigma and difficulties in access surrounding other therapeutic interventions.

These results support the use of improvisation beyond the theater to improve social and personal interactions in a variety of settings. They suggest that the fact that improvisation is unscripted (versus scripted) seems to be important in explaining its benefit for increasing uncertainty tolerance and feeling good (as in Experiment 2). Although most human interactions do not involve literal scripts, the use of a script helps offset the novelty of a laboratory study by providing some predictable or highly structured grounding for the tasks. Thus, these findings highlight two key qualities of improvisational theater: pleasant, intentional encounters with unpredictability (likely causing the increases in uncertainty tolerance and affect in Experiment 2), and co-creative experiences with novelty (likely causing the increases in divergent thinking in Experiment 1) (Felsman et al., 2020). The idea is that improvisation serves as a practice for taking on uncertainties in real life that can then be expanded to all other art forms. Visual and performing arts all have an essential component of interaction with real and imagined audiences, responding to the times and experiences.

How does this manifest in our own lives? In response to threats we react in a range of ways. Beyond the well-known binaries of fight and flight there are also freeze, faint, and fawn (Bracha, 2004). Each response is apt, depending on the threat. Freezing, for example, might help to ensure survival in situations where action might lead to some kind of harm. Fawning might be apt when one encounters forces that are powerful or vindictive. Many threats in the modern world relate not only to physical harm but also to emotionally abusive, neglectful, aggressive, or demeaning human interactions, leading to the innate tendency to respond in ways that ensure we survive in the moment, even if we do not thrive in the long run.

These responses can also be so ingrained in us through chronically stressful or traumatic experiences that we continue to use them even though they have no adaptive purpose beyond a specific time—for example, freezing or fawning when the power differential may no longer exist in the human interaction, or saying "yes" (fawning) when one feels unable to say "no" because previous experiences of saying "no" resulted in deep hurt, rejection, or trauma.

Art-making, especially therapeutic or facilitated self-expression, helps us understand and choose adaptive new ways to respond rather than our unconscious and instinctual ways.

When we struggle, the facilitated support is our scaffold, our splint, our crutch to get us to be whole and self-reliant again. It might be our loved ones or it might be a therapist who pulls us back into the fold of belonging, normalizes our sense of being an outlier, and expands the scope of human experience. To be together and feel safe is defined as co-regulation. Given how deeply interconnected we are as human beings, our inner states radiate through us and impact others. By this I mean that every aspect of our presentation—our posture, our facial expressions, our movements, and even the chemicals we secrete through our skin—communicates how we feel about ourselves and others around us.

As we saw in previous chapters, these signals are almost unconscious responses interpreted simply as approach and avoidance and are then fine-tuned to make meaning and better interpret our responses. Consider the examples of neuroinflammation and the many ways in which the body perceives threats. As we saw in previous chapters, these threats can be minor, everyday challenges of daily living or they can be damaging and destructive to our bodies and our souls. These threats within the body are tackled through a complex series of strategies, including release of energy-boosting and immune-function-regulating cytokines. Together they strive to track the threats being perceived by the brain and the body. If the body responds to threats in this way as a strategic team, why can't we extend this idea to our responses and consider our stance as a warrior protecting and defending the only resources we can claim as our own: our physical health and our psychological well-being? These reactions might manifest in simply sitting together and communicating a feeling of peace and "enoughness": to bring others into our own states or offer our sense of calmness, peace, or support to those who need it. Sometimes we are able to give it; at other times we need to receive it. A colleague refers to this sense of "enoughness" using a Hebrew term, "da ay nu," which roughly translates as "this is enough" (personal communication, Dave Gussak, June 2021). When I sat with my daughter in stillness last year as she worked through her college applications and held her tears and anxieties, I was being that co-regulating presence for her. This year, as I am anxious about multiple new workplace roles and responsibilities (including the agony and ecstasy of writing this book), she is the co-regulating presence, sitting with me. In our efforts to manage our stressors and anxieties, we manifest our warrior selves as well as our warrior communities of support: those who make our tribes.

Adversity comes as a challenge and threat in our lives in both anticipated and unanticipated ways. Adversity can also manifest in the form of feeling a loss that comes from experiencing failure and rejection. All these might be anticipated, but they still feel challenging in the moment when we experience them. In each of these cases, we are confronted with a reality that feels like a wound in emotional, physical, or psychic ways. One aspect is to actively name it. Is it a failure or is it a rejection? Those are two different things. Failure implies an attempt that was unsuccessful for a variety of reasons (e.g., skills, ability, content). A rejection is externally driven and can be rejection of our professional or personal qualities. Either way, it is hard because it denies us a sense of belonging in a relationship or community that we desired to join.

An interesting fact I learned from the animal kingdom was that lions are successful in hunts only one in four times. It is a law of nature and the odds of the predator. Lions also spend a lot of time resting and doing nothing in order to prepare and recover from the stress of hunting. If wounded in the process, they spend time healing. I found this factoid very helpful: It is the law of nature to be unsuccessful most of the time. What does that mean for us? First, it slows us down. We might be upset, licking our metaphorical wounds. What if this slowdown is essential to naming the wound? Is it a bruise, a scrape, or a deep flesh wound that needs attention? What kind of care do we need to recover? Do we need just rest alone, or do we need interpersonal or professional support? In order to determine that, we have to be able to recognize and name our wounds. To recognize the wound is also to recognize its qualities: Is it a recurring wound or was this the first time? Is it acute or chronic—for example, is it a deep wound that has occurred from a one-time event or a chronic wound that does not seem to heal or is not allowed time, care, and resources to heal?

Physical and emotional pain and distress are not dissimilar. Sadness and heartbreak literally impair our memory and functioning (Verhallen et al., 2021). These emotional experiences function to slow us down and make us rest and conserve energy so we can heal and recover. The pain and struggle are real. In a study of emotional pain as a result of romantic rejection, Kross et al. (2011) found that the brain region associated with affective aspects of physical pain is activated for these participants. They focused specifically on an unwanted rejection that elicits a powerful reaction and sought to examine if the network of brain regions that support the affective but not the sensory components of physical pain underlie both experiences. Participants included those who had recently experienced an unwanted breakup; they were asked to view a photograph of their ex-partner as they thought about being rejected. Although it is painful even to imagine how difficult it must have been for the participants to engage in this study, the findings are very telling. Using functional magnetic resonance imaging (fMRI), the researchers found that the brain regions that support the sensory components of physical pain (secondary somatosensory cortex; dorsal posterior insula) became active in both social rejection and physical pain. This activation of the secondary somatosensory cortex and dorsal posterior insula was compared with physical pain from a database of over 500 published studies. Activation in these regions was highly diagnostic of physical pain, with positive predictive values of up to 88%. These results highlight the very real experiences of pain, distress, and hurt that we feel in our bodies and minds. A big part of healing is to be able to diagnose, recognize, and name what is painful for us. Only when we can identify our pain can we potentially come up with panaceas. Having strategies to cope with failure thus gives us some tools to deal with these expected challenges and uncertainties in our life (Figure 9.1).

Adversity that is traumatic

The preceding examples were ways to respond to everyday rejection and failure. Koban et al. (2021) highlighted the importance of the self in context, especially as mental health and physical health are interconnected such that somatic physiology and high-level cognition interact in ways that affect well-being. The brain systems include the ventromedial prefrontal cortex (PFC) and the default mode network (DMN). This interaction allows for predictive control over behavioral and peripheral physiology, including autonomic, neuroendocrine, and immune function. Disorders of mental and physical health associated with the ventromedial PFC and DMN could benefit from interventions focused on understanding and shaping mindsets and beliefs about self, illness, and treatment.

Sometimes we make choices and decisions that put our body and soul at a high likelihood of danger and distress. Other times, we might be hit by external disasters beyond our control or anticipation. Stress, trauma, and adversity force us to confront and sense of safety and demand of us a survival response. Some stress is beneficial to get us moving and not stagnate. It pushes us to flex our cognitive and physical muscles and problem-solve. But chronic stress can lead to trauma, which I think of as an extreme stress response that fundamentally threatens our lives. When we are faced with more difficult and challenging experiences, experiences that threaten our fundamental sense of safety and life, the impact of trauma can be debilitating and if not addressed overwhelming to manage. When we have experienced mental and physical distress, it also affects how we remember and respond to memories and our own life story narrative. In a study comparing autobiographical narratives in healthy versus depressed patients, the researchers found that patients with depression felt greater sadness when thinking of sad memories and less joy when reflecting on happy memories compared with healthy adults (Kim & Yoon, 2020). Clearly, there are limits to being able to handle everything ourselves. Using the home improvement analogy, for some repairs and updates we need to enlist professional help and support: These professionals provide a scaffolding that supports us as we try to rebuild and heal.

Although uncertainty affects all of us, levels are clearly disproportionate around the world, if we consider disease burdens, poverty, discrimination, and violence in society. Our responses might vary by context, but we draw on our creative capacities and narratives to activate our ability to survive and recover from adversity (Metzl, 2009). In a qualitative study comparing responses to natural disasters in Talca, Chile (earthquake), and New Orleans, Louisiana (hurricane), Bender et al. (2015) found that participants in both sites used creative expression and narratives as coping responses. The difference was that in Chile, the creative works were used as a source of income, while in New Orleans they were used as a form of emotional processing. In addition, the narratives that accompanied the art-making process in Chile were more future-oriented; in New Orleans the emphasis was more on spirituality and humor.

Wallace (2021), in an essay on the "morphability" of the self, further suggests that our selves are constantly changing and shaped by experiences, interactions, and relationships and as such might even be imagined as a network. In times of trauma, often the way the brain and body manage the overwhelming assault on selfhood is by dividing up the experience into discrete sensations and parts.

As I mentioned in Chapter 7, creative expression can be treated as akin to home improvement. There are things we can do competently for our health and well-being to sustain the functioning of this mind/body home. But when the distress and pain are beyond our capacity to self-heal, we do need to get support and help. Kearney (2007) further recognized that forming a narrative allows us to gain a sense of agency over the adverse experience, to be able to sequence it and make sense of it in a way that integrates it with our life stories. As seen repeatedly in this book and in the reported studies, artistic expression helps us find this narrative; it gives us words for unnamed sensory experiences; it allows us to organize and process what is not part of normal or typical life experiences. Narrative is thus the accompanist. However, when we struggle to express ourselves in narrative, a facilitating person like a psychotherapist can help support, sublimate, and move forward us from a survival mode to one that helps us thrive.

Creative thinking, or entering the realms of uniqueness and novelty, runs the legitimate risk of being perceived as abnormal and outside the traditional norms of society. Acar and Runco (2012) explored this question of the connection between psychoticism and creativity. In their meta-analysis of 32 studies (representing 6,771 participants), the authors found that psychoticism was associated with measures of uniqueness that were not always the same as creativity but offered conceptual understanding of the thin line that can distinguish original thinking from mental illness. Kusters (2020) also warned against an overemphasis on language and linguistics as a way to understand the human condition as a unique development of the 20th century and invites us to consider the many ways in which we can know of and accept the human condition, including our deep interconnectedness with each other.

What makes art therapy therapeutic in times of distress?

The therapeutic power of creative expression in an art therapy session lies in the multidimensionality of the arts: the nonlinearity and timelessness that allow the process to hold several metaphors, associations, and meaning concurrently. This creative expression and the unlocking of the imagination lead to a sense of agency that might previously not have been available to a patient/client. Each condition or cluster of symptoms might result in different mechanisms and pathways of change. These mechanisms and pathways of change vary by individual, by the clinical needs, and by the context of care. For example, in the case of an individual struggling with feelings of incompetence and inefficacy, the process of making art involves solving problems and serves as a trial run for practicing the ability to gain mastery. For individuals who have experienced trauma, verbal expression is often not an option (van der Kolk et al., 1996; Walker et al., 2016) since the verbal expressive part of the brain tends to be impaired (Rauch et al., 1997). Thus, being able to say the unsayable becomes really critical in such situations. For elderly individuals for whom social isolation might be an issue, the emphasis might be on social integration and expression through the creative and expressive arts therapies (Dunphy et al., 2019). Similarly, the art therapy session could be the therapeutic element for an individual struggling with the ability to manage and contain emotional reactions and to effectively channel these struggles through sublimating the emotions in the artwork instead of harming self or others.

A question that is often asked of art therapists is which patients/clients are best served by the unique contributions of art therapy. The evidence from clinical practice indicates that art therapy is particularly suited for patients who have experienced trauma, identity struggles, physical and psychological stressors, and developmental challenges. Trauma can be overwhelming, which affects how it is integrated into long-term memory and in turn into the personal life story narrative. For individuals who struggle to articulate their lived experiences, challenges, and struggles, art therapy can help initiate expression that leads to reflection, articulation, and a better understanding of their experiences, which allows them to better integrate their experiences into a life narrative that feels empowering and manageable. In working with pediatric oncology patients, Councill (2015) argued that art therapy promotes self-discovery and emotional and sensory integration; it thus allows young people a safe arena in which to practice skills that can help them confront and transcend life's challenges.

In my own clinical interactions, I remember a young woman who started the session feeling a deep sense of loss of hope and covered the page in black ink. She viewed the image for a while and then added cherry blossoms that were reminiscent of the time of the year. Through engaging in an authentic representation of her emotional state at the start of the session, she was also able to create a layer of new imagery that brought her to the physical present, contrasting the pink and white of the blossoms with the underlying darkness. Art therapy helps contain and externalize positive and negative emotions, thereby offering patients/clients an alternative visual perspective of their condition: breaking the cycle of rumination and providing hope for a possibly fulfilling future.

Over the past several decades, art therapists have gone on to work with a range of populations, including those facing developmental challenges and impacts of adverse events (Tripp, as cited in King, 2016), in part due to the value of creative, symbolic communication in the reconsolidation of traumatic memories and emotional regulation. Although art therapy is increasingly well known and established as a clinical services profession, research in the field is needed to better understand the mechanisms of change and how art therapy assessments and interventions impact patient/client outcomes.

If seen from the intersection of evolutionary neurobiology and biopsychosocial-spiritual aspects of human development, art therapy takes into account the human instinct for survival and the capacity to develop life story narratives. As seen in Chapter 7, I refer to this framework as Adaptive

Response Theory (ART) (Kaimal, 2019). It is relevant to individual and group contexts, with the point being that when we create in a safe and facilitative environment with others, we practice imagination, self-expression, problem-solving, playfulness, joy, and the safety of social belonging. Such a setting becomes then a fertile ground to grow resilience and new ways of being, be-cause it normalizes learning from vulnerability and mistakes.

Art therapy for patients and caregivers in medical settings

Many of my studies begin with healthy adults and then extend to clin-ical populations. Given our initial promising findings with adults and with funding from the National Endowment for the Arts Research Labs program, we were able to examine if patients and caregivers facing chronic stress re-lated to cancer treatment would benefit from art therapy. We set up the study in collaboration with the radiation oncology unit of a large urban hospital and offered patients and caregivers individual sessions of coloring or free art-making with an art therapist. The sessions were set up to be about 45 minutes long; participants completed several standardized measures of psychological functioning before and after the session. We found that any opportunity for creative self-expression was beneficial, and participants felt more positive, less stressed, less anxious, and more self-confident. Caregivers in particular felt less burnout in their work. See Figures 9.2 and 9.3.

There can also be visible changes in physical symptoms through a facili-tated art-making session. A patient came in recently for a session of art therapy as part of one of our research studies. He had had surgery for a brain tumor that left him with limited control of his dominant hand. He would hold his right hand with his left hand at the beginning of the session to guide it. In his case, art therapy was a form of relaxation and social reconnection. Once he felt comfortable, relaxed, and safe, he also gained a sense of mastery and self-efficacy. At the end of the session, he was able to use his right hand without support and to write freely. I asked him if he noticed this change and why he thought it had occurred. His response was that he felt less anxious, he felt good, and he was relaxed at the end of the session; all of these factors helped him with his ability to write and to use his right hand. We could argue that this was the result of feeling comfortable in the session, which could occur in any therapeutic context. However, given that art therapy involves verbal interac-tion and some form of "making," we might conjecture that multiple activities, processes, outcomes, and systems are at play in a session. The outcomes of

Figure 9.2. Artwork by a patient undergoing radiation treatment depicting her visualization of her tumor breaking up
(*Source*: Kaimal et al., 2019)

Figure 9.3. Artwork by a patient undergoing cancer treatment and his effort to "hold on" to his world
(*Source*: Kaimal et al., 2019)

individual sessions might be focused on intrapersonal (within the individual) change, whereas the outcomes in group art therapy sessions might result in more interpersonal (group-level) transformations. In my workshops and presentations, I find often that group art-making breaks through the proverbial ice quickly and catalyzes the activation of interpersonal interactions and socialization. The art product offers an externalized object for discussion and mutual engagement as well as a rich resource for learning about each of the group members.

Building on the idea that art-making and art therapy help us express and process the parts of our experiences for which we might not yet have words, in cancer care (in particular the anxiety, uncertainty, and related distress around recurrence of the illness), processing emotions and existential concerns becomes especially important for quality of life after medical treatment. Czamanski-Cohen et al. (2019) propose that emotional awareness and acceptance are key. Survivorship is the stage of treatment in cancer care that occurs after active medical care has ceased and the patient is either in remission or awaiting follow-up care. During those stages there is anxiety and fear about the return of cancer, and patients experience a range of emotions related to the trauma of treatment and existential questions related to what can be a terminal illness. In examining the impact of an 8-week intervention among patients with breast cancer in the survivorship (post-treatment) stage compared with sham sessions without a therapist, the facilitated sessions resulted in significantly improved emotional processing, which in turn was associated with better health outcomes (Czamanski-Cohen et al., 2019).

It is not just patients who can benefit; caregivers are often a neglected group since they experience both the physical and emotional burnout of caregiving with minimal recognition of their own needs. In a study comparing art-making and narrative expression among caregivers of patients in palliative care (Kaimal et al., 2020b), we found that collage helped caregivers identify both the validating and the challenging parts of caregiving. Although there were no statistically significant differences, and both narrative sessions and art-making resulted in positive outcomes, making a visual often helped caregivers to contain the complex, contradictory, and at times ambivalent feelings associated with the demands of the role.

Many aspects of physical and psychological functioning can be influenced using facilitated creative visual self-expression as a doorway. In assessing the perception of visual art, Lauring et al. (2019) found that patients with Parkinson's disease reported greater emotionality when appraising art, possibly related to the role of dopamine release unique to the symptoms of the disease as well as activation of reward pathways. In another study that examined the impact of art therapy on the visual acuity and functioning of patients with Parkinson's disease, Cucca et al. (2021) found that engaging in a 20-week art therapy intervention improved the patients' visual perception and thus their ability to navigate and move safely through physical spaces. Compared with age-matched controls, fMRI tracking indicated that those who received the art therapy intervention had improved functional connectivity between the attentional and executive networks of the brain as well as in the primary visual cortex.

Art therapy interventions also have demonstrated positive outcomes for depression. In a randomized controlled trial, Nan and Ho (2017) performed a 6-week intervention examining the impact of clay-based art therapy versus arts only. The results indicated that on measures of well-being and on the ability to express oneself, the art therapy group showed significantly better outcomes compared with the arts-only control group.

Art therapy for traumatic brain injury and PTSD in the military

One of the origins of art therapy as a profession was through serving military service members, especially through the two world wars, who had what was then referred to as "shell shock" (today known as PTSD). It is well established that trauma affects the speech centers of the brain, which makes traditional talking therapies less than ideal as a form of therapy. In fact, Steenkamp et al. (2020) found that popular verbal psychotherapies such as cognitive-behavioral therapy and cognitive-processing therapy might not be adequate for some populations. Thus, nonverbal forms of therapy like art therapy are ideally suited to address the challenging symptoms of psychosocial functioning following trauma. In a recent systematic review of 20 papers on art therapy and PTSD, Schnitzer et al. (2021) found that art therapy helped with reducing the symptoms, processing traumatic memories, fostering a holistic view of self, and increasing well-being, accompanied by a positive view of self. In particular, the authors asserted the valuable contributions of art therapy to dealing with symptoms of avoidance and feelings of guilt and shame, which are not readily addressed in talking therapies.

For clients who might struggle to understand and share their psychosocial experiences, the use of metaphors in the visual arts helps provide distance and perspective to talk about their experience. Through recent research funding support from Creative Forces (National Endowment for the Arts), my colleagues and I have found that art-making can help address identity issues emerging from traumatic brain injury ("Who am I now after this debilitating injury?"), help with experiencing positive emotions ("I felt good after a long time creating something with my hands"), and help with being able to say the unsayable ("I am able to share things in drawings and metaphors that let me eventually start to express and communicate what I have struggled to share previously"). These forms of expression allow for increased eventual verbalization and authentic communication.

Art therapy for military service members has been found to help reduce self-imposed barriers around self-expression and what is good or bad art and instead focus on what we want to share and what is needed to live a fulfilling life. In allowing for self-expression of unsayable, shameful, taboo topics through the visual form of art, it allows doorways to open up in underlying challenges. Jones (2016) in particular refers to these struggles as disenfranchised grief: grief that has not been allowed expression. Over time, it reveals that underlying a trauma is a deep sense of grief and loss. Given the opportunity to begin to address inner struggles through visual metaphors that provide distance and perspective, service members slowly begin to be able to communicate more openly and with more words, even aspects of their experience that they did not previously have words for (Kaimal et al., 2019). In fact, in addition to being more able to name their emotional experiences, they are literally able to use more words to express themselves. The art-making in the art therapy sessions helps forge a pathway back from the isolation and alienation that many service members feel post-deployment to a sense of belonging and agency.

In our studies we have also found the actual visual imagery to be indicative of sources of resilience or risk. For example, fragmented imagery (cut-up, disintegrated, or broken images) tended to be associated more with psychological risk compared with integrated images (like a metaphor or symbol of group belonging, like to a military unit or region), which were associated with indicators of improved psychological health. Being able to express challenges visually was associated with later well-being, suggesting that the act of naming and identifying ongoing challenges put the service member on a pathway to adaptive functioning later (Berberian et al., 2019; Kaimal et al., 2019; Kaimal, Walker et al., 2018; Landless et al., 2018). See Figures 9.4 and 9.5.

We further explored what art provides that speech does not in a study focused on trying to better understand and represent the experiences of a neglected veteran population, namely those with Gulf War illness. In addition to interviews, we asked the veterans to create collages using magazine cutouts on canvases (Malhotra et al., 2021). Collage elicitation informed by art therapy

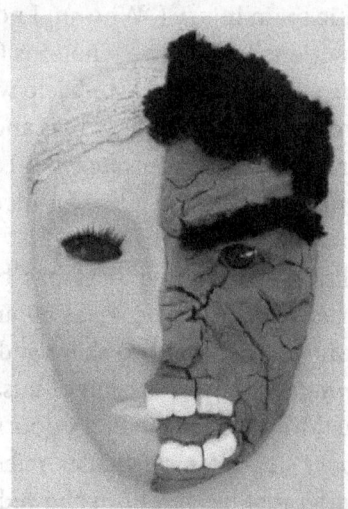

Figure 9.4. Mask made by a service member representing two sides of himself (*Source*: Kaimal, Walker, et al., 2018b)

Figure 9.5. Artwork created by a service member in memory of a comrade killed in action. The artwork made during art therapy group became a way to pay respect and process grief and loss.
(*Source*: Jones et al., 2017)

was used as a data-gathering approach with 14 veterans to understand their Gulf War illness experience as part of a larger overall qualitative research study. As they created these images, they shared aspects that might not have been captured in interview narratives alone. The interviews were often pages long and full of chronological details. The collages, however, offered something different: an additional dimension to their expressed experiences. In these collages they shared what Gulf War illness meant for them. Some summarized the entire experience in one visual image: a synthesis of the range of psychological and biological symptoms. Others found and shared something new in the visuals that the words had not captured. Finally, some veterans used the visual to highlight the most salient aspects of the illness and how it had impacted their lives.

The visual expression allowed them to represent their condition in a way that was different and complementary to the verbal. Collage in particular is a simple technique and a way to express oneself, allowing for spontaneity, metaphorical thinking, uncovering lived experiences, and new affective responses. Just as our experience of life is multisensory and multimodal, this method became a way to elicit and record lived experiences in ways that were not limited by words alone. Even though the session was not art therapy, the methods were derived from art therapy practice. We trained the local data collector in ways to collect data that are sensitive to and responsive to veterans while offering ongoing support for issues that might emerge.

Post-traumatic growth

I wrote my dissertation on the topic of how children experience depression in their parents (Kaimal & Beardslee, 2015, 2018). It was inspired by family stories of loss, depression, and trauma that led to generational patterns of physiological, psychosomatic psychological ill health. By examining how children spoke about it, I discovered a framework. The children either (a) focused on themselves (usually at younger ages) such that they only recognized how parental depression impacted them, usually by either denying any impact or identifying negative impact, (b) recognized that depression affected both themselves and their parents, with sometimes conflicting thoughts on the impact, or (c) recognized how depression was an illness that affected their parents and viewed it with acceptance and compassion. In each of these ways of experiencing, they found a way to cope, but how they framed it and integrated it into their lives differed. When they viewed it only from their own point of view, they were unable and/or unwilling to see it as an illness and tended to make the whole experience monolithic. With the second and third perspectives, there was a deeper understanding of how the illness can affect the individual's functioning and their families. They were able to better inter-twine the collective and the individual stories, taking perspective, and seeing things from multiple points of view. Some of this is a natural part of growing up, and it is also facilitated by making sense of the experience with a therapist who helps guide alternative perspectives and points of view.

One of the compelling aspects of human functioning is our capacity to cope and respond to the most adverse of situations. The concept of post-traumatic growth (PTG), although widely known throughout history, was coined as a construct by Tedeschi and Calhoun (1996). Unlike short-term trauma treatments that might offer temporary or no sustained change or relief from symptoms, PTG reflects moving past the trauma into a new phase and way of life by building on existing and newly identified strengths. Tedeschi and Calhoun (1996) defined it as being different from resilience. Resilience is about being able to survive adversity and bounce back to what you were be-fore; PTG is about being transformed by the adverse experience into a ver-sion of yourself that is different and operates at a different level than before. It is a recognition of our inherent adaptability, strengths, and assets as human beings.

The transformations might be spiritual, personal physical strengths, new appreciation for life, new purpose, and new focus and possibilities, none of which would have been conceivable prior to the traumatic experi-ence. It is about having new perspectives, self-awareness, and interpersonal awareness; understanding and managing triggers; and holding a compas-sionate stance toward self and others. The self is shaped and defined by the experiences that could have and maybe did lead to post-traumatic stress but also led to transformation and growth. PTG is not to be confused with "toxic positivity," which forces platitudes and simplistic tropes, nor is it about minimizing grief and loss. PTG is instead about self-led awareness and reconciliation from an intensely painful period in one's life. It is very likely that there are predisposing traits that affect our capacity for PTG. In survivors of Hurricane Katrina, Dunn et al. (2014) found that variants in the gene *RGS2* significantly interacted with levels of exposure to the hurricane to predict PTG. *RGS2* is linked to fear-related disorders, such as PTSD, panic disorder, and anxiety. However, the authors proposed cau-tion in attributing all PTG to genetics, because so much of our adult self is defined by developmental experiences and not necessarily by genetic predispositions alone.

Relatedly, Taleb (2014) coined the term "antifragility," meaning the capacity to be fortified rather than defeated by adversity. Fragility is the likelihood of breaking easily. He refers to resilience as robustness of the ability to bounce back to the way things were before the stressor, thereby being able to retain one's state prior to the distressing events. He defines antifragility as the ability to be strengthened by adversity, not just the ability to resist challenges and difficulties. For example, when plants and trees encounter wind, they learn to bend and twist with the wind, which in turn helps them grow stronger at points that need to be stronger (such as the trunk) and flexible (at the crown), not just to survive the storm. A body-based analogy is that of changes in muscles as a result of workouts. Muscles break down every time we engage in physical exercise, but the workout makes them stronger for the future and almost transformed by the experience. Similarly, the idea of hormesis is that a small amount of a poison or harmful substance or experience helps build immunity to larger doses (Taleb, 2014, p. 37). This is also the idea underlying "eustress," which involves small doses of challenges that strengthen us, versus distress, which involves challenges that are painful and debilitating (Selye, 1951).

To overcome hardship and challenges is to gain a sense of mastery. It is a mastery that is different from reading about or seeing other people's experiences. It is the lived and embodied confidence of knowing that, having braved a storm and made it through, we might be stronger for it. Of course, as seen in the preceding case examples of military PTSD, people are not always transformed in positive ways after intense trauma. We might, however, find solace in a seed of hope within us in the larger context of human experiences that nothing is new and nothing we struggle or suffer through is something others have not been through in the past. As seen in Chapter 4, the arts hold these memories for us of struggles, joys, and extremes of human experiences, past and present.

In a recent conversation, a friend and I spoke about the connections between the humanities and medicine. I said, "Isn't hope the perfect manifestation of neuroplasticity?" She agreed, and the more we talked about it the more I realized the interconnectedness of all aspects of our functioning. Through the humane idea of hope, we connect back to the material and fundamental elements of the biology of our body. The idea that the brain and our beings are open and receptive to change is a fundamental aspect of our coping. It is how we function each day through uncertainties and unexpected developments in our lives. Ironically, the things we worry about are probably not the things we *should* be worrying about.

We can move through difficult parts of ourselves by first acknowledging them and then drawing on our ability to have connectedness, creativity, courage, and clarity. To see our challenges and difficulties as parts of ourselves that need healing and compassion, we can move forward with our most whole selves. In viewing our responses as adaptations, the parts that are difficult are often those we developed to cope with a challenge at one time but have since lost their purpose and now exist in a context in which they are not needed anymore. However, because they were developed to serve a survival role, they are not easily extinguished. I think often of PTSD symptoms or their triggers as being these parts: They are trying to protect and serve us instinctively but are not necessarily helpful anymore because the trauma that birthed these responses no longer exists.

Interestingly, the idea of PTG can also be related to humor (Boerner et al., 2017). Both crying and laughter release endorphins, our body's natural painkiller. We know that the DMN is implicated in creativity and that the temporal association regions are involved in the processing of humor. In a study looking at the differences in cortical activity, the researchers designed a study to compare the MRI scans of professional comedians ($n = 12$), amateur comedians ($n = 9$), and non-comedians ($n = 17$), focusing on these particular regions of interest. All participants underwent MRI scans that used surface-based morphometry to measure cortical surface area and cortical thickness (Brawer & Amir, 2021). The more professional the comedian, the greater was the stretching of the cortical area, indicating the ability to make remote connections across brain regions and ideas. If we think about humor as associating unconnected things, this creativity can perhaps be seen as a form of adaptive creative coping.

Kashdan and Biswas (2014) write about the unseen value of so-called negative emotions. For example, they argue that emotions and attitudes that are typically considered dark or negative have potential upsides. For example, narcissism is typically associated with selfishness and manipulation. The authors suggest that we reframe narcissism and view it as a form of self-worth and self-love gone too far: that at its core it is about loving and valuing oneself. Similarly, they refer to depression and anger as valid states that allow us to take action or conserve resources; both are relevant tools in the arsenal of options. I often think of related difficult emotions, what they embed, and how they can be useful for us. They exist to help us survive, and we can change them to help us thrive. For example, what if we reimagined the power of under-rated mental states: states that if harnessed can be a source of new ways of being, coping, and creating? These are some of my favorite examples distilled down to fun equations that I once squeezed into a tweet:

Boredom = Health + safety + time

Indifference = Fewer distractions

Spite = Energy + something to prove

Procrastination = Distilled + fully baked ideas

Sad mood = Energy conservation + Focus

Anger = Action

Guilt = Implicit power.

These emotions remind me how fungible and flexible our thinking can be and how much can be reframed over time by shifting our perspective. These are not platitudes; rather, these are ways to conceptualize possible outcomes of experiences beyond survival alone.

Creative self-expression helps us capture and contain a range of often contradictory and confusing emotions that form the landscape of human experience. In particular, creative practices help us see the challenges of recognizing and expressing negative emotions while also experiencing concurrent affirming and positive mental states. As seen in this chapter, this is immensely valuable in helping us successfully weather times of stress, adversity, and trauma. We might be able to engage in these practices by ourselves, but in the absence of these resources, trained professionals can help us tap into these sources of creative strength within us.

Key takeaways

In this chapter, I highlighted how creative self-expression helps us manage, respond to, and process chronic stressors, adversity, and trauma. In cases of extreme threats to our well-being and life itself as we know it, regaining our sense of self and feeling healed and safe again in the world often needs the support of others such as therapists. In ancient times, it was indigenous healers who used natural medicine, but in modern times, it manifests in a range of helping professions. Art therapy practice, the main focus of this chapter, presents as a hope of neuroplasticity to negotiate and change as needed. Humans are essentially expecting challenges and are prepared at the brain level to change as needed and adapt. We might need help when we are debilitated by life-threatening traumas, but we can help each other find our way back to being and living the lives that we seek.

PART IV

PREPAREDNESS

Implications for current and future work in arts, health, and well-being

I shared in Part I some of the landscape of historical and theoretical foundations of arts, creative self-expression, health, and well-being. Part II covered some of the physiological and psychological processes and outcomes of creative visual self-expression, and Part III included examples of how creative expression has a valuable role in mitigating the distress surrounding adversity.

So you might well ask at this point, "What can I do with all this, and what does it mean for my present and future?" To be prepared is to be positioned to better respond to uncertainties and challenges. To integrate creative practices into our lives is to be a prepared creator/warrior, unafraid to enter the fray. When we feel equipped with biopsychosocial coping tools and proficient in their applications, we are better able to respond to the adversities that will inevitably come our way. To be able to express ourselves becomes a foundation for anticipating, responding to, and being well prepared to face life's challenges and adversities, just like a warrior might train their body to perform optimally including but not only for combat. As empowered responders and creators, we can learn and transform the our life experiences, interactions, and actions.

In this last section, I will share how to translate all this research into practice and outline what remains to be done in terms of further learning. Chapter 10 includes strategies for making space and time and setting intentions for engaging in creative practices that can promote health and well-being. Chapter 11 includes reflections on innovations and potential new areas for creative expression and practice.

The way we respond to challenges can range from using distraction to cope in the moment, to problem-solving, to practicing making adaptive changes in our everyday lives. As seen in previous chapters, an emerging evidence base suggests that arts practices and creative arts therapies can help improve our quality of life and address mental health challenges at the individual and community levels. The metaphorical quality of the arts helps us share and communicate the complexity and range of human experiences. As new digital tools and technologies become available, we are increasingly able to transcend some of the expressive limitations and enable humans to connect across space and time.

10

The prepared warrior

Creative expression, health, and well-being in modern society

> The object of art is not to make salable pictures. It is to save your-self . . . to make yourself alive. Most people remain all of their lives in a stupor. The point of being an artist in that you may live.
>
> **Sherwood Anderson**

> It takes tremendous energy to push down the pain of trauma. To heal to channel that energy elsewhere into compassion.
>
> **Gabor Maté**

Terrain map: In this chapter, I provide an overview of how we might integrate the art and science of creative well-being into everyday life. I will discuss how we can manage our well-being and tackle the future, including the uncertainties, adversities, and challenges that are bound to come our way as part of life. Self-expression and creativity is in our hands, both literally and metaphorically. As we emerge from the pandemic and its impacts, being reflective and responsive to stress and adversity will be essential. Akin to any other skill, creative well-being practices can also be learned. I will share my views on personalized practices, including reflective and contemplative approaches and the role of creative expression in biopsychosocial/sexual/spiritual well-being.

Harnessing the power of creative expression, health, and well-being into our lives

During the summer of the pandemic, one of the few places we could safely visit was the ocean. In 2020, while walking on the beach, we encountered a most unexpected sight: a stranded monarch butterfly (Figure 10.1). My daughter warned me not to touch it because my touch would adversely affect the butterfly and also because it contained a poison that was dangerous

The Expressive Instinct. Girija Kaimal, Oxford University Press. © Oxford University Press 2023.
DOI: 10.1093/oso/9780197646229.003.0011

Figure 10.1. August 2020: Monarch on the beach

for its predators, though not for humans. Regardless, this magical and unexpected sight encouraged us to push out the sand from under the butterfly. To our surprise it was alive and able to move up to a drier part of the beach a few feet away. We hope it was lucky enough to dry out and to be released from the sand. As I think of the butterfly, I think of this also as a year of incubation—a year during which we were forced to stay in and challenge ourselves to do better and grow out of our cocoons, to see what we could be if we allowed ourselves to keep pushing at that cocoon and strengthen our wings to eventually fly out as butterflies. We had to help each other without touching each other, which seemed especially appropriate for the year of social distancing.

So what does all this mean for us in modern life and for our future? The year 2020 was a time of global shifts. A nationwide survey conducted by the Kaiser Family Foundation (2021) found that the pandemic increased anxiety, depression, and substance use among U.S. adults, with the greatest increases among youth aged 18 to 24 years. The world experienced the slowdown and destruction of many small businesses and service industry occupations as a result of COVID, as well as the distress that comes from discrimination and social disparities.

The pandemic brought the world to a standstill but also connected us all through the shared experiences. This intense time felt like a year of transformative growth and change. According to Grant (2021), what we missed in the year of the pandemic was the sense of collective joy and sense of rapture we typically feel in a shared experience with others. Now more than ever, we need the active engagement of what Richards (2007) referred to as everyday creativity: the simple choices and acts that advance our survival and well-being.

In a study examining this very idea of creative engagement during COVID-19, Tang et al. (2021) found that there were interesting similarities and differences between responses from a sample ($N = 1,420$) of adult employees in China, Germany, and the United States. Across the sample, COVID-19 was associated with creative engagement, and those who reported creative growth also reported the most positive emotions and well-being. Interestingly, the outcomes of creative engagement well-being were more pronounced for the study participants from China than from other places considered more individualistic, such as the United States and Germany. The authors posit that the collectivist orientation potentially activated the desire for social connections through creative means.

Social isolation such as that precipitated by COVID has its own challenges. A recent study by Tomova et al. (2020) found that the way we crave food is similar to the way we crave social interaction: The part of the brain that modulates hunger is the same as the one that processes the sense of loneliness. Chronic social isolation and loneliness can diminish physical and mental health. The study enrolled 40 healthy adults and had them engage in 10 hours of social isolation one day and 10 hours of fasting another day. At the end of each day, participants underwent functional magnetic resonance imaging (fMRI) while doing a cue-induced task to measure their neural responses to social cues and food cues. The social cues were color images showing groups of people as they met, talked, laughed, and smiled. The food cues were images of highly palatable foods. Both sets of cues were paired with verbal descriptions and were individually tailored to the participants' preferred foods and modes of social interaction. After isolation, the participants reported decreased happiness and increased social craving, loneliness, discomfort, and dislike of isolation. After fasting, participants reported decreased happiness and increased food craving, hunger, discomfort, and dislike of fasting. The researchers found that social craving after isolation was more variable across participants than food craving after fasting. Analysis of the fMRIs showed that food craving and social craving evoked both shared and unshared neural responses. A small structure in the midbrain called the substantia nigra pars compacta and the ventral tegmental area (SN/VTA) responded to both food cues after fasting and social cues after isolation. The SN/VTA consists mostly of dopaminergic neurons, which are nerve cells that create the brain chemical dopamine. SN/VTA activity was higher in people who self-reported greater levels of wanting either food or social interaction after the 10 hours of deprivation. In other parts of the brain, including the striatal and cortical regions, neural responses differed between craving food and craving social interaction.

Both fasting and social isolation narrowed and focused the brain's motivational response to the specific type of deprivation. The main takeaway was that positive social interactions are indeed a basic human need and acute loneliness is an unpleasant state that motivates people to repair what is lacking, similar to hunger.

In this year of forced separation of human beings, in-person gatherings were replaced by online meet-ups. The challenge during COVID-19 and in general with so many disembodied online interactions is the potential for misunderstandings and miscommunications. Despite our best intentions, when words are shared without context and nonverbal signals like facial expressions and body language, we are setting ourselves up for conflict and misunderstanding. Our emotions might feel hardwired, but the more we process and make sense of them, the more we can manage them. In fact, positive emotions can be nurtured in systematic ways and are not a monolith but rather a range of states, including awe, pride, nurturant love, nostalgia, flow, and contentment.

At the beginning of the pandemic, I was invited to do lectures and webinars on how to cope with the unprecedented changes in our lives. I highlighted the need for everyday creative expression in any form: art, music, dance, culinary arts, gardening, whatever gets you inspired and able to "make." I asked attendees how things would change if we allowed ourselves a space and time to fully be ourselves and to accept ourselves. What would that look like? Could we name that for ourselves through the tools available to us? And if we needed help, would we know how to seek it out? In my clinical work and research I always say this:

> There is no right or wrong in this space. I will not be judging the artwork, and I would encourage you also not to do that, and really use the process of self-expression to learn about yourself and enjoy that experience. Enjoy the creative experience, and don't judge the quality of the artwork in any way. Your art and your reflections reflect back to you and connect your story with others who you share it with.

I say these lines to ensure psychological safety and to ensure that the space I provide invites a sense of belonging and normalization of our the creative expressive capacity.

How did I practice some of what I preached? I spent a good part of the year learning to simultaneously manage my work, mentor my students, support my research team, and nurture my children and family, while also playing a leadership role in my professional association. All these pieces are really hard when regular routines are disrupted. As the norm became to stay at home for the year, I had to figure out ways to hold a sense of safety and normalcy for myself and for those I care about in my personal and professional life. I did this by recognizing slowly that I needed a space of my own that included physical solitude in terms of time to think, write, and do the intellectual work that fulfills me. I had to find pockets of space and time that gave me uninterrupted creative and expressive opportunities. In addition, I had to help support these spaces for my children and my students. So I retained regular weekly meetings and scheduled times with my research laboratory team, and they had the option to visit me or to email me any other time. We decided to go for a few big grant proposals, but other than that, most of our time was spent writing and doing any research we could do without human contact. This also meant that I pushed my students and laboratory team to take breaks and work from wherever they were and sent them small care packages as they struggled, especially those who lived alone, to help manage their moods and their ability to function without the reassurance of human company.

I realized that I was being more compassionate than usual, and then I noticed that they were working hard regardless of the challenges. I think my compassion meter just went up for the future with or without COVID. There is no reason to be difficult or unkind. People do their best work when we hold them with love and challenge them to push themselves. It is hard to give critical feedback online, which meant that I had to learn to do it carefully and productively and use every skill I had in my facial expression toolkit to communicate effectively. Smiles, emojis, and time to talk all help with this, as do affirmations and recognition of effort and hard work, even if the end results might not always be what we seek. I was trying to be available without burdening everyone with too much two-dimensional interaction on Zoom. I am grateful for all of them and how they rallied together to make our work happen despite all the challenges.

Tackling challenges of the unknown

What are ways to tackle challenges of the unknown: the certainty of uncertainty? One way to tackle uncertainly is to have a sense of purpose. The German philosopher Nietzsche referred to this as the human ability to be able to tolerate anything if we know why. When we have a sense of purpose, we know what we are living for every day. It might be having a specific job in a community or an identity that serves as a valued role. Purpose need not be grand; it can be as simple as caring for dependents, working at a fulfilling job, volunteering, or doing any activity that helps us feel like our contributions make a difference in the world (Gitlin, 2017). Our purpose might change over time, but having a purpose can help reduce the anxieties that come from not knowing what our actions need to be every day. Purpose plants a seed of motivation and action within us that gives us a compass, so to speak, to deal with the daily unknowns as best we can. It gives us focus and helps direct our energies toward this purpose. How do we, then, find and actualize purpose? How can purpose lead us to creative and effective action? Can it be led by experiences and imagination? Sometimes our purpose might be straightforward and handed to us (e.g., parenting), but at other times we might struggle to find it or we might need to words toward it. It does not help us determine the best ways to achieve it. To learn to recognize and accept these changes as natural parts of our being is essential to our well-being.

To be able to name what we are experiencing, both with words and images, goes a long way toward self-awareness. When I have a difficult day, I allow myself to rest. I also try to take care of myself with things I know will help me feel better: a walk, songs, good food, a cup of chai brewed with fresh ginger, and the right to be cozy and quiet in my corner of the world. I might write to a friend, doodle, talk with family, or watch a show. Sometimes I do nothing and simply allow all sensations to run their course through my mind and body. All of these items make up my checklist of healing solutions. I also read, see, and listen to others' works on what I might be struggling with to better understand the cause of the distress and why I am bothered. This step in turn prepares me to face this challenge better in the future. I am often reminded that there are evolutionary reasons for a low mood: to slow action and make us reflect. Without that slowing and processing, there is no chance to respond differently.

With respect to coping, a recent Netflix show that I saw comes to mind. It was about the international war crimes trial that occurred in the 1940s to address the war crimes of Japan, akin to the similar tribunal that occurred for Nazi war crimes in Nuremberg. The judges, all men and representing a range of countries, speak briefly in one episode about the ways in which they deal with the stress of their job: gardening, playing the violin, taking walks on the beach. These activities kept them from succumbing to substance use as a coping strategy and ensured that they could function effectively as judges. In response to our stressful lives, we often say "X" or "Y" helps us decompress, de-stress, or clear our head. Such activities are the ones we feel competent in, ones that bring us joy. They are our sanctuary: our place to feel safe and in control of our own goals, actions, and destiny.

As described in previous chapters, the facets and impacts of creative self-expression are a uniquely human way of responding to challenges and working our way through them. In many ways, the practice of creative self-expression enhances our creative abilities. As with any other body part, the more we use our imagination, the more we strengthen it and are able to flex it. To engage in the playful exploration of art-making allows us to practice and flex our imagination: to step into the aesthetic experiences we enjoy and to be in a zone of stretching, processing, and integrating our life experiences, thoughts, and interactions. This discipline allows us to turn our focus away from malaise.

During the COVID pandemic, there were many news stories that referenced previous forms of societal isolation during the time of the plague and the Spanish flu. There were references to how Isaac Newton discovered calculus during the time he had to be home from Cambridge due to the plague (National Trust, 2021), and Shakespeare wrote his plays at this time. It is not an accident that the accomplishments relate to men: It is well known that COVID affected women's productivity and employment far more than those of men. Despite the anxiety and uncertainty of this time, it is possible to consider the slowed-down activity and reframe isolation as a time to value solitude. This is not always possible with young children or dependents in the home, but in theory, being forced to shelter and be distant from others can be a time to reflect and allow the brain to wander and daydream.

This might seem contradictory, given all the evidence that loneliness has been associated with many negative health outcomes and that sustained loneliness, especially that due to external circumstances rather than to a desire for solitude, can be deeply harmful to health and well-being. The one potential upside of loneliness is perhaps the deepening and development of the default mode network (DMN). As we saw in previous chapters, being by oneself and allowing oneself to simply "be" engages the DMN and sparks a free flow of ideas and imagination (Spreng et al., 2020). The DMN is implicated in mental representations of ourselves across time and space, our sense of self and identity, prospecting and planning about an envisioned future, imagination, and creative thought as well as simulating thoughts, social interactions, memories of personally significant places, and events (Andrews-Hanna et al., 2014). It is not easy to be restorative and reflective rather than ruminative and depressive, and to be able to know and understand that which helps us instead of bringing us down is no mean task.

Our creative and expressive pursuits connected with our free imagination and connected to some form of making something real and tangible might be our expressive instinct and our unique way to communicate and connect with our imaginary other: our witness and audience to our existence. When we create and make real that which lies in our imagination and in our reflections in solitude, we allow ourselves first to view/witness the external manifestation of our inner states and then perhaps bridge to others we miss and seek to connect with. I think of the sharing of artwork and food and other things we make in our everyday lives, and especially during COVID, as reflecting this impulse. We first express our inner state in all its ambivalence and chaos and then connect with the larger pool of the human experience.

Learning the skills of personalized health and well-being

Pursuing and practicing health and well-being is a skill. It can be learned and practiced through understanding our own triggers, processes, and needs. It is a skill that we can be trained to understand. In previous chapters I spoke about the findings from different forms of self-expression. I want to highlight here further the role of contemplative, generative, and reflective practices. This is not to say that mindfulness is always helpful or beneficial; in a recent study, Poulin et al. (2021) warn that mindfulness alone and out of social context can promote self-centered behaviors. and our actions and intentions might lead us selfishly inward rather than in prosocial ways. They attribute this to the transplantation of mindful practices from the interconnected communities where it originated and allowed for thoughtful attention to self and others. Engaging in artistic practices can help us become better attuned to ourselves, but we need to be mindful that it does not turn us into selfish beings only interested in our own well-being.

Let me share a related anecdote about one of the oldest forms of martial art forms, which comes from the southern state of Kerala, India. It is called Kalaripayattu, or the Kalari approach. Kalari was a form of training using all parts of the body as well as a range of wooden and metal weapons. The practice is said to have inspired other east Asian martial art forms such as karate. In addition to the combat techniques, it also involves a regimen of wellness, medicine, and treatment rooted in Ayurveda and natural methods of massage and treatment. As with many other art forms, these methods were banned during British rule in India, and many teachers and practitioners died, leaving behind only a small part of the method. But there has been an increasing revival of this method and recognition that martial art forms are layered multiple forms that produce both physical fitness and a deep understanding of ourselves and our opponents. This knowledge in turn enables us to tackle challenges effectively.

A favorite example is one shared with me by my father about the final test of the warriors after they have completed training. In order to graduate, the warrior is covered in oil and made to walk through a dark corridor. The warrior expects to be attacked in that dark corridor and to be tested on their skills. However, there is a trick embedded in the process. When attacked, the warrior is expected to demonstrate perfect reactivity. They must respond in such a way that the oil on his body falls on the opponent's weapon but the weapon does not scratch their skin or cause injury. If the warrior responds too fast, there will be no oil, indicating a premature reaction time, but if they respond too slowly, then it could result in an injury or cuts on the skin. Clearly, the training requires a very high level of responsivity and reflexes.

Similarly, the Buddhist philosopher Thich Nhat Hanh (2014, p. 297) discusses how the beauty of the lotus is intricately connected to the mud in which it grows. The mud is essential for the lotus to bloom; it is from the seeming metaphorical mess that the lotus knows how to grow and thrive. Roy (1945) further suggested that what matters is not what we make, but what we become, although perhaps what we make is a part and extension and result of what we become. The eventual aim is to become that which we wished for, hoped for, or became through chance and circumstance.

If we think about adversity as a challenge or an enemy, then aren't we all warriors fighting to protect ourselves and defend our health and well-being? If we tap into methods and ways that have been refined and developed over time, doesn't that put us in the best position to overcome the adversity?

Futterman-Collier and Wayment (2019) talk about the nuances of how art-making can help us. They suggest a framework to identify critical factors associated with well-being in the context of a personalized art-making task and referred to it as PEARLS (P = personalized art-making, E = engaging, A = arousing, R = reducing rumination, and LS = life satisfaction). In their study with 216 participants engaged in different art tasks, they found that it was not distraction alone that helped participants; rather, it was quiet ego contemplation that helped shift them from a ruminative to reflective perspective as well as improved positive mood. They randomly assigned 216 participants to one of four art-making conditions, designed to enhance either negative or positive mood through a focus on rumination or growth. The findings highlight the need for and role of contemplative practices in enhancing the creative expressive experience and decreasing self-focus. Our experimental study further supports our theoretical PEARLS model. In the context of personalized art-making activities, high flow, high arousal, and low rumination are essential for mood repair to occur; positive mood may be facilitated by activities and mindsets that reduce self-focus and orient the individual toward growth and transcendence.

Finding our unique sanctuaries and oases: space, time, expressive intentions, and creative expression

Arguably, one of the outcomes of the COVID pandemic has been reduced distractions and increased time to examine our boundaries and that which is important to us. Isolation need not always be a negative. Bowker et al. (2017) found that not all aspects of social withdrawal had negative outcomes. Especially in emerging adulthood, higher levels of unsociability were associated with higher levels of creativity. Perhaps our instincts for creative communication need this time of incubation and free imagination to be innovative and make creative connections.

Our challenge in the world of online distractions will be to find ways to focus and rest our simple primitive brains that are unused to so much stimulation. A friend and I decided a few months ago to meet at a set time every month and discuss our thinking on various aspects of life, philosophy, and Eastern and Western spiritual traditions. It began with our shared interests and experience in Indian philosophical traditions and connections to artistic practice but evolved to talking about psychological theories and how we manage our lives. One of the insights that came from one of those conversations was the conceptualization of our homes as ashrams. Ashrams are spaces for spiritual renewal and service; the word conjures up images of structured, disciplined living in bucolic retreats. We imagined through COVID that our homes and our living spaces could be our retreats: our ashrams. In these spaces we might engage in mindful reflection, learning, intentional giving, and creative expression. For me, this can be through waking up after a good night's sleep and mindfully starting the day with quiet cups of coffee. I then proceed to consider the structure of the workday, meals, writing, interacting, and serving those in my life, including my family, my students, and the mundane activities that maintain the home (cleaning, cooking, laundry), all of which are forms of service. Finally, I make time for creative work and time to reflect in my study/ studio. This is a boundary I have set: spaces and a corner that allow for safe uninterrupted time. I will explain each aspect about space, time, expressive intention, and creative expression.

Space

One of the unique aspects of art-making and artworks is the ability to hold multiple perspectives and emotions concurrently. The making process can induce physical relaxation, focus, and distraction. Depending on the needs and context of the individual, it can provide insight, reflective space, and transformative outcomes in life. A foundational element, I believe, is space: physical and mental space to allow one's creative capacity to survive and flourish. For me this happens in what I refer to as my study/studio, which is a space I guard zealously (Figure 10.2). It is quiet and has all my art materials, laptop, reading materials, comfortable places to lie down as well as chairs to give ergonomic support. I am surrounded by art made by my children and memories of people I have known and loved. I have next to my desk a scratch-off map that is a humbling reminder of so much I haven't seen of the world: so many countries to visit and so few that I have! This corner is my oasis, my sanctuary. It is the place where I meditate, reflect, connect, and write. I also have a view of my backyard from the window as well as a few succulents that bask in the morning light that comes in through the window. Together these elements bring a sense of peace and safety.

Time

There is a story of the traveler who once met a person trying to saw a branch off a tree. The traveler noticed that the saw was blunt and told the person that he might be more effective if he stopped to sharpen the saw. The person replied, "I have no time to sharpen my saw."

Figure 10.2. My study/io space for creative and restorative activities

After physical spaces that offer us sanctuary and refuge to refuel our beings, the next element is time. There are no rules, of course, but I believe it helps to have structured time for such endeavors. I usually have some art project open and ongoing in my workspace. It could be a big mural or it could be a small work. Either way, I know it is there and waiting for me whenever I am ready for it. Some days I might add a few marks and other days I might add hours of work. It all depends on how much time and energy I have and feel the need for. This also becomes my reflective practice on my own terms. Because some works stay in progress for months and others finish in a single setting, the outcomes vary, as does the reflection. What I do allow myself is the time for things to cook and simmer as they need. Some pieces evolve over time into unexpected outcomes, whereas others emerge fully formed. Either process is acceptable, and all forms of expression and processing become part of creative exploration and learning.

Expressive intention

The third element I think of in ensuring creative well-being is the intention we bring to it. An aspect to consider is whether the work is for intrapersonal learning, expression and processing, or if it is meant for a larger or specific external audience. My artwork at present is not a source of income or livelihood for me; rather, it is a form of giving and sharing. In recent years, as I moved into clinical practice and research, I found that art-making was best positioned in my life as a way of making sense and making my way through life's struggles. I often give away my artwork and give away any proceeds from sales to charity. "Artruism" is how I think of it. It might be artwork for a friend's home, or hand-made cards for all occasions, or gifts or thank-you symbols. Regardless, it is the one part of my life that I have tried to decouple from any external demands and expectations. My daughters tell me that when I engage in these artistic works, I shout less around the house. I smile and think, "Isn't that a positive outcome for overall family quality of life?"

I recognize that my choices are a form of privilege. However, for many individuals and communities around the world, especially in indigenous communities and traditional heritage crafts, art-making is a source of income (Sharma & Vijay, 2021). These works of art represent longstanding skills honed and refined over generations. As seen in Chapter 3, arts can be deeply intertwined with well-being, providing a source of livelihood and continuity of cultural heritage. As a society it is something we need to attend to when we think about well-being as being interconnected among us all as human beings.

It also reminds me of the idea of right action in Buddhism, as articulated by Thich Nhat Hanh. He refers to it as "anything we do to lessen the suffering of the world and the community" (2014, p. 78). To me, the act of art-making is also a form of self-compassion, to make sure I make time and space and have a place in the universe to reflect and fully be myself. Thich Nhat Hanh (2014, p. 81) talks about this in the context of meditation, but I believe this applies fully to creative practices. He refers to it as transforming suffering into happiness and making peace with our suffering, treating it tenderly and looking deeply at the roots of our pain. The art of suffering and the art of happiness are intertwined and require that we nourish happiness daily, with acknowledgment, understanding, and compassion for ourselves and for those around us. The intention and space we bring can transform us and those around us. Artistic works provide an added gift in the form of the written work or the visual piece to help us reflect, appreciate, and own our place in this world and our unique contributions to it.

Intention can also manifest in our ability to be generative rather than restrictive. An example I think of is my interactions with a mentor almost 10 years ago. He taught me the difference between setting boundaries as distancing and restrictive versus setting boundaries as transformative. At that time I was just starting out as a scholar, and he was someone I had admired for many years as one of the first people to connect physiological health and authentic self-expression. I pondered for many days and sent him an email asking if he would be a mentor on this proposal I was writing. He wrote me back a few lines the same night, and I remember them to this day because it set the model for me on how to say "no" that was kind while also protecting myself from overwhelming commitments. This is what he said: "At any other time, I would have loved to work with you. But I am now retired and trying to stay focused on a couple of projects. I do have a suggestion for someone who is available and could help you. Trying contacting person X. All the best in your research." I liked how he started out: He validated me and assured me of the worth of what I was proposing, This was so important to me at that time as a no-name scholar just starting out. He then told me why he could take on anything, because of his prior commitments. But he did not leave it at that: He recognized my search for a mentor and suggested someone that I could work with. It was not about his ego; rather, it was about offering help that would be helpful to those other than him. As we move through our lives and examine the future, our ability to understand and support each other will be paramount to our well-being as well as that of the upcoming generation.

Creative expression

The fourth element is to take this further into expression that becomes mean-ingful. We are able to often do this when we are attentive to ourselves and others: To be able to recognize and be compassionate to our own needs and accept the concurrent joy and distress that exists all around us. Winch (2014) refers to it as being able to provide emotional first aid to ourselves. The ability to be adaptable means being able to recognize both the threats and our crea-tive imaginative potential to engage with them effectively. This involves rec-ognizing and responding in ways that are manageable for us in the short and long term. This might mean initial distraction to survive the moment; then, when we have summoned enough resources, we will be able to face and cope with the challenges such that they are integrated into our ongoing narrative. Figure 10.3 summarizes these strategies: responding in the moment (distrac-tion; seeking alternative enjoyment, including receptive experiences), naming distress (with self and others), accepting the cause and source, and planning for responses should distress recur.

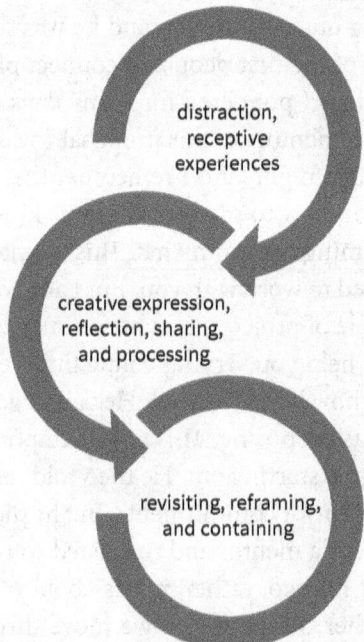

Figure 10.3. Continuum of health with receptive and creative self-expression

How do I choose my expressive option?

A question I get often is where to begin and how to choose an expressive form. For me, visual art and writing were natural expressive forms, mostly because I felt successful and also able to communicate through these formats. You might say I am biased about the benefits and value of arts because I have been a lifelong artist. My daughter, who is a mathematician, has found the arts to be very difficult because she feels judged on her expertise. I cannot count the number of times adult participants in my research studies have told me about the moment they decided that art was not for them; it usually had to do with a casual or disparaging comment about their skills by a friend, a teacher, or a family member. Some were told that they were not skilled enough in the arts and should pursue something else. How many times have we succumbed to this pressure to move away from doing things we might enjoy because we were not adequately skilled?

So is everyone an artist? If we define being an artist as being able to express yourself visually, in music, in dance, in drama, in poetry, I would say yes, all of us are. And to seek inspiration, it would be helpful to return to our childlike states. Consider what forms of expression are joyful and playful and also allow you to reflect and learn about yourself and others as you engage in the creative practices. The answer might lie in photography, culinary arts, dance, pottery, and so forth. Each of us has a preferred form of creative self-expression that we steadily dampened down and ignored over time as we grew older and developed unnecessarily unreachable personal standards and expectations. Certainly, some individuals have more technical skills than others, but that does not detract from the idea of universal artistic capacity. Creative and artistic self-expression is a means to process and communicate without the burden of aesthetic excellence. Since we know that all humans are inherently creative, translating it into an artistic work is a real possibility and everyone is capable of self-expression.

The role of a witness/audience: ourselves and others

As human beings we are primed to be attuned to social interactions. We are shaped by our interactions with others, and our life story is verily written everyday as we encounter both the new and the familiar. Our expressions might be mundane (everyday interactions) or metaphorical (through our artistic expression). As seen in Figures 1.2 and 4.3, we mostly are the first witnesses to our expression, and then we invite others to witness and be our audience. Especially when we are representing difficult experiences, the need to be seen accurately by witnesses is important. Coping and responding effectively is not easy; it always hurts to be rejected and or to lose something that was meaningful and valuable to us. But when faced with difficult days, sharing our creative works with others means completing the loop of imagination, self-expression, and feeling a sense of belonging.

The challenges of online relational exchanges pushed me to explore new art media, different from any I typically have used. As with writing, artistic options that we might consider even serendipitously help us manage and understand ourselves. In my case it was using the phone camera and playing with filters and composition. I found, through the visual images that stared back at me, the specific triggers that affect me and make me reactive to specific behaviors and actions. Through this process, I was able to name what sets me off and what makes me feel happy and fulfilled. I shared these images and my writings with a dear friend, and she gave me perspective. Having her view and read my works helped give me a sense of being seen and heard through the process. As seen in Chapters 1 and 4, without having someone as a witness/ viewer/audience, it is hard to process and integrate our experiences into a co-herent and evolving life story narrative.

In our modern digital age, this witness and audience might be both those we interact with every day in person and those who are kindred spirits but live miles away from us. Some of my peers and I share artwork and poetry with each other using WhatsApp. There even are virtual exhibitions now fully curated online. We have the opportunity to connect in many different ways, and the doorways that bring us to each other, help us feel less isolated, and offer us a forum to communicate and feel understood will necessarily advance our well-being. Through tele-mental health or individual communications, or with community connections, sharing our work and having witnesses for our metaphorical expressions is a gift to our sense of self and our life story and helps us to feel less threatened and alone.

Connecting back to nature as a metaphor for life itself

Being connected to our environment means being better connected to our senses and fully engaged in receptive and expressive experiences. Recent research indicates the many health benefits of physical access to nature in terms of receptive healthful benefits. Being in nature has been found to reduce stress

(Kabisch et al., 2017) and to improve creativity and skills in problem-solving (Atchley et al., 2012), as well as to decrease anxiety and rumination and to improve working memory (Bratman et al., 2015). The acts of walking and being in nature were found to improve cardiovascular health, reduce blood pressure, and enhance self-esteem (Barton et al., 2012). Patients in hospitals have reportedly recovered faster when they are able to view a nature scene (Brown et al., 2013). Despite the many opportunities of living in a city (e.g., access to jobs and resources), urban dwellers who lived near a park had better health outcomes that those who did not (Van den Bosch & Odesang, 2017). Given our evolutionary roots, from being hunter-gatherers and even settled agriculturists not long ago, our brains are familiar with and expect the healthful benefits of natural surroundings. Even exercising is proposed to have greater benefits when conducted out in nature rather than in the sterile and non-stimulating indoor setting of a gym.

Most of these experiences are receptive, in that the benefits that accrue from being or responding to nature serve as a stimulus. Natural environments like pathways and trails, including those in forests, might encourage movement—but do they enhance creative self-expression? What happens to us in these settings that generates the reported health benefit? How does nature inspire health and well-being, and does it promote action? We can intentionally connect the natural environment and creative expression, including ephemeral practices such as those we read about in Chapter 3 on indigenous art forms, in order to reap the benefits from both. A way to examine and explore that further is to dive into our own ancestral roots and to work with media and approaches from our communities of origin and cultural heritage.

Nature offers us endless creative metaphors: life cycles, stages of development, adaptations, roles, and being invaluable parts of a larger interdependent whole. Everything in nature blooms at its own time, but everything gets done. The slow natural processes and experiences in nature can serve as a counterbalance to the speed and superficiality of social media and our online lives. In my own artworks, I use natural media as my inspiration and "canvas." I use found objects (objects with potential that are lying around unused) and repurposed materials to create my art projects. I rarely buy art canvases anymore. My artistic goal is to return us to our roots in creative expression, when we were interconnected with others and living closer to nature and natural colors, textures, and objects.

Our current challenges are to reconcile our digital lives and real lives in ways that enhance rather than diminish. Digital expressive options, including social media, can be a way to enhance a sense of belonging and kinship but can also cause a false sense of disembodied relationality. Current digital and expressive tools offer a range of ways in which to cope, including through sharing creative works and combining analog and digital art. The main challenge is being able to recognize the distress we feel and how we might best respond to these emotions. Some stress and distress requires us to step away from the experience and respond by the distraction of seeking alternative forms of enjoyment or pleasure. It might require us to physically and metaphorically be in a different space and activity. At other times, avoidance through distraction might not be helpful; in that case, we need to delve deep into the experience to better understand and accept it. Writing and artwork to process the experience helps with this, as does talking with a trusted friend, therapist, or family member. This emotional processing helps us better understand ourselves and prepare more effectively for similar distressing experiences in the future. Most importantly, as seen in the studies on adversity and trauma, and returning to the home repair analogy, we must be able to recognize when we need professional help to address our injuries and damage from life's challenges.

Key takeaways

Much of managing our health and well-being involves first being able to recognize our needs, making space for them in our life, and ensuring we engage in activities and experiences that meet these needs. Creating space and time with intention is key. Like the story of the blunt saw, to be effective and to thrive, we need time to reflect, process, and hone our skills. Creative expression and connecting to natural environments further enhance these aspects. And most important is recognizing when we need professional help and support during challenges in life when we are not able to manage our needs ourselves. As we know from physiological evidence, to our brain, mental and physical ailments are similar. Thus, getting help for mental challenges needs to be as acceptable as getting help for physiological diseases.

11
What lies ahead?

Research and practices for the future

Life is not what you alone make it. Life is the input of everyone who touched your life and every experience that entered it. We are all part of one another.

Yuri Kochiyama

We must be willing to let go of the life we have planned so as to have the life that is waiting for us.

Joseph Campbell

We are only as wise as the awareness of our ignorance.

Socrates

Terrain map: My aim with this book was to cover theory, historical perspectives, and research on the role of creative self-expression (mainly visual art) in our lives. To see the value of our innate creative potential and to use our imaginative skills to engage in self-expression is to be able to survive and thrive. Creative materials, strategies, and tools exist to tell our stories in word and image, democratizing creative capacity in the process. Each day is then the start of a new quest, adding learning through experiences to the continuing tale that is our collective and individual human journey. We are in a new world of art media at the intersection of digital tools and societal transformation. Art can helps us at the individual level and could transform communities through the same principles of communication, empathy, and metaphors. New forms of expression and new research tools await us in preparing the next generation of creative individuals, art therapists, and arts and health workers. There is an emerging and robust body of research on arts and health. However, much remains to be known and understood.

The Expressive Instinct. Girija Kaimal, Oxford University Press. © Oxford University Press 2023.
DOI: 10.1093/oso/9780197646229.003.0012

Figure 11.1. Artwork made in virtual reality

Accepting and living creatively with uncertainty and ambiguity

As seen in Chapter 1, uncertainty is a given for us all as humans, even though it might vary depending on our unique context and circumstances, including where we are born and where we live. Fromm (2010) wrote about the vulnerabilities of humans as well their creative potential as being sprung from the same expanded consciousness. He referred to our vulnerabilities and struggles with the unknown as a unique attribute of living beings and yet different compared with those of animals, who function at a more instinctual level. As humans, that which causes us distress and worry is the very thing that also gives us foresight and sensitivity. Even though we do not know the future and never will, we can approach it with a clear understanding of our present and asking the right questions that will impact our future. This comes from carefully knowing and recognizing what we fear and worry about in terms of knowledge, beliefs, emotions, and cognitive concerns. Furthermore, to live every day means knowing that our stressors will never go away, and to be human means regularly facing challenges. Our uncertain futures promise to concurrently bring us opportunities, difficulties, joys, and sorrows. All we can do is be prepared and better understand that which we are drawn to and that which we avoid.

In addition, the challenges we encounter might not even be entirely new. These challenges might be memories of past traumatic events that we might be forced to encounter as a result of current triggering experiences. To give you a personal example, recently we were in a holiday spot that we go to every year. It is near the ocean and is associated in my mind with rest and fun at the beach collecting shells and playing in the waves. I expected that this year, too, we might use these few days away from home and work for respite after a demanding year. Instead, I was met with an unexpected experience. Although happy to make the trip, my daughter burst into tears as soon as we reached our apartment. She cried quietly, and as I inquired why, she told me that she was reminded of the time the previous year when she was treated poorly by a classmate during a group project. The apartment and our being here triggered the memory of that traumatic time, and she was convulsed in sobs as she was reminded of an incident that literally occurred a year ago. I let her cry her heart out, and we decided that we could use this time to rewire some of those associations. Since the apartment reminded her of a time when she felt undermined, we knew it was time to replace that memory with a new one. After she was able to externalize her distress (first through physical tears and then narrative), she spend the rest of the time at the beach being her playful teen self: trying out the boogie board, working on a summer course, and watching television shows. I asked her a few days later how she felt, and she neither cried nor mentioned the triggering event again. We reflected together that the trigger was now hopefully replaced with memories of learning new things, enjoying time together, and forming new associations to the place, delinked from a previously distressing experience. In this case it was not necessarily creative self-expression per se but rather the opportunity for physiological self-expression (through tears) to a witness (her mother) and being able to clearly articulate her distress in words that likely helped her move into remaking that narrative with new, fulfilling, and enjoyable experiences that helped her reframe and move past the traumatic memories of the previous year.

In many ways, we are constantly reworking our stories and our perceptions of ourselves, letting go and reimaging new versions of our identities over time. Each new experience or memory of it shifts our sense of self a little bit, fortifying us as best we know to new futures. Sometimes we over-prepare and shut ourselves out of new experiences; other times we don't learn or prepare enough and we get hurt again.

New tools and areas for further research

Writer and poet Mary Oliver (2019) once said that the most regretful people on earth were those who felt the call to creative work, felt their own creative power restive and uprising, but gave to it neither power nor time. To prepare ourselves and those we know, to draw from our creative and innovative capacities be it to be seen, to be heard, to practice imagination, to be understood, or to problem-solve, is to care and advance each other's experiences of fulfillment. More research is needed to better understand the influences on and impacts of our innately creative lives.

Systematic reviews indicate that much of the current research is not rigorous enough (De Witte et al., 2021; Schnitzer et al., 2021), and we need to better understand the various ways in which art can and cannot address our human needs. I do not mean to sound simplistic or Pollyanna-ish here. Art-making and artists, as we saw in Chapter 2, have their share of misperceptions and marginalization. Interacting with colleagues from the traditional sciences, I see every day that the struggle is real, with the result that arts-based interventions are typically not taken seriously. In addition, to be considered of value in modern health care systems, we need studies to document the health outcomes and cost benefits of creative expression as well as better understanding personalized care: knowing how and when different arts practices, including those we undertake ourselves and those we do with the facilitation of others, promote health.

That said, it is very possible, as we have seen in previous chapters, that self-expression alone is not a prerequisite for well-being. Art is not always a cure-all or helpful, and art-making alone is not the answer. If unprocessed and difficult emotions and thoughts emerge and are not processed effectively, self-expression can be like a fire that burns down the house. We need to better understand and continue to examine when and how self-expression is healthful and which approaches best suit us based on our individual skills, needs, and differences. Relatedly, there are interesting differences of note too between artists and non-artists in terms of the extent of externalization of internal mental states, and these add nuance to the evidence on the benefits of engaging in visual self-expression. The act of creating engages multiple brain regions and seems to help with many aspects of functioning, both cognitive and emotional. Much remains, however, to be understood about the complex interactions involved in self-expression, including by ourselves and with others. Emerging technologies, including mobile imaging options, allow us to get closer to tracking the functioning of the human brain, especially when it engages in creative expressive experiences.

A challenge in analyzing arts-based self-expression is operationalizing data collection tools and measures. Many of the changes seen in facilitated sessions such as those led by art therapists are tracking what we refer to above as "personalized small c creativity": the transformative process of human imagination to see our lives in new ways. With technological advancements in knowledge and the tools of neurobiology, changes as a result of a session can increasingly be measured physiologically by tracking neuroinflammatory markers, heart rate and skin conductance, relational synchrony in patient and therapist, activation of creative and relaxed brain states, activation of brain centers of language and metaphor for communication, regulation in cortical and limbic activity, connectivity, empathy, and activation of reward pathways. Each of these constructs might also be examined for subjects with specific diagnoses and demographic characteristics and artistic experience as well as in various contexts (individual or group art therapy, short- and long-term approaches). The measures are naturally limited in scope, and none to date can capture the complexity of the human interaction and creative expressive process, but we can take small steps toward capturing some aspects of multi-layered experience.

Additional areas of research include examining neurotransmitters and how we might control their levels through intentional activities and choices. For example, Foo et al. (2021) in animal studies found that mice can be trained to control their release of dopamine. As we saw in research on art-making and reward perception, creative self-expression can potentially be a way for humans to manage and respond to the joyful aspects of dopamine release. Areas of inquiry can focus on the effects of not just the excitatory hormones like dopamine and endorphins but also the ones that calm us down and inhibit neuronal firing. The role of hormones such as GABA (gamma-aminobutyric acid) that serve to inhibit neuronal firing could be an area for further study and research, especially in cases where we as humans are overstimulated and unable to down-regulate our responses to stressors (Jie et al., 2018). Lowering GABA levels will affect the functions of the amygdala and will activate overly fearful responses. Medications like benzodiazepines (e.g., Valium) work by mimicking GABA. Thus, the role of GABA in reducing these responses that affect our functioning is of note and relevant to consider, particularly for those at risk of anxiety disorders, phobias, and post-traumatic stress. Even as we recognize our expressive instincts, in the current context of information overload and access to provocative messaging, such inhibitory functions are especially salient.

Psychedelics and how they impact sensory perceptions and therefore neural pathways represent an area that is ripe for exploration. At the intersection of health and creative experiences, psychedelic compounds like psilocybin have been found to improve dendritic number and size, which is impli-cated in experiences of depression. Akin to virtual reality (VR; Kaimal et al., 2021), which upends our synaptic wiring and resulting sensory experiences, psychedelics work to challenge our perceptions of reality and, as a result, potentially modify our worldview (Shao et al., 2021). Shao et al. (2021) found that sustained change is possible with psychedelics, indicating their ability to shift neural connections even with a single dose. New tools and interventions also highlight the potential to enhance neuroplasticity in the brain through activating chemicals such as ketamine and light flickering at 60 Hz to impact neuronal activity and connectivity (Venturino et al., 2021).

Mobile brain imaging technologies (King & Kaimal, 2019) like electroencephalography (EEG) and functional near-infrared spectroscopy (fNIRS) are contemporary tools that offer ways to measure brain activity in measuring brain dynamics in real-world environments. These technologies could help to elucidate how art-making within the therapeutic relationship engages the brain and could provide scientific data to measure mechanisms of change and outcomes of clinical art therapy interventions. In particular, these tools will enable measurement of synchrony in brain activity between individuals in order to assess therapeutic outcomes as well as interpersonal alignment. These tools allow for measurement in naturalistic settings and offset self-report data with more concrete measurements, allowing for a deeper understanding of human brain functioning. Applications in arts practices are so far limited, so this topic is well positioned for further inquiry.

Moreover, not all creative work is in the artistic domain, and research innovations on the intersection of arts with health disciplines is another area for further inquiry. Beyond our individual selves, our minds and bodies are deeply intertwined and these are further interconnected with our environment, our nutritional intake, and our circadian rhythms. Each experience connects us with inner and external elements. Thus, where we live, what we eat, and how much we sleep are all connected to our well-being, which in turn affects all aspects of our physical and psychological health. These social and structural determinants of health map onto our health trajectories (U.S. Department of Health and Human Services, 2021; World Health Organization, 2021).

Our bodies are literally changing every few years. Why not support this change through all the ways in which we thrive both in mind and body? In addition, the microbiome is deeply interconnected to with our psychosocial health. In animal studies, Wu et al. (2021) have demonstrated how mice with diversity in their gut microbiome were able to respond more effectively to social contexts and to stress and had lower levels of stress hormones compared with mice with more limited microbiomes. These interconnections between our nutritional habits and health outcomes are an area for further study. Being outdoors and doing simple activities like walking in natural settings are well established to promote well-being. It can feel overwhelming, but to be led by a sense of discovery that includes significant time to rest and recuperate is essential. Rest, sleep, and even the quality of our dreams (Wamsley, 2021) advance our abilities to survive and thrive. As we age, our physiological abilities and needs might change too, but the desire to express ourselves does not. We need to be open to the many ways for self-expression. For example, in addition to traditional definitions of artistic practice, culinary and horticultural arts and body-based expression are potential forms of self-expression.

New media connecting our digital and physical worlds

A particular point of note that defines our present and will likely define our future as well is the ubiquitous presence of digital interactions and communications. These include social media, messaging, and online interactions, which have been particularly heightened during COVID. Our digital selves, however disembodied, desperately seek to connect with other human beings. No matter how much we isolate, we need to and want to belong to our communities and tribes (Dunphy et al., 2019). We want to be seen, heard, and valued as unique individuals while also feeling the safety and belonging of being part of an accepting community. It is hard to do this, given that much has to be extrapolated from the awkwardness of online communications that are limited to written word exchanges without the context of nonverbal and human connection. Being online in this disembodied sense of community does not seem to affect our perceptions and expectations of positive future events, but it aggravates our anxieties of negative events, including exacerbation of obsessive-compulsive and anxious behaviors (Jezzini et al., 2021; Monosov, 2017). Being able to regulate ourselves in terms of ready access to digital tools and events is essential. Moreover, the author Michael Easter (2021) suggests that we have become less creative over time because we are inundated with digital entertainment and options. He argues that our intellectual and creative capacities have declined because we are too comfortable and our lives are too easy in the Western world; we don't have time to be bored and to allow thoughts to flow unhindered: the seeds of creative expression.

The intersection of digital augmented realities and real-world objects is already a part of museum exhibits and can continue to help us envision and connect digital and real worlds. One of the advantages of digital technologies might be their role in helping with expressive options and access. Self-expression, that safety valve of our mental lives, might not always need motor functions. This will be especially relevant to individuals with limited physical functioning. Moreover, as with all things created for individuals with disabilities, this can help everyone. New tools and methods to capture the lived experience of humans as well as physiological indicators of change and impact are being developed each day. Emerging neural technology that can connect brain activity to expressed speech offers an incredible avenue for creative expression, health, and well-being, allowing for expression not necessarily mediated by motor capacity and skills. Moses et al. (2021) in a study demonstrated how a paralyzed individual was able to communicate using a brain interface technology. Although these technologies are in nascent stages, future expressive capacities can be imagined and may further enhance the quality of life for individuals with expressive limitations.

As we proceed into the 21st century, the idea of using media and technology in arts-based psychotherapies is also expanding. There are increasingly successful clinical telehealth options in the creative arts therapies. Clinicians and researchers, including our lab, are exploring the role of VR in expanding our notions of what is possible and are encouraging movement and immersion in artistic expression.

Digital interactive expressive environments can foster a sense of creativity and connection. In a previous study, based on a secondary analysis of the 2012 Survey of Public Participation in the Arts administered by the National Endowment for the Arts, we had found that increasing proportions of people in the United States were using digital media for creating, archiving, and sharing their art. COVID has accelerated the support for and increase in use of digital media by art therapists for their own art and has highlighted the need for research and education on best practices for use of digital media (Kaimal et al., 2016c). Unlike traditional art media, digital artforms allow for "undoing" and changing what we do, which means we can both document and reverse creative actions. Although the lack of tangible object is a concern in digital environments, a potential way to overcome that is to print out work, including in two-dimensional and three-dimensional formats.

A recent development in digital environments is the emergence of VR and augmented reality expression (Figure 11.2). VR expands our digital experience from two dimensions to three dimensions, immersing our heads (the seat of all our senses) into new digital spaces. Immersive experiences can potentially enhance memory and learning (Safaryan & Mehta, 2021). These experiences can include recreations of places and spaces that we cannot or have not been able to visit in real time. VR allows us to simulate these movements of the body, albeit in a disembodied way. The VR experience can be so lifelike that participants can sometimes feel disoriented and experience motion sickness. Once that discomfort is mastered or managed

Figure 11.2. Art-making in VR

(mainly by sitting or removing the headset as needed), VR can be an existentially transformative tool. It becomes a novel experience challenging the laws of physics (being able to move through objects and defying gravity, for example), it can enhance mood, and it can encourage movement and learning (inadvertently).

Our studies, including those in collaboration with the International Arts + Mind Lab at Johns Hopkins University, indicate that the use of novel media such as VR can break down many of the fears around art-making. Instead, it becomes a space for discovery. It provides an as-yet-uncharted territory where we can imagine and capture new dimensions and ways to understand our inner lives and our interactions with others, along with helping us to grapple with our uncertain futures. In our studies we have found that participants are also less resistant to or intimidated by art-making in VR because there is limited precedent around perceived skills in this context (Kaimal et al., 2019). In a series of recent studies we examined how relatively healthy adult participants responded to different types of visual self-expression in VR. Overall we found that the participants enjoyed the creative expressive option much more than rote tasks (Kaimal et al., 2020a). This was independent of whether they felt they had any artistic skills. Participants' affect, self-efficacy, satisfaction with life, and sense of creative agency were all improved as a result of engaging in VR art-making. Participants made simple images, including fantasy scenes, memories, everyday objects, and nature scenes.

Of note from this study is the finding that rote tracing engages the pre-frontal cortex. This finding can be adapted to real life practices staying focused and in the present. Thus, rote tasks can be a way of engaging our executive functioning and decision-making. Things like mindless doodling, tracing, or simple coloring can be considered rote tasks that do not require much analysis but still keep us focused and on task. In addition in this study (Kaimal et al., 2021), we also examined the effect of introducing a calming fragrance into the room during the arts tasks. Outcomes were found to trend toward being enhanced with the fragrance. Integrating multisensory experiences could be an area for further exploration as well. Perhaps some forms of support could be provided by artificial intelligence (AI) tools that can support self-expression, akin to guided imagery in music or meditation directives.

Going forward, traditional ideas of artworks, art media, and how these are created and shared are being upended with the rise of non-fungible tokens (NFTs). NFTs are digital or physical works that are sold in cryptocurrency and stored as specific tokens on blockchains. The intersection of physical and digital art with monetary alternatives is a fascinating new area of expression. NFTs are an interesting development, countering the ideas around savings and banks, which have been the traditional reserves to reduce financial uncertainties. To deposit funds in the cryptocurrency world, using NFTs is not just about owning art but also links to the idea of long-term financial security. It comes with its challenges, including questions about copyrights and energy usage, but is nevertheless a new expressive medium with creators and patrons.

Art-making is also encountering expression with AI algorithms that can recreate art that looks like it is made by a human as well as predict our preferences based on prior likes and dislikes. There is increasing evidence that there are ways to predict our aesthetic preferences. In a recent study, an AI algorithm was able to predict participants' preferences based on their reported previous choices of, for instance, different European-inspired art genres such as Impressionism and Cubism (Ligaya et al., 2021). Viewing our preferred artwork can be creatively inspiring, perhaps a reminder of what we enjoy and inviting us to a familiar place of safe play. In a series of studies, participants' creative written responses were better in terms of both quality and quantity of words after viewing their preferred artwork (Welke et al., 2021). The authors further surmised that being in the presence of their preferred art forms moved the study participants to transcendence and inspiration in complex ways.

Can creative expression bring us back from our isolation?

Dunbar (1992) proposed that on average most humans have a community of 150 to 200 people ("Dunbar's number"), which tended to be the size of the average village. This is the size of our community on average on terms of acquaintances, friends, family, and so forth. Most of the digital native generation (those born in the 21st century) have a social media life that sometimes replaces the real-world hangouts of yore. Our worlds are expanding in literal and figurative ways with digital media options, VR communications, and even holographic options. The year of the pandemic changed us and continues to change ways of living that we had pursued unquestioningly until 2020. In particular, social distancing confused our brains and made us wary and emotionally ambivalent about things that are fundamentally part of who we are as humans, deeply socially connected beings. Studies are finding that people are eager to return to work and be in proximity with others while also struggling with the repercussions of social starvation, which, as we have seen, is akin to literal hunger and starvation. These forms of deprivation affect our brain in terms of hippocampal functioning, emotion regulation, and cognitive functioning (Stahn et al., 2019).

Finding the right setting for us on the social thermostat is key to well-being, and we need to learn what that might be for us in the context of reduced travel and gatherings, more time spent with a smaller group of individuals, and extended time spent in online interactions. Isolation makes us more sensitive to rejections and perceived exclusions, and this in turn exacerbates feelings of fear, sadness, and loneliness. One of the unfortunate side effects of COVID and our enforced distancing has been the emergence of moral extremism and harshness, oddly mirroring the physical distancing from each other (Henderson & Schnall, 2021). In a study examining the judgments made by individuals worried about COVID, the authors found increased harshness and moral condemnation. Across three studies ($N = 913$), conducted in 2020 as the pandemic started to unfold in the United States, the researchers found that individuals who were worried about contracting the infectious disease made harsher moral judgments than those who were relatively less worried. This effect was not restricted to transgressions involving purity but extended to those involving harm, fairness, authority, and loyalty, and remained when controlling for political orientation. These findings add to the growing literature that concrete threats to health can play a role in abstract moral considerations, supporting the notion that judgments of wrongdoing are not based on rational thought alone. We must work hard to be sensitive and not succumb to instinctive tribal responses that our brains readily default to in times of distress and threat.

COVID and the resultant fatalities have further highlighted the intense disparities present in society. Differences in access to health care and vaccines and even the privileges of remote work brought to the fore the work we need to do as a society to bring more equity. Those in jobs that could be done remotely were able to work from home. But even within this privilege lay other disparities; for instance, in a family with heterosexual parents, mothers might be burdened more than fathers with juggling responsibilities of the home and childcare. Recent research has found that women took on the responsibilities of managing and planning for uncertainties and uncertainty mitigation in the lives of their children (Daminger, 2019).

What is our role as humans in such a time in society? The arts hold up a mirror to society and ourselves. They can at all levels serve as a reminder of what has been and what can be. The author Iris Murdoch (1999) referred to the arts as being clarifying; as such being, they are the enemy of tyrants because tyrants seek to mystify. The arts—both our expression at the individual level and in society—allow us to continually be able to view and course-correct. As we saw in Chapter 7, we might sometimes use creative expression effectively by ourselves; at other times, when our stressors are overwhelming, we need skilled professionals who can support us through our vulnerabilities and help us cope and adapt through adversity. Some years ago I did a series of workshops with human resources professionals in companies that reported struggles with communication. In these sessions I shared research and did some simple experiential exercises using scribble drawing exercises. Scribble drawings are a widely used technique in the field of art therapy that are by design meant to reduce inhibitions and fears around artistic merit. By inviting participants to scribble freely, the drawing tasks allow for the earliest developmental form of visual expression: namely, making marks on a paper with no plan or effort to represent anything, just simply moving freely and allowing the movement of the hand and arm to make marks on a surface. This act of free expression tends to loosen up individuals by removing the pressure to make any sort of visual image; instead, they can get into the mindset of play and exploration. By intentionally eliminating any expectation of mastery, the scribble drawing exercise has, in my experience, been consistently effective in empowering participants to be open, trusting, and vulnerable. This in turn helps them to engage in authentic self-expression when they start creating with intention and sharing their works. This to me is the power of self-expression: It is a shortcut to ourselves and each other. It is a way to communicate when words become inadequate, jaded, or meaningless. Art might not be a panacea, but it can get us to connect so we might work together to learn, trust, care for, and support each other.

Some traumas can never be fully resolved. Sapolsky (2003) asserts that conditions like post-traumatic stress disorder rewire the brain in such fundamental ways that there is no complete recovery: We can only learn to manage ourselves and the symptoms over time. At the intergenerational level, Menakem (2017) talks about racialized trauma sitting in our bodies and how this needs to be acknowledged and recognized if we are to heal ourselves and our communities. For communities who have faced years and perhaps centuries of marginalization, exclusion, and cultural appropriation, the cycle of trauma is complex and multigenerational. According to Arslanbek et al. (2022), artistic works from indigenous and traditional communities can connect us back to the historical knowledge, beliefs, and community bonds that can inform collective understanding. Martin (2020) refers to the ongoing need to expand beyond having artists that are of the dominant culture, including the artforms themselves, and privileging of perspectives beyond European and White artistic traditions. Broadening our understanding and valuing of a range of artistic practices past and present is the need of the hour and future. The interplay of historical arts practices in the context of current societal exchanges all open for further inquiry such that we retain the insights and wisdom of our ancestors while also integrating new knowledge and innovation.

The paradox of the future lies in the concurrent presence of the past in terms of tangible physical art and digital artforms and practices. On the one hand, there is potential for technological innovation, communication, and expression through a range of new digital tools. In parallel is a movement toward the use of sustainable practices, such as mending and creating by remembering and restoring. Practices like patchwork quilting or the Japanese artform of sashiko embody this spirit. Sashiko is the repair of torn or damaged fabrics by creating entirely new patterns in the mending of this fabric. Creative practices handed down over generations that are ways to repair, upcycle, mend, and connect artifacts of everyday life are a reminder to us to sustain and maintain rather than replace (Rachlin, 2019). Relatedly, by expanding the conceptualization of art media and art-making, we might examine many different ways to engage in multisensory expression, including integrating physical and natural materials with new digital technologies.

Arts engages our senses. This implies a very real connection between arts engagement and sensuality. Relatedly sexual well-being is a portal to whole-body health. Our well-being is intertwined with the universe both literally in terms of chemical elements and interactive processes of intake and expression of signals from our bodies. Connecting further with history and indigenous ways of knowing further deepens our connection and rootedness in this world. Contemplative creative practices remind us that connecting to ourselves means paradoxically also connecting with the broader ideas of humanity. The idea of brahman and atman (humans being part of the larger universe) in Hinduism is the same idea as that of the Sufi mystic Rumi, who said, "You are not a drop in the ocean; you are the ocean in a drop." The ideas of detachment in Buddhism are not contrary to Western attachment theory. They are both about the ability to care without being possessive: to love and to simultaneously be able to let go. By exploring the similarities inherent in seemingly different cultures, we can find treasure troves of insights we need to better understand and value each other.

Art is also a way to archive as we move forward. For instance, the Governor's Office in Pennsylvania initiated a project to archive photographs from citizens during the pandemic. Such an archive exists for the Spanish flu of 1918; the difference is that the archive is digital. Just as art helps us imagine, it also serves as a reminder of what we have learned from the past. Such archives serve as our collective history and can be a way to bring together communities.

The arts sector broadly has been hard hit by COVID, especially the performing arts. But many forms of expression, including teaching and learning in smaller communities and pods, have emerged, as have alternative outdoor options and venues. We see throughout history that, humankind always finds a way, whether moving outdoors or imagining new methods to collaborate using digital technologies. Much research remains to be done to better understand how care providers and health systems might work together in integrative ways, including bringing in historical, cultural, and humanities perspectives in meaningful ways.

Accepting the journey

One of the things I desired most as a child growing up in India was to travel the world. At that time, and even now, I am very aware how the opportunity to travel is itself a manifestation of deep privilege. The excitement of a new place and traveling is inevitably combined with the intense aloneness of unfamiliarity. Travel forces us out of our comfort zones and encourages us to gain perspective. To have distance is to see things in a new light. When we fly, take a train, or ride in a car for long distances, we see different parts of our world and in that unfamiliar space we are forced to confront assumptions we might have held about things we know and things we don't. These new experiences and reflections add to our world. It reminds me of the quote by Mark Twain (1869):

> Travel is fatal to prejudice, bigotry, and narrow-mindedness, and many of our people need it sorely on these accounts. Broad, wholesome, charitable views of men and things cannot be acquired by vegetating in one little corner of the earth all one's lifetime.

Many women have also told me that travel gives them a much-needed respite from the responsibilities of caring for family members or workplace colleagues and supervisees. Very often, traveling paradoxically teaches us more about what we know and take for granted than what we think we are going to see in the new place. A game I like to play with myself is to see if I planned for and packed everything. Invariably I forget something that was familiar at home, and then my trip becomes a time to adapt to the absence of a familiar and comforting item. It pushes me out of safety and predictability to innovate and problem-solve.

In Hindi there is a word, jugaad, that means to be gutsy and improvise with limited resources. Radjou et al. (2012), in their book on the principle of jugaad define it as the ability to creatively problem-solve, to do better with less, and to expect challenges and adversity as a part of life itself. The good news is that our brains are incredibly adaptable, and we can reverse these non-normative experiences with awareness and conscious effort. As we have seen, our brains strive to change and survive despite the most devastating of traumas. We need to stay honest about all we know and experience and see, and we must be able to see this in others: both strengths and vulnerabilities. Difficult experiences can be shared through the metaphor of the arts. Our instinct to express, when shared in this inclusive metaphorical form, brings out our core attributes: our imagination and possible futures that are yet to be.

I began this book as a journey and invited you to travel with me. It was a journey that traversed time and space forwards and back with memories interspersed with art and science. This brings me to the story of Goddess Parvati from Indian mythology that I mentioned in Chapter 1. Parvati is one of the three main goddesses who are the feminine counterparts of the gods Shiva (symbolizing destruction), Vishnu (symbolizing life), and Brahma (symbolizing creation). Parvati is the partner of Shiva, Lakshmi that of Vishnu, and Saraswati that of Brahma. Lakshmi is considered the goddess of wealth, and Saraswati is the goddess of learning. Parvati is known for many things, including for her power as Shakti, the feminine counterpart to Shiva. She is known as the mother of two prominent figures in Indian mythology, Ganesha and Kartikeya. My mother used to recite her names on Fridays as a form of a prayer ritual. The text was called the *Lalitha Sahasranamam*, which translates to mean "1,000 names for Parvati." Parvati can be many different selves: the demure Gauri, the fierce warrior Durga, and the deathly demoness Kali. (Fun fact: My name literally means "daughter of the mountains" and is one of the many names of Parvati, the daughter of Himavan, the king of the Himalayas.)

As I wrote about emotions, mental states, and our ability to manifest and express them, I came to realize that Parvati represents this aspect of our many possible selves. To be able to tap into each of those selves and manifest a range of emotions and forms of expression is her unique strength. She demands her space and allows nobody to enter it. She offers a heroine's journey that allows for us to be all that we can and need to be. Myths and stories make up the narratives in our lives—the words that shape who we are and hold the inner narrative of our unique life story. This connection between verbal and nonverbal expression represents how we make sense of the world, negotiate the adversities that come our way, and integrate them in our life scripts and schemas. To me, this story represents our many possible selves: each aspect is valid and real and represents parts of ourselves that exist and manifest as needed and as a challenge arises in life. Some moments require discipline and focus, others require warrior-like strategy, and yet others require equanimity and grace. We have in us infinite capacity to manage, understand, and respond to signals from within and outside our bodies. Our brains, bodies, and creative capacities and the stories of our lives are all inevitably intertwined. Our stories are our journeys, and they will unfold in new and unexpected ways. To match the self with the challenge at hand is a way to approach the uncertainties of our lives. As we look forward, we have the resources and assurances from the past leading us to continuing discovery.

Key takeaways

The idea that creative expression, arts, and health can be interconnected is a revelation to many. The evidence is, however, compelling, and although much remains to be done in exploring art media and conducting research, the idea that we are all fundamentally creative and expressive beings is fairly certain. The struggle to recognize the value of making time and space for creative expression is real, and continued research, sharing, and exploration are the needs of the future. More work remains to be done, but there is now a foundation that we could build upon.

Afterword

The journey story as metaphor

I began this book with an invitation to you, my reader, to join me on this journey. Preparing and packing for journeys for me always begins with trepidation. How do I take the comforts and necessities of a familiar and safe home in a carry-on bag or at most a suitcase? What is essential? What is not? No matter how carefully I pack and how much I prepare for the uncertain future trip, there is always something forgotten. As with all journeys, there are things we might prepare for, and yet we know we will encounter surprises. We prevail often because it is our human wont to improvise, such that each forgotten element becomes a way to creatively problem solve through the unexpected.

As I wrote this book, many metaphors and analogies came to mind to me throughout the process. The process of writing was like slipping into a personal fantasy journey. My computer, myself in my corner in my room or in my backyard. It felt like a special portal I stepped into each day, connecting ideas, thoughts, lessons learned: gathering words and images to create an offering for the reader. The metaphors first were those of exploration and setting out on a journey. It was a journey not only of the actual writing but also of sharing what I have wanted to write about connecting personal reflections, professional insights, and lessons learned through lived experiences as well as deliberate investigation. I had a map and some tools of space and time to set out on this quest. Then I found that I needed to battle ongoing challenges of negotiating multiple roles and responsibilities while carving out the precious time to write and think and rinse and repeat that cycle. Despite my fantasy of retreating into a cave in the woods to write in a focused way, life was not something that allowed me to go that way.

As the book evolved, I began to be able to externalize the ideas I wanted to share from my journey: things I had seen, learned, and experienced. As the journey unfolded, it offered nature as a metaphor with all its accompanying associations of maps, terrains, beings, landscapes of arts and creative expression, and health, including going back in time into historical recreations and remembering our past embedded in rocks and cave drawings. In writing about neuroinflammation, for example, the metaphor that emerged was of the warrior: a creative one striving to optimize capacity and strength.

Figure A.1. All the office I want and need is a writing space in nature.

My journey metaphor extended now to being a forager, a hunter-gatherer, collecting raw materials to distill and interpret for my reader. The metaphor now turned to that of a kitchen. The book and its chapters to me felt like preparing a multicourse meal. The chapters were outlined and the book was taking shape; it reminded me of working through the recipes, chopping, cooking, and baking as needed, and laying out a table for beloved guests to share and partake. I thought about the sequencing of the dishes, and each chapter in my mind represented a unique dish. It consisted of reflections on a topic and, though it related to the whole meal, it was just one of several courses. I truly imagined this book, then, as a conversation as we then hung out and discussed the ideas and research. I imagined our conversations, discussions, and debates and hoped that the travels felt nourishing and sated some epistemic hunger. I hoped there was food for thought, even if some dishes weren't your favorite.

My goal with the offerings in the book was to be able to share what I had seen and known to be true, and to empower us all to harness the healthful and productive possibilities of creative self-expression. Sometimes things are said best through metaphors and analogies because they invite us to view with multiple perspectives. As with all art, these metaphors exist in what we view as well as what we create. If you made it this far, you have traversed this road with me. You have seen the possibilities, perhaps seen new sites, and maybe will travel again or set out on roads of discovery of your own.

This brings me to my final metaphor, which was the beginning of much of my professional life: fibers and yarn. My journey started alone on a quest, but this thread was spun into a larger block. Eventually our journeys lead us to each other, and together we weave and carry our individual yarns in the collective weave of the human story.

I hope you learned something new and perhaps view the purpose of art and self-expression anew. And if this journey was successful, perhaps you will seek out and sustain your own creative practices, whatever they might be. I hope this book and journey through it fulfills the best purposes of journeys: to travel, to learn, and perhaps to see the familiar in a new light. We can never know what lies ahead, but we can be prepared by knowing ourselves and bringing our fully responsive and expressive selves, along with what we know about our unique needs to survive and thrive in this world. I hope you will let me know what you think, and I would love to hear your metaphors and analogies: where your story meets mine and where it might build off on its own.

Acknowledgments

The idea for this book began with a combination of requests. The first was a comment my parents made several years ago about their not being able to understand my academic writing because of all the jargon. The second was a request at a keynote lecture I gave in Utah in 2019. The lovely organizer asked me if I had a book to share that might summarize many of the ideas I had spoken about. I did not at that time, but the need for a text that reached beyond the restricted academic journal context seemed necessary and the ideas I wanted to share with a larger audience slowly began to incubate. I have wanted to share the benefits of creative expression with a wide audience and I am so grateful to be able to do it now with this book.

I am grateful to Dr. Dave Gussak who cheered and guided me all through the writing and initially connected me with Sarah Harrington at Oxford University Press, who in turn connected me with my amazing editor, Dana Bliss. Thank you, Dana, for your generous and gentle support throughout this process. You have the incredible ability to communicate creative and critical feedback with kindness and humor, for which I am eternally grateful. It has been a pleasure to work with you in the past two years. Thank you Sarah Ebel and Rebin Alex for timely guidance and responsivenes through the entire production process.

Thank you to my dear friends Juliet King, Dr. Einat Metzl, and Dr. Iva Fattorini for encouraging and supporting me to pursue the intimidating task of writing a single-authored book. Thank you, Juliet, for talking me off the ledge on numerous occasions when I have doubted myself. Einat, thank you for our exchanges with art and words, and, for your insightful feedback. You all model for me how to critique while holding each other with love and compassion.

To Pam Fried, who has helped me with editing over the years and continues to offer gentle, incisive, and helpful advice.

To my brilliant students, Dr. Marygrace Berberian and Bani Malhotra. Your hard work, kindnesses, humility, and dedication inspire me to keep at it! Thank you for your energy and commitment to helping with the references for this manuscript. Technically I might be the teacher, but my students have taught me more than they know: Asli, Katrina, Kendra, and so many more, thank you for our work together and in the world.

To all my research colleagues. We are able to do things in the world only because we work together. Thank you for bridging the languages of different disciplines and being willing to explore and learn with each other.

To my parents, who have supported and encouraged my (ad)ventures, more so as a girl. Thank you for celebrating my explorations, and for encouraging me strive to my heart's content. Thank you to my father for your teaching us that writing can be a form of legacy and memory, and for your pride in our heritage and striving toward excellence. To my brothers, who taught me how to not take myself too seriously.

Thank you to my husband, who has helped support all my aspirations for decades and is an example of how spouses can break generational cycles in order to help women and girls live fulfilling lives.

My deepest love and gratitude goes to my extraordinary daughters, who have been so patient with a mommy who has been disappearing into her headphones and computers for the past year. To you, I am insanely grateful. Thank you for learning to be so self-sufficient and creative in making your own meals, taking care of your schoolwork, and also feeding me in the process. I am so immeasurably proud of you both and the independent-minded, free-thinking, funny, loving, and generous young ladies that you are. Thank you for being our little tribe, for helping me visualize many of the figures from my scratchy scribbles. Especially through the challenges of an isolated COVID year, your resilience and spirit have inspired us beyond measure. Love you to the ends of space and time.

Glossary

Agency: A psychological term referring to a belief and confidence in one's ability to respond to threats and challenges in the world.

Anti-fragile: The quality of an entity that makes it thrive and transform for the better in conditions of adversity. Unlike resilience, which refers to returning to the previous state once the stressor has been removed, being anti-fragile means the stressor turned the entity into something of greater value than before.

Appropriation: Using or taking cultural and artistic ideas from indigenous communities without permission or respectful understanding of the history of the practice.

Arts in health: A broad term referring to the many ways in which professionals with arts training can serve in health care settings.

Art therapy: A regulated human services and mental health profession that uses visual and verbal self-expression as a form of psychotherapy.

Ashram: A word from Sanskrit originally meaning a place of learning, reflection, and retreat with a guru or teacher.

Associative pathways: Pathways of neurons that help make connections between different brain regions.

Big C creativity: Creative acts or works that are known to have been transformative in human history.

Bindi: Dot-like marks made of vermilion worn at the center of the forehead by women in Hindu communities as a decoration and formerly as a mark of being married.

Biophilia hypothesis: The biological connection to nature that is innate to all humans and living beings.

Blackfoot: American Indian and First Nations tribes from Montana (United States) and Alberta (Canada).

Causal coherence: Consistency around logical links between ideas in a piece of writing.

Charkha: Spinning wheel used in India and of special significance during the Indian Freedom movement.

Control group: The participants in an experimental research study who do not receive the main intervention or treatment (also see *treatment group*).

Co-regulation: The experience of being interconnected with another human being in regulating emotion together.

Creative agency: Confidence in one's ability to be creative and imaginative.

Creative arts therapies: An umbrella term for the disciplines of art therapy, music therapy, dance movement therapy, drama therapy, and poetry/bibliotherapy.

Default mode network (DMN): A system of brain structures that includes the ventromedial prefrontal cortex, posterior cingulate cortex, and regions in the medial temporal and parietal lobes, such as the hippocampus. The DMN is associated with personal reflection, imagination, and daydreaming.

Distress: Stressful experiences that are difficult and challenging to endure.

Dopaminergic pathways: Pathways that when activated are associated with dopamine release.

Electroencephalography (EEG): A technological tool that tracks brain wave activity using electrodes placed on the scalp.

Emergent literacy: Beginning knowledge of written words as seen in preschool children.

Emergent numeracy: Beginning knowledge of numbers as seen in preschool children.

Endorphins: Hormone released by the body as a natural painkiller.

Enteroception: The perception of sensation from inner organs in the body (e.g., rumbling in an empty stomach).

Ethnoscience: Systematic valuing and understanding of indigenous and traditional knowledge systems.

Eustress: Stressful experiences that are helpful to optimize performance and development.

Expressive arts therapies: A form of psychotherapy that engages multiple artforms in conjunction to serve patient health needs.

Expressive experiences: Experiences that include and involve self-expression in words, sound, visual art, movement, or any kind of performance that results in an externalization of inner states.

Failure: The internal feeling or experience of having been unsuccessful at an task or effort.

Flow: The feeling of being lost in an activity that is both enjoyable and adequately challenging.

Fragile: The psychological state of being vulnerable to destruction in the event of threatening or adverse events.

Functional magnetic resonance imaging (fMRI): A brain imaging technique that uses blood oxygenation levels to track activation patterns.

Functional near-infrared spectroscopy (fNIRS): A mobile brain imaging technology that uses infrared light to track blood flow during different tasks.

Gulf War Illness: An illness defined by toxic exposure during the 1990–91 Gulf War and the resulting impact on veterans' physical and psychological functioning.

Haiku: A three-line form of poetry, originally from Japan, that uses the syllable structure of 5-7-5 for each line of the poem.

Henna: A form of temporary skin decoration used in Central and South Asia using a paste made from the leaves of the henna plant.

Hormesis: The development of immunity to a poison or destructive force by building resistance to it in small doses (e.g., vaccines for illnesses that in small doses trigger an effective immune response).

Ikebana: A Japanese style of flower decoration that integrates symbolic, philosophical, and aesthetic elements.

Improvisation techniques: Creative techniques that require spontaneous responses that are not planned but are derived in the moment as a response to expressions by another person.

Interoception: Sensory perception of signals and sensations from within the body. It is a broader term than enteroception, which is specific to organs within the body.

Jugaad: A Hindi term used to refer to creative problem-solving in situations of limited resources.

Kantha: A form of embroidery from western India that uses a simple running stitch and is often used to upcycle and layer old fabrics into quilts.

Karma yoga: A form of yoga practice that focuses on service to others in a community.

Kolam: A form of floral decoration from Tamil Nadu, India, using rice flour. The style has simple elements of dots and lines and is meant to be both a decorative element and a spiritual offering connecting to nature.

Malayalis: People of the southern state of Kerala, India.

Mandala designs: Designs that originated in South Asia among Hindu and Buddhist communities as a form of creative meditative practice.

Meaning-making: Associating words and personal relevance to experiences.

Meditation: The act of paying attention and focusing the mind and thoughts.

Mindfulness: Paying intentional attention to experiences in the moment, especially as they relate to input from our senses.

Mini c creativity: Creativity associated with the choices and actions we engage in every day, especially ones that have interpersonal relevance and learning.

Mirror neurons: A type of neuron that connects the visual and motor cortices and responds to external stimuli reactively and prior to conscious meaning-making.

Negativity bias: The evolutionary tendency to notice and remember negative events as a way to enhance survival.

Neuroception: The sense that assesses information on the threats in one's environment. Also called *nociception*.

Neuroplasticity: The quality of neuronal networks in the brain to grow new networks and connections to adapt to human actions and needs.

Oxytocin: A hormone released by the body during the formation of deep attachments, primarily between mothers and children but also between peers and sexual partners.

Parasympathetic nervous system: Works to support body activities at rest such as relaxation, activating metabolism, digestion, and removal of toxins.

Post-traumatic stress disorder: A sustained experience of being impacted by a traumatic event long after it has ceased; symptoms range from hypervigilance to numbness.

Proprioception: The sense of knowing how the body is positioned in the space around it.

Rabari community: A nomadic community that lives in the state of Gujarat in western India.

Rangoli: A form of floor decoration created in many parts of India especially, during festive or special community celebratory occasions.

Receptive experiences: Experiences that involve viewing, listening, or receiving sensory input without any active expressive components.

Rejection: The experience of being denied something by an external force or entity; unlike failure, which feels more like an internal assessment.

Resilience: The psychological ability to bounce back to a normative or baseline state after a non-normative stressful experience.

Salience network: The networks of the brain associated with paying attention and focus, including the prefrontal cortex.

Sashiko: A traditional Japanese embroidery style used to repair torn or damaged fabrics by creating an entirely new pattern in the mending of this fabric.

Self-regulation: The ability to recognize and manage one's self adaptively through awareness of inner mental states and responses to external stimuli.

Small c creativity: Acts of exploration, imagination, and creative expression that we generate as we negotiate the challenges of life.

Social prescriptions: Recommendations by medical providers to participate in arts and culture in order to promote holistic health and well-being in patients.

Somatosensory: Referring primarily to the sense of touch.

Spanda: Originally from the Sanskrit, it refers to the pulse or vibration pulse associated with creative energy.

Structured art media: In art therapy, refers to the use of art media that are harder in form and easier to control, such as pencils and markers.

Sympathetic nervous system: Activates the body into physical action and responds to external stimuli and threats.

Temporal coherence: Consistency around the sequencing of events and of time in a piece of writing.

Thematic coherence: Consistency around an idea or theme in a piece of writing.

Treatment group: The participants in an experimental research study who receive the main intervention or treatment (also see *control group*).

Triggers or triggering events: Sensory or human interactional experiences that remind us of past unresolved traumas and wounds. Triggers can be completely unrelated to the event but are powerful in that the activated memories can be intense, overwhelming, and painful to manage.

Valence: The emotional leaning of an experience.

Weaves: Fabrics made of woven threads. Can also refer to the metaphorical interweaving of ideas and experiences, as in stories.

Yoga: A form of health practice that originated in India and combines breathing, physical movement, and meditative practices for physiological and spiritual well-being.

References

Acar, S., & Runco, M. A. (2012). Psychoticism and creativity: A meta-analytic review. *Psychology of Aesthetics, Creativity and the Arts*, 6(4), 341. https://doi.org/10.1037/a0027497

Albright, T. D., & Stoner, G. R. (2002). Contextual influences on visual processing. *Annual Review of Neuroscience*, 25, 339–379. https://doi.org/10.1146/annurev.neuro.25.112 701.142900

Alter-Muri, S. (2020). The body as canvas: Motivations, meanings, and therapeutic implications of tattoos. *Art Therapy*, 37(3), 139–146. https://doi.org/10.1080/07421656.2019.1679545

Alter-Muri, S. B., & Vazzano, S. (2014). Gender typicality in children's art development: A cross-cultural study. *The Arts in Psychotherapy*, 41(2), 155–162. https://doi.org/10.1016/j.aip.2014.01.003

American Art Therapy Association. (2018). www.arttherapy.org

American Psychiatric Association. (2021). *Stress in America: One year later a new wave of pandemic health concerns*. https://www.apa.org/news/press/releases/stress/2021/sia-pandemic-report.pdf

Anda, R. F., Butchart, A., Felitti, V. J., & Brown, D. W. (2010). Building a framework for global surveillance of the public health implications of adverse childhood experiences. *American Journal of Preventive Medicine*, 39(1), 93–98. https://doi.org/10.1016/j.amepre.2010.03.015

Andrade, J. (2010). What does doodling do? *Applied Cognitive Psychology*, 24, 100–106. https://doi.org/10.1002/acp.1561

Andrews-Hanna, J. R., Smallwood, J., & Spreng, R. N. (2014). The default network and self-generated thought: Component processes, dynamic control, and clinical relevance. *Annals of the New York Academy of Sciences*, 1316(1), 29–52. https://doi.org/10.1111/nyas.12360

Aristotle. (1963). *Poetics*, 111, A. Everyman Library Translation, 12f.

Arslanbek, A., Malhotra, B., & Kaimal, G. (2022). Indigenous and traditional arts in art therapy practices: Value, meaning, and clinical implications. *The Arts in Psychotherapy*, 77, 101879. https://doi.org/10.1016/j.aip.2021.101879

Askenase, M. H., & Sansing, L. H. (2016). Stages of the inflammatory response in pathology and tissue repair after intracerebral hemorrhage. *Seminars in Neurology*, 36(3), 288–297. https://doi.org/10.1055/s-0036-1582132

Atchley, R. A., Strayer, D. L., & Atchley, P. (2012) Creativity in the wild: Improving creative reasoning through immersion in natural settings. *PLoS One*, 7(12), e51474. https://doi.org/10.1371/journal.pone.0051474

Aubert, M., Setiawan, P., Oktaviana, A. A., Brumm, A., Sulistyarto, P. H., Saptomo, E. W., Istiawan, B., Ma'rifat, T. A., Wahyuono, V. N., Atmoko, F. T., Zhao, J.-X., Huntley, J., Taçon, P. S. C., & Brand, H. E. A. (2018). Palaeolithic cave art in Borneo. *Nature*, 564(7735), 254–257. https://doi.org/10.1038/s41586-018-0679-9

Ayaz, H., Onaral, B., Izzetoglu, K., Shewokis, P. A., McKendrick, R., & Parasuraman, R. (2013). Continuous monitoring of brain dynamics with functional near infrared spectroscopy as a tool for neuroergonomic research: Empirical examples and a technological development. *Frontiers in Human Neuroscience* 7(871), 1–13. http://dx.doi.org/10.3389/fnhum.2013.00871

Babouchkina, A., & Robbins, S. J. (2015). Reducing negative mood through mandala creation: A randomized controlled trial. *Art Therapy*, 32(1), 34–39. https://doi.org/10.1080/07421656.2015.994428

Balasubramanian, D. (2021, May 29). Our inheritance from the Neanderthals. *The Hindu.* https://www.thehindu.com/sci-tech/science/our-inheritance-from-the-neanderthals/arti cle34678437.ece

Baldwin, C. L., Roberts, D. M., Barragan, D., Lee, J. D., Lerner, N., & Higgins, J. S. (2017). Detecting and quantifying mind wandering during simulated driving. *Frontiers in Human Neuroscience, 11,* 406. https://doi.org/10.3389/fnhum.2017.00406

Baldwin, J. (2013). *The fire next time.* Vintage Books (reissue).

Baron, R. A., & Thomley, J. (1994). A whiff of reality: Positive affect as a potential mediator of the effects of pleasant fragrances on task performance and helping. *Environment and Behavior, 26*(6), 766–784. https://doi.org/10.1177%2F0013916594266003

Barton, J., Griffin, M., & Pretty, J. (2012). Exercise-, nature- and socially interactive-based initiatives improve mood and self-esteem in the clinical population. *Perspectives in Public Health, 132*(2), 89–96. https://doi.org/10.1177/1757913910393862

Baumgartner, H. M., Cole, S. L., Olney, J. J., & Berridge, K. C. (2020). Desire or dread from nucleus accumbens inhibitors reverse by same site optogenetic excitations. *Journal of Neuroscience, 40*(13), 2737–2752. https://doi.org/10.1523/JNEUROSCI.2902-19.2020

Beaty, R. E., Benedek, M., Kaufman, S. B., & Silvia, P. J. (2015). Default and executive network coupling supports creative idea production. *Scientific Reports, 5*(1), 1–14. https://doi.org/10.1038/srep10964

Beaty, R. E., Kenett, Y. N., Christensen, A. P., Rosenberg, M. D., Benedek, M., Chen, Q., Fink, A., Qiu, J., Kwapil, T. R., Kane, M. J., & Silvia, P. J. (2018). Robust prediction of individual creative ability from brain functional connectivity. *Proceedings of the National Academy of Sciences USA, 115*(5), 1087–1092. https://doi.org/10.1073/pnas.1713532115

Beerse, M. E., Van Lith, T., & Stanwood, G. D. (2019). Is there a biofeedback response to art therapy? A technology-assisted approach for reducing anxiety and stress in college students. *SAGE Open, 9*(2), 2158244019854646. https://doi.org/10.1177/2158244019854646

Beghetto, R. A., & Kaufman, J. C. (2007). Toward a broader conception of creativity: A case for 'mini-c' creativity. *Psychology of Aesthetics, Creativity, and the Arts, 1*(2), 73–79. https://doi.org/10.1037/1931-3896.1.2.73

Belkofer, C. M., Van Hecke, A. V., & Konopka, L. M. (2014). Effects of drawing on alpha ac-tivity: A quantitative EEG study with implications for art therapy. *Art Therapy, 31*(2), 61–68. https://doi.org/10.1080/07421656.2014.903821

Bender, B., Metzl, E. S., Selman, T., Gloger, D., & Moreno, N. (2015). Creative soups for the soul: Stories of community recovery in Talca, Chile, after the 2010 earthquake. *Psykhe: Revista de la Escuela de Psicología, 24*(1), 1–13. https://doi.org/10.7764/psykhe.24.1.641

Berberian, M. G., Walker, M. S., & Kaimal, G. (2019). "Master my demons": Montage paintings by active-duty military service members with traumatic brain injury and post-traumatic stress. *Medical Humanities, 45,* 353–360. https://doi.org/10.1136/medhum-2018-011493

Berridge, K. C., & Kringelbach, M. L. (2013). Neuroscience of affect: Brain mechanisms of pleasure and displeasure. *Current Opinion in Neurobiology, 23*(3), 294–303. https://doi.org/10.1016/j.conb.2013.01.017

Biederman, I., & Vessel, E. A. (2006). Perceptual pleasure and the brain: A novel theory explains why the brain craves information and seeks it through the senses. *American Scientist, 94*(3), 247–253.

Boerner, M., Joseph, S., & Murphy, D. (2017). The association between sense of humor and trauma-related mental health outcomes: Two exploratory studies. *Journal of Loss and Trauma, 22*(5), 440–452. https://doi.org/10.1080/15325024.2017.1310504

Bolwerk, A., Mack-Andrick, J., Lang, F. R., Dörfler, A., & Maihöfner, C. (2014). How art changes your brain: Differential effects of visual art production and cognitive art evaluation on functional brain connectivity. *PLoS One, 9*(7), e101035. http://dx.doi.org/10.1371/jour nal.pone.0101035

Boras, E., Slevin, M., Alexander, M. Y., Aljohi, A., Gilmore, W., Ashworth, J., Krupinski, J., Potempa, L. A., Al Abdulkareem, I., Elobeid, A., & Matou-Nasri, S. (2014). Monomeric C-reactive protein and Notch-3 co-operatively increase angiogenesis through PI3K signalling pathway. *Cytokine, 69*(2), 165–179. https://doi.org/10.1016/j.cyto.2014.05.027

Bowker, J. C., Stotsky, M. T., & Etkin, R. G. (2017). How BIS/BAS and psycho-behavioral variables distinguish between social withdrawal subtypes during emerging adulthood. *Personality and Individual Differences, 119*, 283–288. https://doi.org/10.1016/j.paid.2017.07.043

Bracha, H. S. (2004). Freeze, flight, fight, fright, faint: Adaptationist perspectives on the acute stress response spectrum. *CNS Spectrums, 9*(9), 679–685. https://doi.org/10.1017/s1092852900001954

Bratman, G. N., Dailey, G. C., Levy, B. A., & Gross, J. J. (2015). The benefits of nature experience: Improved affect and cognition. *Landscape and Urban Planning, 138*, 41–50. https://doi.org/10.1016/j.landurbplan.2015.02.005

Brawer, J., & Amir, O. (2021). Mapping the "funny bone": Neuroanatomical correlates of humor creativity in professional comedians. *Social Cognitive and Affective Neuroscience, 16*(9), 915–925. https://doi.org/10.1093/scan/nsab049

Brockington, G., Moreira, A. P. G., Buso, M. S., da Silva, S. G., Altszyler, E., Fischer, R., & Moll, J. (2021). Storytelling increases oxytocin and positive emotions and decreases cortisol and pain in hospitalized children. *Proceedings of the National Academy of Sciences USA, 118*(22), e2018409118. https://doi.org/10.1073/pnas.2018409118

Brown, B. (2015). *Daring greatly: How the courage to be vulnerable transforms the way we live, love, parent, and lead.* Penguin.

Brown, D. K., Barton, J. L., & Gladwell, V. F. (2013). Viewing nature scenes positively affects recovery of autonomic function following acute mental stress. *Environmental Science and Technology, 47*(11), 5562–5569. https://doi.org/10.1021/es305019p

Brown, E. D., Garnett, M. L., Anderson, K. E., & Laurenceau, J. P. (2017). Can the arts get under the skin? Arts and cortisol for economically disadvantaged children. *Child Development, 88*(4), 1368–1381. https://doi.org/10.1111/cdev.12652

Brown, E. D., & Sax, K. L. (2013). Arts enrichment and preschool emotions for low-income children at risk. *Early Childhood Research Quarterly, 28*(2), 337–346. https://doi.org/10.1016/j.ecresq.2012.08.002

Bruner, J. (1986). *Actual minds, possible worlds.* Harvard University Press.

Bubic, A., Von Cramon, D. Y., & Schubotz, R. I. (2010). Prediction, cognition and the brain. *Frontiers in Human Neuroscience, 4*, 25. https://doi.org/10.3389/fnhum.2010.00025

Cappelorn, N. J., Hannay, A., Kangas, D., Kirmmse, B. H., Rumble, V., Söderquist, K. B., & Pattison, G. (2008*). Kierkegaard's journals and notebooks (Volume 2: Journals Ee-Kk).* Princeton University Press.

Center for Mental Health. (2019). Toronto hospital opens sweat lodge for aboriginal patients. *White Wolf Pack.* http://www.whitewolfpack.com/2016/06/toronto-hospital-opens-sweat-lodge-for.html?fbclid=IwAR2Rk3Dq-EavL5YoyIM4Tzs_dERi6W92vTu2onRlDBQA96A8YUHk3TM81-U&m=1

Cesari, M., Kritchevsky, S., Baumgartner, R., Atkinson, H., Pennix, B., Lenchik, L., Palla, S. L., Ambrosius, W. T., Tracy, R. P., & Pahor, M. (2005). Sarcopenia, obesity, and inflammation—results from the Trial of Angiotensin Converting Enzyme Inhibition and Novel Cardiovascular Risk Factors study. *American Journal of Clinical Nutrition, 82*(2), 428–434. https://doi.org/10.1093/ajcn/82.2.428

Chamberlain, R., Drake, J. E., Kozbelt, A., Hickman, R., Siev, J., & Wagemans, J. (2019). Artists as experts in visual cognition: An update. *Psychology of Aesthetics, Creativity, and the Arts, 13*(1), 58. https://doi.org/10.1037/aca0000156

Chamberlain, R., McManus, C. I., Brunswick, N., Rankin, Q., Riley, H., & Kanai, R. (2014). Drawing on the right side of the brain: A voxel-based morphometry analysis of observational drawing. *Neuroimage, 96*, 167–173. https://doi.org/10.1016/j.neuroimage.2014.03.062

Chatterjee, A. (2004). Prospects for a cognitive neuroscience of visual aesthetics. *Bulletin of Psychology and the Arts, 4*, 56–60.

Chatterjee, A., & Vartanian, O. (2014). Neuroaesthetics. *Trends in Cognitive Sciences, 18*(7), 370–375. https://doi.org/10.1016/j.tics.2014.03.003

Chatterjee, A., & Vartanian, O. (2016). Neuroscience of aesthetics. *Annals of the New York Academy of Sciences, 1369*(1), 172–194.

Chaudhry, S. R., & Gossman, W. (2021). Biochemistry, endorphin. StatPearls. https://www.ncbi.nlm.nih.gov/books/NBK470306/

Chen, F., Xu, Y., Wang, J., Yang, X., Cao, H., & Huang, P. (2020). Relaxation effect of patchouli alcohol in rat corpus cavernous and its underlying mechanisms. *Evidence Based Complementary and Alternative Medicine, 2020*, Article ID 3109069. https://doi.org/10.1155/2020/3109069

Chilisa, B. (2012). *Indigenous research methodologies.* Sage.

Clark, A. (2014). *Surfing uncertainty: Prediction, action, and the embodied mind.* Oxford University Press.

Coburn, A., Vartanian, O., & Chatterjee, A. (2017). Buildings, beauty, and the brain: A neuroscience of architectural experience. *Journal of Cognitive Neuroscience, 29*(9), 1521–1531. http://dx.doi.org/10.1162/jocn_a_01146

Collier, A. F. (2011). The well-being of women who create with textiles: Implications for art therapy. *Art Therapy, 28*(3), 104–112. https://doi.org/10.1080/07421656.2011.597025

Collier, A. F. (2012). *Using textile arts and handcrafts in therapy with women.* Jessica Kingsley.

Comas-Díaz, L. (2021). Afro-Latinxs: Decolonization, healing, and liberation. *Journal of Latinx Psychology, 9*(1), 65–75. https://doi.org/10.1037/lat0000164

Cooney, J. (2001). Conference Presentation. In 5th Annual Society for the Study of Childhood in the Past conference: *Child Labour in the Past: Children as Economic Contributors and Consumers.* University of Cambridge.

Costa, V. D., Tran, V. L., Turchi, J., & Averbeck, B. B. (2014). Dopamine modulates novelty seeking behavior during decision making. *Behavioral Neuroscience, 128*(5), 556–566. https://doi.org/10.1037/a0037128

Councill, T. (2015). Art therapy with children. In D. E. Gussak & M. L. Rosal (Eds.), *Wiley handbook of art therapy* (pp. 242–251). John Wiley & Sons.

Councill, T. D., & Ramsey, K. (2019). Art therapy as a psychosocial support in a child's palliative care. *Art Therapy, 36*(1), 40–45. https://doi.org/10.1080/07421656.2019.1564644

Crook, A. (2021, January 28). *The future of art according to Shirin Neshat* [video]. Artsy. https://www.artsy.net/series/artsy-editors-future-art/artsy-editorial-future-art-shirin-neshat

Crowe, N. (1995). *Nature and the idea of a man-made world: An investigation into the evolutionary roots of form and order in the built environment.* MIT Press.

Csikszentmihalyi, M. (1990). *Flow: The psychology of optimal experience* (1st ed.). Harper & Row.

Csikszentmihalyi, M. (1996). *Creativity: Flow and the psychology of discovery and invention.* Harper Collins.

Cucca, A., Di Rocco, A., Acosta, I., Beheshti, M., Berberian, M., Bertisch, H. C., Droby, A., Ettinger, T., Hudson, T. E., Inglese, M., Jung, Y. J., Mania, D. F., Quartarone, A., Rizzo, J.-R., Sharma, K., Feigin, A., & Ghilardi, M. F. (2021). Art therapy for Parkinson's disease. *Parkinsonism & Related Disorders, 84*, 148–154. https://doi.org/10.1016/j.parkreldis.2021.01.013

Czamanski-Cohen, J., & Weihs, K. L. (2016). The Bodymind Model: A platform for studying the mechanisms of change induced by art therapy. *The Arts in Psychotherapy, 51*, 63–71.

Czamanski-Cohen, J., Wiley, J. F., Sela, N., Caspi, O., & Weihs, K. (2019). The role of emotional processing in art therapy (REPAT) for breast cancer patients. *Journal of Psychosocial Oncology*, 37(5), 586–598. https://doi.org/10.1080/07347332.2019.1590491

Daminger, A. (2019). The cognitive dimension of household labor. *American Sociological Review*, 84(4), 609–633. https://doi.org/10.1177/0003122419859007

Dance, A. (2021, February 9). *How the arts can help you to craft a successful research career*. *Nature* (Career Feature). https://www.nature.com/articles/d41586-021-00334-2?mc_cid=cee506ec94&mc_eid=76d1018f76

D'Argembeau, A., Cassol, H., Phillips, C., Balteau, E., Salmon, E., & Van der Linden, M. (2014). Brains creating stories of selves: The neural basis of autobiographical reasoning. *Social Cognitive and Affective Neuroscience*, 9(5), 646–652. https://doi.org/10.1093/scan/nst028

Davies, C., Knuiman, M., & Rosenberg, M. (2015). The art of being mentally healthy: A study to quantify the relationship between recreational arts engagement and mental well-being in the general population. *BMC Public Health*, 16(1), 1–10. https://doi.org/10.1186/s12889-015-2672-7

Deaver, S. (2009). A normative study of children's drawings: Preliminary research findings. *Art Therapy: Journal of the American Art Therapy Association*, 26(1), 4–11. https://doi:10.1080/07421656.2009.10129309

De Dreu, C. K., Greer, L. L., Van Kleef, G. A., Shalvi, S., & Handgraaf, M. J. (2011). Oxytocin promotes human ethnocentrism. *Proceedings of the National Academy of Sciences USA*, 108(4), 1262–1266. https://doi.org/10.1073/pnas.1015316108

DeMoraes, C. G. (2013). Anatomy of visual pathways. *Journal of Glaucoma, 22*, S2–S7. https://doi.org/10.1097/IJG.0b013e3182934978

Dewey, J. (1923). *Democracy and education: An introduction to the philosophy of education*. Macmillan.

De Witte, M., Orkibi, H., Zarate, R., Karkou, V., Sajnani, N., Malhotra, B., Ho, R. T. H., Kaimal, G., Baker, f. A., & Koch, S. C. (2021). From therapeutic factors to mechanisms of change in the creative arts therapies: A scoping review. *Frontiers in Psychology, 12*, 678397. https://doi.org/10.3389/fpsyg.2021.678397

Dissanayake, E. (2000). *Art and intimacy: How the arts began*. University of Washington.

Dissanayake, E. (2001). *Homo aestheticus: Where art comes from and why*. University of Washington Press.

Dissanayake, E. (2003). Retrospective on Homo aestheticus. *Journal of the Canadian Association for Curriculum Studies*, 1(2), 7–11.

Dissanayake, E. (2015). *What is art for?* University of Washington Press.

Dixon, D. (2019). How to approach works by morally bad artists. *Art Aesthetics*. https://www.artaesthetics.net/publications/2019/5/26/conflicted-art-how-to-approach-works-by-morally-bad-artists

Dodson, B. (1987). *Sex for one: The joy of self-loving*. Harmony Books.

Donato, A. (2020, August 19). Trauma therapy sees artists of colour turning to art practices of their cultures. *Huffpost*. https://www.huffingtonpost.ca/entry/trauma-therapy-art-bipoc-canadians_ca_5f1b371fc5b6128e6825aa23

Doom, J. R., Seok, D., Narayan, A. J., & Fox, K. R. (2021). Adverse and benevolent childhood experiences predict mental health during the COVID-19 pandemic. *Adversity and Resilience Science, 2*, 193–204. https://doi.org/10.1007/s42844-021-00038-6

Doran, R. P. (2017). Restorative aesthetic pleasures and the restoration of pleasure. *Australasian Philosophical Review*, 1(1), 73–78. https://doi.org/10.1080/24740500.2017.1296399

Doty, R. L., & Kamath, V. (2014). The influences of age on olfaction: A review. *Frontiers in Psychology, 5*, 20. https://doi.org/10.3389/fpsyg.2014.00020

Dougherty, D. (2012). The maker movement. *Innovations: Technology, Governance, Globalization*, 7(3), 11–14.

Dubow, E. F., Boxer, P., Huesmann, L. R., Landau, S., Dvir, S., Shikaki, K., & Ginges, J. (2012). Cumulative effects of exposure to violence on posttraumatic stress in Palestinian and Israeli youth. *Journal of Clinical Child and Adolescent Psychology, 41*(6), 837–844. https://doi.org/10.1080/15374416.2012.675571

Duff, M. (2019). *In narrative therapy, Maori creation stories are being used to heal.* https://www.stuff.co.nz/national/102115864/in-narrative-therapy-mori-creation-stories-are-being-used-to-heal?fbclid=IwAR0QLK9XLOOH6g4Ta1FzUIc6I6KgSg7ARoU_u5Jn5ipx20sZRYFaPBwfz_w

Dunbar, R. I. (1992). Neocortex size as a constraint on group size in primates. *Journal of Human Evolution, 22*(6), 469–493. https://doi.org/10.1016/0047-2484(92)90081-J

Dunn, E. C., Solovieff, N., Lowe, S. R., Gallagher, P. J., Chaponis, J., Rosand, J., Koenen, K. C., Waters, M. C., Rhodes, J. E., & Smoller, J. W. (2014). Interaction between genetic variants and exposure to Hurricane Katrina on post-traumatic stress and post-traumatic growth: A prospective analysis of low income adults. *Journal of Affective Disorders, 152*, 243–249. https://doi.org/10.1016/j.jad.2013.09.018

Dunphy, K. F., Baker, F.A., Dumaresq, E., Carroll-Haskins, K., Eickholt, J., Ercole, M., Kaimal, G., Meyer, K., Sajnani, N., Shamir, O. Y., &, Wosch, T. (2019). Creative arts interventions to address depression in older adults: A systematic review of outcomes, processes and mechanisms. *Frontiers in Psychology.* https://doi.org/10.3389/fpsyg.2018.02655

Dutton, D. (2010). *The art instinct: Beauty, pleasure, and human evolution.* Bloomsbury Press.

Easter, M. (2021). *The comfort crisis: Embrace discomfort to reclaim your wild, happy, healthy self.* Rodale Books.

Ehlers, S., & Kaufmann, S. H. (2010). Infection, inflammation, and chronic diseases: Consequences of a modern lifestyle. *Trends in Immunology, 31*(5), 184–190. https://doi.org/10.1016/j.it.2010.02.003

Ehrlichman, H., & Bastone, L. (1992). The use of odor in the study of emotion. In S. van Toller & G. H. Dodd (Eds.), *Fragrance—The psychology and biology of perfume* (pp. 143–159). Elsevier Applied Science.

Einstein, A. (1930). What I believe. Living Philosophies XIII. *Forum and Century (1930–1940), LXXXIV*(4), 192.

Elkis-Abuhoff, D. L., & Gaydos, M. (2018). Medical art therapy research moves forward: A review of clay manipulation with Parkinson's disease. *Art Therapy, 35*(2), 68–76. https://doi.org/10.1080/07421656.2018.1483162

English, M., Kaplan, G., & Rogers, L. J. (2014). Is painting by elephants in zoos as enriching as we are led to believe? *PeerJ, 2,* e471. https://doi.org/10.7717/peerj.471

Estrella, K. (2005). Expressive therapy: An integrated arts approach. In C. A. Malchiodi (Ed.), *Expressive therapies* (pp. 183–209). Guilford Press.

Fadelli, I. (2021, April 2). Researchers find that rare rewards amplify dopamine responses during learning. *Medical Xpress/Neuroscience.* https://medicalxpress.com/news/2021-04-rare-rewards-amplify-dopamine-responses.html

Fancourt, D., & Finn, S. (2019). What is the evidence of the role of the arts in health and well-being? A scoping review. *World Health Organization Health Evidence Network Synthesis Report, 67.* https://www.euro.who.int/en/publications/abstracts/what-is-the-evidence-on-the-role-of-the-arts-in-improving-health-and-well-being-a-scoping-review-2019

Farago, J. (2021, April 2). What a tiny masterpiece reveals about power and beauty. *New York Times.* https://www.nytimes.com/interactive/2021/04/02/arts/design/shah-jahan-chitarman.html?referringSource=articleShare&fbclid=IwAR0uE5Y1Le9vhDfM_z4F33yfVB4Aq689oOT4GILvfYQwudYKt8mPcqwqB-w

Farahbakhsh, Z. Z., & Siciliano, C. A. (2021). Neurobiology of novelty seeking. *Science, 372*(6543), 684–685. https://doi.org/10.1126/science.abi7270

Felsman, P., Gunawardena, S., & Seifert, C. M. (2020). Improv experience promotes divergent thinking, uncertainty tolerance, and affective well-being. *Thinking Skills and Creativity, 35*, 100632. https://doi.org/10.1016/j.tsc.2020.100632

Ferrari, M., & Quaresima, V. (2012). A brief review on the history of human functional near-infrared spectroscopy (fNIRS) development and fields of application. *NeuroImage, 63*, 921–935. http://dx.doi.org/10.1016/j.neuroimage.2012.03.049Grossmann

Fincher, S. F. (1991) *Creating mandalas for insight, healing, and self-expression*. Shambhala.

Fiske, E. B. (Ed.). (1999). *Champions of change: The impact of the arts on learning*. Arts Education Partnership.

Foo, C., Lozada, A., Aljadeff, J., Li, Y., Wang, J. W., Slesinger, P. A., & Kleinfeld, D. (2021). Reinforcement learning links spontaneous cortical dopamine impulses to reward. *Current Biology, 31*(18), P4111–P4119. https://doi.org/10.1016/j.cub.2021.06.069

Franklin, M. F. (2018). *Art as contemplative practice: Expressive pathways to the self*. SUNY.

Friston, K. (2005). A theory of cortical responses. *Philosophical Transactions of the Royal Society B: Biological Sciences, 360*(1456), 815–836. https://doi.org/10.1098/rstb.2005.1622

Fromm, E. (2010). *The revolution of hope: Towards a humanized technology*. American Mental Health Foundation.

Fujiwara, N., & Kobayashi, K. (2005). Macrophages in inflammation. *Current Drug Targets Inflammation & Allergy, 4*(3), 281–286. https://doi.org/10.2174/1568010054022024

Futterman-Collier, A., & Wayment, H. A. (2019). Enhancing and explaining art-making for mood-repair: The benefits of positive growth-oriented instructions and quiet ego contemplation. *Psychology of Aesthetics, Creativity, and the Arts, 15*(2), 363–376. https://doi.org/10.1037/aca0000286

Futterman-Collier, A. D., Wayment, H. A., & Birkett, M. (2016). Impact of making textile handcrafts on mood enhancement and inflammatory immune changes. *Art Therapy, 33*(4), 178–185. https://doi.org/10.1080/07421656.2016.1226647

Gabora, L., O'Connor, B. P., & Ranjan, A. (2012). The recognizability of individual creative styles within and across domains. *Psychology of Aesthetics, Creativity, and the Arts, 6*(4), 351. https://doi.org/10.1037/a0030193

Genc, H., & Saritas, S. (2019). The effects of lavender oil on the anxiety and vital signs of benign prostatic hyperplasia patients in preoperative period. *Explore, 16*(2), 116–122. https://doi.org/10.1016/j.explore.2019.07.008

Gibbons, A. (2021). When modern humans met Neanderthals. *Science, 372*(6538), 115–116. https://doi.org/10.1126/science.372.6538.115

Gilbert, J., Knight, R., & Blakeslee, S. (2017). *Dirt is good: The advantage of germs for your child's developing immune system*. St. Martin's Press.

Gilligan, C. (1982). *In a different voice: Psychological theory and women's development*. Harvard University Press.

Gitlin, L. N. (2017, December, 21). *Leading a purposeful life in health and in sickness: What gets you out of bed in the morning?* Thrive Global. https://thriveglobal.com/stories/leading-a-purposeful-life-in-health-and-in-sickness/

Glazek, K. (2012). Visual and motor processing in visual artists: Implications for cognitive and neural mechanisms. *Psychology of Aesthetics, Creativity, and the Arts, 6*(2), 155. https://doi.org/10.1037/a0025184

Gotschall, J. (2013). *The storytelling animal: How stories make us human*. Mariner Books.

Gould, S. J. (1997). The exaptive excellence of spandrels as a term and prototype. *Proceedings of the National Academy of Sciences USA, 94*(20), 10750–10755. https://doi.org/10.1073/pnas.94.20.10750

Grant, A. M. (2017). *Originals: How non-conformists move the world*. Penguin.

Grant, A. (2021, July 10). There's a specific kind of joy we've been missing: Guest essay. *New York Times: Sunday Review*. https://www.nytimes.com/2021/07/10/opinion/sunday/covid-group-emotions-happiness.html

Great Big Story. (2018, January 1). *The Link Between Japanese Samurai and Real Indigo* [Video]. https://www.youtube.com/watch?v=Aj5oA0YxCi0

Greenberg, D. M., Decety, J., & Gordon, I. (2021). The social neuroscience of music: Understanding the social brain through human song. *American Psychologist, 76*(7), 1172–1185. https://doi.org/10.1037/amp0000819

Greene, M. (1994). Carpe diem: The arts and school restructuring. *Teachers College Record, 95*, 494–507.

Greene, M. (2007). *Imagination and the healing arts*. Maxine Greene Institute. https://maxinegreene.org/uploads/library/imagination_ha.pdf

Güner, F. (2020, December 10). Why decolonising museums is not enough. *Fisun Güner Writing About Art*. https://fisunguner.com/why-decolonising-museums-is-not-enough/

Guyer, P. (2017). A complex of pleasures: Comment on "The Pleasure of Art" by Mohan Matthen. *Australasian Philosophical Review, 1*(1), 40–49. https://doi.org/10.1080/24740500.2017.1296382

Gussak, D. E. (2021). *The frenzied dance of art and violence*. New York: Oxford University Press.

Habermas, T., & Bluck, S. (2000). Getting a life: The emergence of the life story in adolescence. *Psychological Bulletin, 126*(5), 748. https://doi.org/10.1037/0033-2909.126.5.748

Hackman, D. A., & Farah, M. J. (2009). Socioeconomic status and the developing brain. *Trends in Cognitive Sciences, 13*(2), 65–73. https://doi.org/10.1016/j.tics.2008.11.003

Haiblum-Itskovitch, S., Czamanski-Cohen, J., & Galili, G. (2018). Emotional response and changes in heart rate variability following art-making with three different art materials. *Frontiers in Psychology, 9*, 968. https://doi.org/10.3389/fpsyg.2018.00968

Hair, N. L., Hanson, J. L., Wolfe, B. L., & Pollak, S. D. (2015). Association of child poverty, brain development, and academic achievement. *JAMA Pediatrics, 169*(9), 822–829. https://doi.org/10.1001/jamapediatrics.2015.1475

Haller, M., Case, J., Crone, N. E., Chang, E. F., King-Stephens, D., Laxer, K. D., Weber, P. B., Parvizi, J., Knight, R. T., & Shestyuk, A. Y. (2018). Persistent neuronal activity in human prefrontal cortex links perception and action. *Nature Human Behaviour, 2*(1), 80–91. https://doi.org/10.1038/s41562-017-0267-2

Halligan, P. W., & Oakley, D. A. (2021). Giving up on consciousness as the ghost in the machine. *Frontiers in Psychology, 12*, 1237. https://doi.org/10.3389/fpsyg.2021.571460

Hardiman, M., Rinne, L., & Yarmolinskaya, J. (2014). The effects of arts integration on long term retention of academic content. *Mind, Brain and Education, 8*(3), 144–148. https://doi.org/10.1111/mbe.12053

Hass-Cohen, N., Findlay, J. C., Carr, R., & Vanderlan, J. (2014) "Check, change what you need to change and/or keep what you want": An art therapy neurobiological-based trauma protocol. *Art Therapy, 31*(2), 69–78. https://doi.org/10.1080/07421656.2014.903825

Hayes, S. (2014). Foreword. In J. Stoddard & N. Afari (Eds.), *The big book of ACT metaphors: A practitioner's guide to experiential exercises and metaphors in Acceptance and Commitment Therapy* (pp. ix–xi). New Harbinger.

Hays-Grudo, J., & Morris, A. S. (2020). *Adverse and protective childhood experiences: A developmental perspective*. American Psychological Association.

Heckman, J. J. (2006). Skill formation and the economics of investing in disadvantaged children. *Science, 312*(5782), 1900–1902. https://doi.org/10.1126/science.1128898

Heller, A. S., Shi, T. C., Ezie, C. C., Reneau, T. R., Baez, L. M., Gibbons, C. J., & Hartley, C. A. (2020). Association between real-world experiential diversity and positive affect relates to hippocampal–striatal functional connectivity. *Nature Neuroscience, 23*(7), 800–804. https://doi.org/10.1038/s41593-020-0636-4

Helm, C. W., Cawthra, H. C., De Vynck, J. C., Helm, C. J., Rust, R., & Stear, W. (2019). Patterns in the sand: A pleistocene hominin signature along the South African coastline? *Proceedings of the Geologists' Association, 130*(6), 719–740. https://doi.org/10.1016/j.pgeola.2019.08.004

Henderson, R. K., & Schnall, S. (2021). Disease and disapproval: COVID-19 concern is related to greater moral condemnation. *Evolutionary Psychology, 19*(2), 1–10. https://doi.org/10.1177/14747049211021524

Hetland, L., Winner, E., Veenema, S., &, Sheridan, K. (2007). *Studio thinking: The real benefits of visual arts education*. Columbia University Press.

Heyes, C., & Catmur, C. (2022). What happened to mirror neurons? *Perspectives on Psychological Science, 17*(1), 153–168. https://doi.org/10.1177/1745691621990638

Hoffer, E. (1951). *The true believer: Thoughts on the nature of mass movements*. New York: Harper and Row.

Hoffmann, D. L., Standish, C. D., García-Diez, M., Pettitt, P. B., Milton, J. A., Zilhão, J., Alcolea-González, J. J., Cantalejo-Duarte, P., Collado, H., De Balbín, R., Lorblanchet, M., Ramos-Muñoz, J., Weniger, G.-C., & Pike, A. W. (2018). U-Th dating of carbonate crusts reveals Neandertal origin of Iberian cave art. *Science, 359*(6378), 912–915. https://doi.org/10.1126/science.aap7778

Hoffmann, J. D., & Russ, S. (2016). Fostering pretend play skills and creativity in elementary school girls: A group play intervention. *Psychology of Aesthetics, Creativity, and the Arts, 10*(1), 114.

Holcomb, P., & Grainger, J. (2006). On the time course of visual word recognition. *Journal of Cognitive Neuroscience, 18*, 1631–1643. https://doi.org/10.1162/jocn.2006.18.10.1631

Horgan, J. (2019, December 19). Can philosophy make you happy? Philosopher Catherine Wilson thinks the ancient sage Epicurus can provide guidance for our modern scientific age. *Scientific American.* https://blogs.scientificamerican.com/cross-check/can-philosophy-make-you-happy/

Hovane, M. (2017). *Ikebana: The Japanese "way of the flower."* https://www.zenvita.com/blog/ikebana-the-japanese-way-of-the-flower.html

Huotilainen, M., Rankanen, M., Groth, C., Seitamaa-Hakkarainen, P., & Makela, M. (2018). Why our brains love arts and crafts. *FormAkademisk: Research Journal of Design and Design Education, 11*(1), 1–17. https://doi.org/10.7577/formakademisk.1908

Husk, K., Elston, J., Gradinger, F., Callaghan, L., & Asthana, S. (2019). Social prescribing: Where is the evidence? *British Journal of General Practice, 69*(678), 6–7. https://doi.org/10.3399/bjgp19X700325

Iacoboni, M. (2009). Imitation, empathy, and mirror neurons. *Annual Review of Psychology, 60*, 653–670. https://doi.org/10.1146/annurev.psych.60.110707.163604

Iyer, M. (2018). *Rangoli, culture and art therapy: Integrating a tradition within clinical practice*. Unpublished Master's thesis. Singapore: LaSalle University.

Izard, C. E., King, K. A., Trentacosta, C. J., Morgan, J. K., Laurenceau, J. P., Krauthamer-Ewing, E. S., & Finlon, K. J. (2008). Accelerating the development of emotion competence in Head Start children: Effects on adaptive and maladaptive behavior. *Development and Psychopathology, 20*(1), 369–397.

James, V. L. (2019, July 15). Migrant women fleeing violence find beauty and healing in embroidery. *America: The Jesuit Review.* https://www.americamagazine.org/faith/2019/07/15/migrant-women-fleeing-violence-find-beauty-and-healing-embroidery?fbclid=IwAR0AL7F8ZOawb9hCXLlfddmija6xf1rNXYNAuUqDWrOufsbJ1l1cGiLlLWk

James, W. (1890). *The principles of psychology*. Harvard University Press.

Jamison, K. R. (2015). *An unquiet mind: A memoir of moods and madness* (Vol. 4). Pan Macmillan.

Jezzini, A., Bromberg-Martin, E. S., Trambaiolli, L. R., Haber, S. N., & Monosov, I. E. (2021). A prefrontal network integrates preferences for advance information about uncertain rewards and punishments. *Neuron, 109*(14), P2339–2352. https://doi.org/10.1016/j.neuron.2021.05.013

Jie, F., Yin, G., Yang, W., Yang, M., Gao, S., Lv, J., & Li, B. (2018). Stress in regulation of GABA amygdala system and relevance to neuropsychiatric diseases. *Frontiers in Neuroscience, 12*, 562. https://doi.org/10.3389/fnins.2018.00562

Jones, J. P. (2016). Complicated grief: Considerations for treatment of military populations. In P. Howie (Ed.), *Art therapy with military populations: History, innovation and applications* (pp. 98–110). Routledge.

Jones, J. (2021, April 23). *Did art peak 30,000 years ago? How cave paintings became my lockdown obsession. Guardian Art.* https://www.theguardian.com/artanddesign/2021/apr/23/cave-paintings-art-lockdown-obsession-30-000-years-lascaux

Jones, J. P., Walker, M. S., Drass, J. M., & Kaimal, G. (2017). Art therapy interventions for active-duty military service members with post-traumatic stress disorder and traumatic brain injury. *International Journal of Art Therapy, 23*(2), 70–85. https://doi.org/10.1080/17454832.2017.1388263

Joseph, C. (2006). Creative alliance: The healing power of art therapy. *Art Therapy, 23*(1), 30–33. https://doi.org/10.1080/07421656.2006.10129531

Junkin, J., Kaimal, G., Katz-Terry, J., & Smith, K. (2016). The Art of Growing Leaders program: Supporting identity and leadership development through arts-based self-expression. *Journal of Applied Arts and Health, 7*(3), 327–345. https://doi.org/10.1386/jaah.7.3.327_1

Kabisch, N., van den Bosch, M., & Lafortezza, R. (2017). The health benefits of nature-based solutions to urbanization challenges for children and the elderly–A systematic review. *Environmental Research, 159*, 362–373. https://doi.org/10.1016/j.envres.2017.08.004

Kadohisa, M. (2013). Effects of odor on emotion, with implications. *Frontiers in Systems Neuroscience, 7*, 66. https://doi.org/10.3389/fnsys.2013.00066

Kaimal, G. (2001). *The role of individual art therapy in reducing disruptive behavior in a young adolescent male: A single case experimental study.* Master's thesis, MCP Hahnemann University, College of Nursing and Health Professions, Creative Arts in Therapy Program.

Kaimal, G. (2007). *Emerging adulthood and the perception of parental depression.* Doctoral dissertation, Harvard University Graduate School of Education, Human Development and Psychology program.

Kaimal, G. (2015). Evolving identities: The person(al), the profession(al) and the artist(ic). *Art Therapy, 32*(3), 136–141. https://doi.org/10.1080/07421656.2015.1060840

Kaimal, G. (2019). Adaptive response theory (ART): A clinical research framework for art therapy. *Art Therapy, 36*(4), 215–219. https://doi.org/10.1080/07421656.2019.1667670

Kaimal, G., Ayaz, H., Herres, J. M., Makwana, B., Dieterich-Hartwell, R. M., Kaiser, D. H., & Nasser, J. A. (2017a). fNIRS assessment of reward perception based on visual self-expression: Coloring, doodling and free drawing. *The Arts in Psychotherapy, 55*, 85–92. https://doi.org/10.1016/j.aip.2017.05.004

Kaimal, G., & Beardslee, W. R. (2010). Emerging adulthood and the perceptions of parental depression. *Qualitative Health Research, 20*(9), 1213–1229. https://doi.org/10.1177/1049732310371625

Kaimal, G., & Beardslee, W. R. (2015). The perceived impact of parental depression on the narrative construction of personal identity: Reflections from emerging adults. *Narrative Works, 5*(1), 40–67.

Kaimal, G., Carroll-Haskins, K., Berberian, M. G., Dougherty, A., Carlton, N. R., &, Ramakrishnan, A. (2019). Virtual reality and art therapy: A pilot qualitative study of the novel medium. *Art Therapy, 37*(1), 16–24. https://doi.org/10.1080/07421656.2019.1659662

Kaimal, G., Carroll-Haskins, K., Ramakrishnan, A., Magsamen, S., Arslanbek, A., & Herres, J. (2020a). Outcomes of visual self-expression in virtual reality on psychosocial well-being with the inclusion of a fragrance stimulus: A pilot mixed-methods study. *Frontiers in Psychology, 11*, 3161. https://doi.org/10.3389/fpsyg.2020.589461

Kaimal, G., & Arslanbek, A. (2020c). Indigenous and traditional visual artistic practices: Implications for art therapy clnical practice and research. *Frontiers in Psychology, 11*, 1320. https://doi.org/10.3389/fpsyg.2020.01320.

Kaimal, G., Drescher, J., Fairbank, H., Gonzaga, A., Junkin, J., & White, G. P. (2016a). Learning about leadership from a visit to the art museum. *International Journal of Education and the Arts, 17*(6), 1–22. http://www.ijea.org/v17n6/index.html

Kaimal, G., Drescher, J., Fairbank, H., Gonzaga, A., & White, G. P. (2014). Inspiring creativity in school leaders: Leadership lessons from the performing arts. *International Journal of Education and the Arts, 15*(4), 1–22. http://www.ijea.org/v15n4/

Kaimal, G., & Gerber, N. (2007). Impressions over time: Community progressive murals in an outpatient HIV/AIDS clinic. *The Arts in Psychotherapy, 34*(2), 151–162.

Kaimal, G., Gonzaga, A. M. L., & Schwachter, V. (2016b). Crafting, health and well-being: National trends and implications for art therapists. *Arts and Health, 9*(1), 81–90. https://doi.org/10.1080/17533015.2016.1185447

Kaimal, G., Carroll-Haskins, K., Topoglu, Y., Ramakrishnan, A., Arslanbek, A., & Ayaz, H. (2021). Exploratory fNIRS assessment of differences in activation in virtual reality visual self-expression including with a fragrance stimulus. *Art Therapy*. https://doi.org/10.1080/07421656.2019.1659662

Kaimal, G., Hommel, S., Seiden, J., & Pisani, L. (2022). Healing and Education Through the Arts (HEART): Outcomes of a 9-month arts-based psychosocial support intervention for 5-year-old children in Malawi. In C. Maguire & A. Holt (Eds.), *Arts and culture in development practice*. Routledge.

Kaimal, G., Jones, J. P., Wang, X., Acharya, B., Dieterich-Hartwell, R., (2019). Evaluation of long- and short-term art therapy interventions in an integrative care setting for military service members with post-traumatic stress and traumatic brain injury. *The Arts in Psychotherapy, 62*, 28–36. https://doi.org/10.1016/j.aip.2018.10.003

Kaimal, G., & Jordan, W. (2016). Do incentive-based programs improve teacher quality and student achievement? An analysis of implementation in 12 charter schools. *Teachers College Record, 118*(7), 1–34. https://vialogues.com/vialogues/play/34969/

Kaimal, G., Mensinger, J. L., & Carroll-Haskins, K. (2020b). Outcomes of collage art-based and narrative self-expression among home hospice caregivers. *International Journal of Art Therapy, 25*(2), 52–63. https://doi.org/10.1080/17454832.2020.1752756

Kaimal, G., Carroll-Haskins, K., Mensinger, J. L., Dieterich-Hartwell, R. M., Biondo, J., & Levin, W. P. (2020d). Changes in Measures of Stress, Affect, Anxiety, Self-efficacy, and Salivary Biomarkers as a Result of Therapeutic Artmaking in Patients Undergoing Radiation Oncology Treatment: A Mixed Methods Pilot Study. *Integrative Cancer Therapies, 19*. https://doi.org/10.1177/1534735420912835

Kaimal, G., Mensinger, J. L., Drass, J. M., &, Dieterich-Hartwell, R. (2017b). Open studio art therapy versus coloring: Differences in outcomes of affect, stress, creative agency and self-efficacy. *Canadian Art Therapy Association Journal, 30*(2), 56–68. https://doi.org/10.1080/08322473.2017.1375827

Kaimal, G., Metzl, E., &, Millrod, E. T. (2017c). Facilitative leadership: A framework for the creative arts therapies. *Art Therapy, 34*(3), 146–151. https://doi.org/10.1080/07421656.2017.1343072

Kaimal, G., Miller, G., Rattigan, M. D., & Haddy, J. (2016c). Implications of national trends in digital media use for art therapy practice. *Journal of Clinical Art Therapy, 3*(1), 6. http://digitalcommons.lmu.edu/jcat/vol3/iss1/6

Kaimal, G., & Ray, K. (2016). Free art making in an art therapy open studio: Changes in affect and self-efficacy. *Arts and Health*, 9(2), 154–166. https://doi.org/10.1080/17533015.2016.1217248

Kaimal, G., Ray, K., & Muniz, J. M. (2016d). Reduction of cortisol levels and participants' responses following artmaking. *Art Therapy*, 33(2), 74–80. https://doi.org/10.1080/07421656.2016.1166832

Kaimal, G., Walker, M. S., Herres, J., French, L. M., & Degraba, T. J. (2018). Observational study of associations between visual imagery and measures of depression, anxiety and stress among active-duty military service members' with post-traumatic stress and traumatic brain injury at the Walter Reed National Military Medical Center. *BMJ Open*. http://dx.doi.org/10.1136/bmjopen-2017-021448

Kaimal, G., Councill, T., Ramsey, K. Cottone, C. A., & Snyder, K. (2019). A conceptual framework for research in art therapy research in pediatric hematology and oncology settings. *Canadian Art Therapy Association Journal*, 32(2), 95–103. https://doi.org/10.1080/08322473.2019.1672453

Kaiser Family Foundation. (2021, May 26). *Mental health and substance use state fact sheets*. https://www.kff.org/statedata/mental-health-and-substance-use-state-fact-sheets/

Kandel, E. (2012). *The age of insight: The quest to understand the unconscious in art, mind and brain*. Random House.

Kaplan, S. (1995). The restorative benefits of nature: Toward an integrative framework. *Journal of Environmental Psychology*, 15, 169–182. https://doi.org/10.1016/0272-4944(95)90001-2

Karayol, R., Medrihan, L., Warner-Schmidt, J. L., Fait, B. W., Rao, M. N., Holzner, E. B., Greengard, P., Heintz, N., & Schmidt, E. F. (2021). Serotonin receptor 4 in the hippocampus modulates mood and anxiety. *Molecular Psychiatry*, 26, 2334–2349. https://doi.org/10.1038/s41380-020-00994-y

Kashdan, T. B., & Biswas-Diener, R. (2014). *The upside of your dark side: Why being your whole self—not just your "good" self—drives success and fulfillment*. Penguin.

Katahira, K., Yamazaki, Y., Yamaoka, C., Ozaki, H., Nakagawa, S., & Nagata, N. (2018). EEG correlates of the flow state: A combination of increased frontal theta and moderate frontocentral alpha rhythm in the mental arithmetic task. *Frontiers in Psychology*, 9, 300. https://doi.org/10.3389/fpsyg.2018.00300

Kaufman, J. C., & Beghetto, R. A. (2009). Beyond big and little: The Four C Model of Creativity. *Review of General Psychology*, 13(1), 1–12.

Kearney, R. (2007). Narrating pain: The power of catharsis. *Paragraph*, 30(1), 51–66.

Kedar, Y., Kedar, G., & Barkai, R. (2021). Hypoxia in Paleolithic decorated caves: The use of artificial light in deep caves reduces oxygen concentration and induces altered states of consciousness. *Time and Mind*, 14(2), 181–216. https://doi.org/10.1080/1751696X.2021.1903177

Kellert, S. R. (1993). Introduction. In S. R. Kellert & E. O. Wilson (Eds.), *The biophilia hypothesis* (pp. 18–25). Shearwater Books/Island Press.

Kellert, S. R. (2003). *Kinship to mastery: Biophilia in human evolution and development*. Island Press.

Killick, S., Curry, V., & Myles, P. (2016). The mighty metaphor: A collection of therapists' favourite metaphors and analogies. *The Cognitive Behaviour Therapist*, 9, e37. https://doi.org/10.1017/S1754470X16000210

Kim, D., & Yoon, K. L. (2020). Emotional response to autobiographical memories in depression: Less happiness to positive and more sadness to negative memories. *Cognitive Behaviour Therapy*, 49(6), 475–485. https://doi.org/10.1080/16506073.2020.1765859

King, J. L. (2016). Art therapy: A brain-based profession. In D. E. Gussak & M. L. Rosal (Eds.), *Wiley handbook of art therapy* (pp. 77–89). Wiley-Blackwell.

King, J. L., & Kaimal, G. (2019). Approaches to research in art therapy using imaging technologies. *Frontiers in Human Neuroscience*, 13, 159. https://doi.org/10.3389/fnhum.2019.00159

King, J. L., Kaimal, G., Konopka, L., Belkofer, C., & Strang, C. E. (2019). Practical applications of neuroscience-informed art therapy. *Art Therapy*, *36*(3), 149–156. https://doi.org/10.1080/07421656.2019.1649549

King, J. L., Knapp, K. E., Shaikh, A., Li, F., Sabau, D., Pascuzzi, R. M., & Osburn, L. L. (2017). Cortical activity changes after art making and rote motor movement as measured by EEG: A preliminary study. *Biomedical Journal of Science &Technical Research*, *1*(4), 1–21. https://doi.org/10.26717/BJSTR.2017.01.000366

Kleinman, A. (1981). *Patients and healers in the context of culture: An exploration of the borderland between anthropology, medicine and psychiatry.* University of California Press.

Klorer, P. G., & Robb, M. (2012). Art enrichment: Evaluating a collaboration between Head Start and a graduate art therapy program. *Art Therapy*, *24*(4), 180–187. https://doi.org/10.1080/07421656.2012.730920

Kneller, J. (2017). Pleasure of art and pleasure of nature: A response to Matthen. *Australasian Philosophical Review*, *1*(1), 85–89. https://doi.org/10.1080/24740500.2017.1296385

Knierim, J. (2020, October 20). Chapter 3: Motor cortex. *Neuroscience Online*. https://nba.uth.tmc.edu/neuroscience/m/s3/chapter03.html

Koban, L., Gianaros, P. J., Kober, H., & Wager, T. D. (2021). The self in context: Brain systems linking mental and physical health. *Nature Reviews Neuroscience*, *22*(5), 309–322. https://doi.org/10.1038/s41583-021-00446-8

Kongtrul, D. (2020). *Peaceful heart: The Buddhist practice of patience*. Shambhala Publications.

Kopytin, A., Bockhorni, R., & Zhou, T. (2019). From Ikebana to botanical arranging: Artistic, therapeutic, and spiritual alignment with nature. *Creative Arts in Education and Therapies*, *5*(2), 96–108. https://doi.org/10.15212/CAET/2019/5/35

Kossak, M. (2021). *Attunement in expressive art therapy: Toward an understanding of embodied empathy*. Charles C. Thomas Publisher.

Kounios, J., & Beeman, M. (2015). *The Eureka factor: Creative insights and the brain*. Random House.

Kragel, J. E., Schuele, S., VanHaerents, S., Rosenow, J. M., & Voss, J. L. (2021). Rapid coordination of effective learning by the human hippocampus. *Science Advances*, *7*(25), eabf7144. https://doi.org/10.1126/sciadv.abf7144

Kragel, P. A., Knodt, A. R., Hariri, A. R., & LaBar, K. S. (2016). Decoding spontaneous emotional states in the human brain. *PLoS Biology*, *14*(9), e2000106. https://doi.org/10.1371/journal.pbio.2000106

Kross, E., Berman, M. G., Mischel, W., Smith, E. E., & Wager, T. D. (2011). Social rejection shares somatosensory representations with physical pain. *Proceedings of the National Academy of Sciences USA*, *108*(15), 6270–6275. https://doi.org/10.1073/pnas.1102693108

Kruk, K. A., Aravich, P. F., Deaver, S. P., & deBeus, R. (2014). Comparison of brain activity during drawing and clay sculpting: A preliminary qEEG study. *Art Therapy*, *31*(2), 52–60. https://doi.org/10.1080/07421656.2014.903826

Krusemark, E. A., Novak, L. R., Gitelman, D. R., & Li, W. (2013). When the sense of smell meets emotion: Anxiety-state-dependent olfactory processing and neural circuitry adaptation. *Journal of Neuroscience*, *33*(39), 15324–15332. https://doi.org/10.1523/JNEUROSCI.1835-13.2013

Kusters, W. (2020). *A philosophy of madness: The experience of psychotic thinking*. MIT Press.

Lacey, S., Hagtvedt, H., Patrick, V. M., Anderson, A., Stilla, R., Deshpande, G., Hu, X., Sato, J. R., Reddy, S., & Sathian, K. (2011). Art for reward's sake: Visual art recruits the ventral striatum. *NeuroImage*, *55*(1), 420–433. http://dx.doi.org/10.1016/j.neuroimage.2010.11.027

Lackie, J. (2010). *A dictionary of biomedicine*. Oxford University Press.

Lakoff, G., & Johnson, M. (2003). *Metaphors we live by*. University of Chicago Press.

Lambert, K. (2008). *Lifting depression: A neuroscientist's hands-on approach to activating your brain's healing power*. Basic Books.

Lambert, P. D., Betts, D., Rollins, J., Sonke, J., & Swanson, K. W. (2017). Arts, health and well-being in America. White paper commissioned by the National Organization for Arts in Health. Retrieved from https://thenoah.net/wp-content/uploads/2019/01/NOAH-2017-White-Paper-Online-Edition.pdf

Landless, B. M., Walker, M. S., & Kaimal, G. (2018). Using human and computer-based text analysis of clinical notes to understand military service members' experiences with therapeutic writing. *The Arts in Psychotherapy, 62*, 77–84. https://doi.org/10.1016/j.aip.2018.10.002

Langer, S. K. (1953). *Feeling and form*. Routledge and Kegan Paul.

Langer, S. K. (1957). *Problems of art*. Charles Scribner's Sons.

Langlois, K. (2018). Why scientists are beginning to care about cultures that talk to whales. *Smithsonian Magazine.* https://www.smithsonianmag.com/science/talking-to-whales-180968698/?fbclid=IwAR0X5dcy2CDphjdBZkhQcrRRJzRVsi0TAHOojwfHx-HLJaEhMCiU8pv2s2U#zxAalVk1yuYZ7bKW.01

Lanza, R. (2020). *The grand biocentric design: How life creates reality*. BenBella.

Lauring, J. O., Pelowski, M., Specker, E., Ishizu, T., Haugbøl, S., Hollunder, B., Leder, H., Stender, J., & Kupers, R. (2019). Parkinson's disease and changes in the appreciation of art: A comparison of aesthetic and formal evaluations of paintings between PD patients and healthy controls. *Brain and Cognition, 136*, 103597. https://doi.org/10.1016/j.bandc.2019.103597

Leavy, P. (2015). *Method meets art: Arts-based research practice*. Guilford.

Lee, S., Parthasarathi, T., & Kable, J. W. (2021). The ventral and dorsal default mode networks are dissociably modulated by the vividness and valence of imagined events. *Journal of Neuroscience*. https://doi.org/10.1523/JNEUROSCI.1273-20.2021

Levick, M. F. (1983). *They could not talk and so they drew: Children's styles of coping and thinking*. Charles C. Thomas Publishers.

Levick, M. (2003). *See what I'm saying: What children tell us through their art* (2nd ed.). Regal Printing Ltd.

Lévi-Strauss, C. (1950). The effectiveness of symbols. In *Structural anthropology*. Basic Books.

Li, Q., Kobayashi, M., Inagaki, H., Hirata, Y., Li, Y. J., Hirata, K., . . . & Kagawa, T. (2010). A day trip to a forest park increases human natural killer activity and the expression of anti-cancer proteins in male subjects. *Journal of Biological Regulators and Homeostatic Agents, 24*(2), 157–165.

Li, Q., Otsuka, T., Kobayashi, M., Wakayama, Y., Inagaki, H., Katsumata, M., Hirata, Y., Li, Y., Hirata, K., Shimizu, T., Suzuki, H., Kawada, T., & Kagawa, T. (2011). Acute effects of walking in forest environments on cardiovascular and metabolic parameters. *European Journal of Applied Physiology, 111*(11), 2845–2853. https://doi.org/10.1007/s00421-011-1918-z

Ligaya, K., Yi, S., Wahle, I. A., Tanwisuth, K., & O'Doherty, J. P. (2021). Aesthetic preference for art can be predicted from a mixture of low-and high-level visual features. *Nature Human Behaviour, 5*(6), 743–755. https://doi.org/10.1038/s41562-021-01124-6

Lilly, K. V., & Venukapalli, S. (2021). How do children respond to different artistic genres? *European Journal of Literature, Language and Linguistics Studies, 4*(4), 46–63.

Liu, C., Chen, H., Liu, C. Y., Lin, R. T., & Chiou, W. K. (2020). Cooperative and individual mandala drawing have different effects on mindfulness, spirituality, and subjective well-being. *Frontiers in Psychology, 11*, 2629. https://doi.org/10.3389/fpsyg.2020.564430

Lobo, Y. B., & Winsler, A. (2006). The effects of a creative dance and movement program on the social competence of head start preschoolers. *Social Development, 15*(3), 501–519. https://doi.org/10.1111/j.1467-9507.2006.00353.x

Loeb, A. (2021, June 9). Creative thinking in both science and the arts is not for the faint of heart. *Scientific American: Behavior & Society Opinion.* https://www.scientificamerican.com/article/creative-thinking-in-both-science-and-the-arts-is-not-for-the-faint-of-heart1/

Lorde, A. (1978). *Uses of the erotic: The erotic as power* (No. 3). Crossing Press.

Lowenfeld, V., & Brittain, W. (1987). *Creative and mental growth* (8th ed.). Macmillan.

Lu, K., Teng, J., & Hao, N. (2020). Gender of partner affects the interaction pattern during group creative idea generation. *Experimental Brain Research, 238*(5), 1157–1168. https://doi.org/10.1007/s00221-020-05799-7

Luby, J., Belden, A., Botteron, K., Marrus, N., Harms, M. P., Babb, C., . . . & Barch, D. (2013). The effects of poverty on childhood brain development: The mediating effect of caregiving and stressful life events. *JAMA Pediatrics, 167*(12), 1135–1142. https://doi.org/10.1001/jamapediatrics.2013.3139

Lund, C., De Silva, M., Plagerson, S., Cooper, S., Chisholm, D., Das, J., Knapp, M., & Patel, V. (2011). Poverty and mental disorders: breaking the cycle in low-income and middle-income countries. *Lancet, 378*(9801), 1502–1514. https://doi.org/10.1016/S0140-6736(11)60754-X

Lusebrink, V. B. (2004). Art therapy and the brain: An attempt to understand the underlying processes of art expression in therapy. *Art Therapy, 21*(3), 125–135. https://doi.org/10.1080/07421656.2004.10129496

Lusebrink, V. B., Mārtinsone, K., & Dzilna-Šilova, I. (2013). The expressive therapies continuum (ETC): Interdisciplinary bases of the ETC. *International Journal of Art Therapy, 18*(2), 75–85. https://doi.org/10.1080/17454832.2012.713370

MacCoitir, N. (2010). *Ireland's wild plants: Myths, legends and folklore.* Collins Press.

Malchiodi, C., & Perry, B. (2008). *Creative interventions with traumatized children.* Guildford Press.

Malhotra, B., Dieterich-Hartwell, R., DeBeer, B., Burns, C., & Kaimal, G. (2021). Collage-based graphic elicitation method for capturing the lived experiences of veterans with Gulf War illness. *Life Sciences, 284*, 119656. https://doi.org/10.1016/j.lfs.2021.119656

Mangin, M., Sinha, R., & Fincher, K. (2014). Inflammation and vitamin D: The infection connection. *Inflammation Research, 63*(10), 803–819. https://doi.org/10.1007/s00011-014-0755-z

Manson, M. (2013). *The subtle art of not giving a f* ck: A counterintuitive approach to living a good life.* Macmillan Publishers Aus.

Marshall III, J. M. (2001). *The Lakota way: Stories and lessons for living. Native American wisdom on ethics and character.* Penguin Books.

Martin, M. M. (2020, December 11). Envisioning my future self: Reflections from a future leader of color. *Artsblog for professionals in the know, American for the Arts.* https://blog.americansforthearts.org/2020/12/11/envisioning-my-future-self-reflections-from-a-future-leader-of-color

Masten, A. (2014). *Ordinary magic: Resilience in development.* Guilford Press.

Matthen, M. (2017a). The pleasure of art. *Australasian Philosophical Review, 1*(1), 6–28. https://doi.org/10.1080/24740500.2017.1287034

Matthen, M. (2017b). Constructing aesthetic value: Responses to my commentators. *Australasian Philosophical Review, 1*(1), 100–111. https://doi.org/10.1080/24740500.2017.1287035

Mayseless, N., Hawthorne, G., & Reiss, A. L. (2019). Real-life creative problem solving in teams: fNIRS-based hyperscanning study. *NeuroImage, 203*, 116161. https://doi.org/10.1016/j.neuroimage.2019.116161

McAdams, D. P. (2001). The psychology of life stories. *Review of General Psychology, 5*(2), 100–122. https://doi.org/10.1037/1089-2680.5.2.100

McMahon, J. A. (2017) From Kantianism to aesthetic hedonism: Aesthetic pleasure revised. *Australasian Philosophical Review, 1*(1), 1–5. https://doi.org/10.1080/24740500.2017.1296403

McWhinnie, H. J. (1991). *The ideology of Vicktor Lowenfeld: A review of research.* https://files.eric.ed.gov/fulltext/ED368621.pdf

Melton, K. K., Larson, M., & Boccia, M. L. (2019). Examining couple recreation and oxytocin via the ecology of family experiences framework. *Journal of Marriage and Family, 81*(3), 771–782. https://doi.org/10.1111/jomf.12556

Menakem, R. (2017). *My grandmother's hands: Racialized trauma and the pathway to mending our hearts and bodies.* Penguin UK.

Merieb, E. N., & Hoehn, K. (2007). *Human anatomy & physiology.* Pearson International.

Metzl, E. S. (2009). The role of creative thinking in resilience after hurricane Katrina. *Psychology of Aesthetics, Creativity, and the Arts, 3*(2), 112–113. https://doi.org/10.1037/a0013479

Michael, J. (1986). Viktor Lowenfeld: Some misconceptions, some insights. *Art Education, 39*(3), 36–39. https://doi:10.2307/3192954

Michel, K. L. (2014, April 19). *Maslow's hierarchy connected to Blackfoot beliefs.* https://lincol nmichel.wordpress.com/2014/04/19/maslows-hierarchy-connected-to-blackfoot-beliefs/

Miller, A. H., & Raison, C. L. (2016). The role of inflammation in depression: From evolutionary imperative to modern treatment target. *Nature Reviews Immunology, 16*(1), 22–34. https://doi.org/10.1038/nri.2015.5

Monosov, I. E. (2017). Anterior cingulate is a source of valence-specific information about value and uncertainty. *Nature Communications, 8,* 134. https://doi.org/10.1038/s41 467-017-00072-y

Monti, A., Porciello, G., Panasiti, M. S., & Aglioti, S. M. (2021). The inside of me: Interoceptive constraints on the concept of self in neuroscience and clinical psychology. *Psychological Research.* https://doi.org/10.1007/s00426-021-01477-7

Moon, C. H. (2011a). Theorizing materiality in art therapy. In C. H. Moon (Ed.), *Materials and media in art therapy: Critical understandings of diverse artistic vocabularies* (pp. 1–49). Routledge.

Moon, C. H. (Ed.). (2011b). *Materials & media in art therapy: Critical understandings of diverse artistic vocabularies.* Routledge.

Moore, A. (2013, October 13). Hedonism. *Stanford Encyclopedia of Philosophy.* https://plato. stanford.edu/archives/win2019/entries/hedonism/

Moses, D. A., Metzger, S. L., Liu, J. R., Anumanchipalli, G. K., Makin, J. G., Sun, P. F., .. . & Chang, E. F. (2021). Neuroprosthesis for decoding speech in a paralyzed person with anarthria. *New England Journal of Medicine, 385*(3), 217–227.

Mosley, T., & McMahon, S. (2020, December 8). Archaeologists uncover trove of Ice Age paintings in Colombian Amazon. *Wbur.* https://www.wbur.org/hereandnow/2020/12/08/ ancient-cliff-art-amazon?utm_term=nprnews&utm_source=facebook.com&utm_campa ign=npr&utm_medium=social&fbclid=IwAR3FaEyaLWTq9JlWI-6OJjNcVmoGWfZbl1 79npp97-yI95P-VYeeu5UU-ow

Murdoch, I. (1999). *Existentialists and mystics: Writings on philosophy and literature.* Penguin.

Nagarajan, V. (2018). *Feeding a thousand souls: Women, ritual and ecology in India, an exploration of the Kōlam.* Oxford University Press.

Nan, J. K., & Ho, R. T. (2017). Effects of clay art therapy on adults outpatients with major depressive disorder: A randomized controlled trial. *Journal of Affective Disorders, 217,* 237–245. https://doi.org/10.1016/j.jad.2017.04.013

Narayan, A. J., Rivera, L. M., Bernstein, R. E., Harris, W. W., & Lieberman, A. F. (2018). Positive childhood experiences predict less psychopathology and stress in pregnant women with childhood adversity: A pilot study of the Benevolent Childhood Experiences (BCEs) scale. *Child Abuse & Neglect, 78,* 19–30. https://doi.org/10.1016/j.chiabu.2017.09.022

Narayana, A. N. (2004). *Yoga Vashistha: The art of self-realization.* Author.

Naseer, N., & Hong, K.-S. (2015). fNIRS-based brain-computer interfaces: A review. *Frontiers in Human Neuroscience, 9*(3), 1–15. https://doi.org/10.3389/fnhum.2015.00003

National Institute of Health/National Cancer Institute. (2020). *NCI dictionary: Interleukin.* https://www.cancer.gov/publications/dictionaries/cancer-terms/def/interleukin

National Institute of Health/National Cancer Institute. (2015, April 29). *NCI dictionary: Chronic inflammation.* https://www.cancer.gov/about-cancer/causes-prevention/risk/chronic-inflammation

National Organization for Arts in Health. (2017). *Arts, health, and well-being in America.* Author.

National Trust. (n.d.). *Year of wonders 1665–1667.* Woolsthorpe Manor: Features. https://www.nationaltrust.org.uk/woolsthorpe-manor/features/year-of-wonders

Newton, E., Edwards, H. G., Wynn-Williams, D., & Hiscox, J. A. (2000). Exobiological prospecting. *Astronomy & Geophysics, 41*(5), 5–28. https://doi.org/10.1046/j.1468-4004.2000.41528.x

Noble, K. G., Houston, S. M., Brito, N. H., Bartsch, H., Kan, E., Kuperman, J. M., . . . & Schork, N. J. (2015). Family income, parental education and brain structure in children and adolescents. *Nature Neuroscience, 18*(5), 773–778. https://doi.org/10.1038/nn.3983

Nussbaum, M. C. (2001). *The fragility of goodness: Luck and ethics in Greek tragedy and philosophy.* Cambridge University Press.

O'Brien, P. D., Hinder, L. M., Callaghan, B., & Feldman, E. (2017). Neurological consequences of obesity. *Lancet Neurology, 16*(6), 465–477. https://doi.org/10.1016/S1474-4422(17)30084-4

Observations. (2020, December 10). Why decolonising museums is not enough. *Elephant.* https://elephant.art/why-decolonising-museums-is-not-enough-10122020/

Oliver, M. (2019). *Upstream: Selected essays.* Penguin Books.

Pahwa, R., Goyal, A., Bansal, P., & Jialal, I. (2018). *Chronic inflammation.* StatPearls.

Pascoe, B. (2015). *The dark emu.* Magabala Books.

Pennebaker, J. (1997a). *Opening up: The healing power of expressing emotions.* Guilford.

Pennebaker, J. W. (1997b). Writing about emotional experiences as a therapeutic process. *Psychological Science, 8*(3), 162–166. https://doi.org/10.1111/j.1467-9280.1997.tb00403.x

Pennebaker, J. W., & Smyth, J. M. (2016). *Opening up by writing it down: How expressive writing improves health and eases emotional pain.* Guilford Publications.

Petitte, T., Mallow, J., Barnes, E., Petrone, A., Barr, T., & Theeke, L. (2015). A systematic review of loneliness and common chronic physical conditions in adults. *Open Psychology Journal, 8*(Suppl 2), 113–132.

Phiri, P., Nkhonjera, J., Mabeti, F., Kamiza, K., & Seiden, J. (2016). *Malawi ELM & HEART endline analysis report.* Save the Children, Lilongwe.

Pinti, P., Scholkmann, F., Hamilton, A., Burgess, P., & Tachtsidis, I. (2019). Current status and issues regarding pre-processing of fNIRS neuroimaging data: An investigation of diverse signal filtering methods within a general linear model framework. *Frontiers in Human Neuroscience, 12*(505), 1–21. https://doi.org/10.3389/fnhum.2018.00505

Plucker, J. A., & Beghetto, R. A. (2003). Why not be creative when we enhance creativity? In J. H. Borland (Ed.), *Rethinking gifted education* (pp. 215–226). Teachers College Press.

Potash, J. S., Chen, J. Y., & Tsang, J. P. Y. (2016). Medical student mandala making for holistic well-being. *Medical Humanities, 42*(1), 17–25. https://doi.org/10.1136/medhum-2015-010717

Poulin, M., Ministero, L., Gabriel, S., Morrison, C., Naidu, E., & Poulin, M. J. (2021). Minding your own business? Mindfulness decreases prosocial behavior for those with independent self-construals. *PsyArXiv.* https://doi.org/10.31234/osf.io/xhyua

Puligandla, R. (1998). Creativity in Advaita Vedanta. *Journal of Indian Philosophy and Religion, 3,* 124–147.

Qi-Yue, Y., Ting, Z., Ya-Nan, H., Sheng-Jie, H., Xuan, D., Li, H., & Chun-Guang, X. (2020). From natural dye to herbal medicine: A systematic review of chemical constituents, pharmacological effects and clinical applications of *Indigo naturalis. Chinese Medicine, 15*(1), 1–13. https://doi.org/10.1186/s13020-020-00406-x

Rachlin, M. (2019). Instead of hiding rips and tears, the visible mending movements turns them into art. https://www.vox.com/the-goods/2019/3/25/18274743/visible-mending-sash iko-mending-fast-fashion-movement?fbclid=IwAR0_aCRHkZJiE7y1AHrpFJaowcQCY2lv tYCtwtIQrXsHdifuMydPYCUafU4

Radjou, N., Prabhu, J., & Ahuja, S. (2012). *Jugaad innovation: Think frugal, be flexible, generate breakthrough growth*. John Wiley & Sons.

Raichlen, D. A., & Alexander, G. E. (2020). Why your brain needs exercise: The evolutionary history of humans explains why physical activity is important for brain health. *Scientific American*. https://www.scientificamerican.com/article/why-your-brain-needs-exercise/

Ramachandran, V. S., & Hirstein, W. (1999). The science of art: A neurological theory of aesthetic experience. *Journal of Consciousness Studies, 6*, 15–51.

Rauch, S. L., Savage, C. R., Alpert, N. M., Fischman, A. J., & Jenike, M. A. (1997). The functional neuroanatomy of anxiety: A study of three disorders using positron emission tomography and symptom provocation. *Biological Psychiatry, 42*(6), 446–452. https://doi.org/10.1016/S0006-3223(97)00145-5

Redwood, S., Gale, N. K., & Greenfield, S. (2012). "You give us rangoli, we give you talk": Using an art-based activity to elicit data from a seldom heard group. *BMC Medical Research Methodology, 12*, 7. https://doi.org/10.1186/1471-2288-12-7

Reser, D., Simmons, M., Johns, E., Ghaly, A., Quayle, M., Dordevic, A. L., . . . & Yunkaporta, T. (2021). Australian Aboriginal techniques for memorization: Translation into a medical and allied health education setting. *PLoS ONE, 16*(5), e0251710. https://doi.org/10.1371/journal.pone.0251710

Richards, R. E. (2007). *Everyday creativity and new views of human nature: Psychological, social, and spiritual perspectives*. American Psychological Association.

Richardson, M., McEwan, K., Maratos, F., & Sheffield, D. (2016). Joy and calm: How an evolutionary functional model of affect regulation informs positive emotions in nature. *Evolutionary Psychological Science, 2*(4), 308–320. https://doi.org/10.1007/s40 806-016-0065-5

Rilke, R. M. (2021). *Letters to a young poet: A new translation and commentary*. Shambhala.

Ripley, D. L., & Politzer, T. (2010). Vision disturbance after TBI. *NeuroRehabilitation, 27*(3), 215. https://doi.org/10.3233/NRE-2010-0599

Rolls, E. T. (2017). Neurobiological foundations of aesthetics and art. *New Ideas in Psychology, 47*, 121–135. https://doi.org/10.1016/j.newideapsych.2017.03.005

Root-Bernstein, R., Allen, L., Beach, L., Bhadula, R., Fast, J., Hosey, C., . . . & Weinlander, S. (2008). Arts foster scientific success: Avocations of Nobel, National Academy, Royal Society, and Sigma Xi members. *Journal of Psychology of Science and Technology, 1*(2), 51–63.

Root-Bernstein, R. S., Bernstein, M., & Garnier, H. (2008). Correlations between avocations, scientific style, work habits, and professional impact of scientists. *Creativity Research Journal, 8*(2), 115–137. https://doi.org/10.1207/s15326934crj0802_2

Rothenhoefer, K. M., Hong, T., Alikaya, A., & Stauffer, W. R. (2021). Rare rewards amplify dopamine responses. *Nature Neuroscience, 24*(4), 465–469. https://doi.org/10.1038/s41 593-021-00807-7

Roy, D. K. (1945). *Among the great*. Nalanda Publishers.

Rozin, P., & Royzman, E. B. (2001). Negativity bias, negativity dominance, and contagion. *Personality and Social Psychology Review, 5*(4), 296–320. https://doi.org/10.1207/S1532795 7PSPR0504_2

Rubin, J. A. (2005). *Child art therapy*. John Wiley & Sons.

Runco, M. (2014). "Big C, little c" creativity as a false dichotomy: Reality is not categorical. *Creativity Research Journal, 26*(1), 131–132. https://doi.org/10.1080/10400419.2014.873676

Runco, M. A., & Jaeger, G. J. (2012). The standard definition of creativity. *Creativity Research Journal, 24*, 92–96. https://doi.org/10.1080/10400419.2012.650092

Russ, S. (2016). Pretend play: Antecedent of adult creativity. *New Directions for Child and Adolescent Development, 2016*(151), 21–32. https://doi.org/10.1002/cad.20154.

Safaryan, K., & Mehta, M. R. (2021). Enhanced hippocampal theta rhythmicity and emergence of eta oscillation in virtual reality. *Nature Neuroscience, 24*, 1065–1070. https://doi.org/10.1038/s41593-021-00871-z

Sapolsky, R. (2003). Taming stress. *Scientific American, 289*(3), 86–95.

Schlegel, A., Alexander, P., Fogelson, S. V., Li, X., Lu, Z., Kohler, P. J., . . . & Meng, M. (2015). The artist emerges: Visual art learning alters neural structure and function. *NeuroImage, 105*, 440–451. https://doi.org/10.1016/j.neuroimage.2014.11.014

Schnitzer, G., Holttum, S., & Huet, V. (2021). A systematic literature review of the impact of art therapy upon post-traumatic stress disorder. *International Journal of Art Therapy, 26*(4), 147–160. https://doi.org/10.1080/17454832.2021.1910719

Schrade, C., Tronsky, L., & Kaiser, D. H. (2011). Physiological effects of mandala making in adults with intellectual disability. *The Arts in Psychotherapy, 38*(2), 109–113. https://doi.org/10.1016/j.aip.2011.01.002

Schubert, E. (2021). Creativity is optimal novelty and maximal positive affect: A new definition based on the spreading activation model. *Frontiers in Neuroscience, 15* (390), 1–15. https://doi.org/10.3389/fnins.2021.612379

Selye, H. (1951). *The physiology and pathology of exposure to stress: A treatise based on the concepts of the general adaptation syndrome and the diseases of adaptation.* Acta.

Semetko, H., & Scammell, M. (2012). *The SAGE handbook of political communication.* SAGE Publications.

Seneca, L. A. (2013). Letter XII, On groundless fears. In *Moral letters to Lucilius, written by L. Annaeus Seneca* (translated by R. M. Gummere).

Shao, L. X., Liao, C., Gregg, I., Davoudian, P. A., Savalia, N. K., Delagarza, K., & Kwan, A. C. (2021). Psilocybin induces rapid and persistent growth of dendritic spines in frontal cortex in vivo. *bioRxiv.* https://doi.org/10.1101/2021.02.17.431629

Sharma, S., & Vijay. P. (2021). Uplifting the grassroots through community entrepreneurship development: A case study of Sualkachi handloom town of Assam (India). *Bioscience and Biotechnology Research Communication (Special issue), 14*(9), 268–271. https://doi.org/10.21786bbrc/14.9.51

Shils, M. E., Shike, M., Ross, A. C., Caballero, B., & Cousins, R. J. (2014). *Modern nutrition in health and disease.* Lippincott Williams & Wilkins.

Shraim, R. (2021, April 23). How philosophy is making me a better scientist. *Nature: Career Column.* https://www.nature.com/articles/d41586-021-01103-x

Singha, S., Warr, M., Mishra, P., Henriksen, D., & the Deep-Play Research Group. (2020). Playing with creativity across the lifespan: A conversation with Dr. Sandra Russ. *TechTrends, 64*, 550–554. https://doi.org/10.1007/s11528-020-00514-3

Slepian, M. L., Chun, J. S., & Mason, M. F. (2017). The experience of secrecy. *Journal of Personality and Social Psychology, 113*(1), 1–33. https://doi.org/10.1037/pspa0000085

Smith, K., Stewart, S., Riddell, N., & Victor, C. (2018). Investigating the relationship between loneliness and social isolation with inflammation: A systematic review. *Innovation in Aging, 2*(suppl. 1), 839–840. https://doi.org/10.1093/geroni/igy023.3128

Smith, Z. (2020). *Intimations: Six essays.* Penguin UK.

Snyder, K., Malhotra, B., & Kaimal, G. (2021). Team value and visual voice: Healthcare providers' perspectives on the contributions and impact of art therapy in pediatric hematology/oncology clinics. *The Arts in Psychotherapy, 75*, 101808. https://doi.org/10.1016/j.aip.2021.101808

Sorokowski, P., Karwowski, M., Misiak, M., Marczak, M. K., Dziekan, M., Hummel, T., & Sorokowska, A. (2019). Sex differences in human olfaction: A meta-analysis. *Frontiers in Psychology, 10*, 242. https://dx.doi.org/10.3389%2Ffpsyg.2019.00242

Spreng, R. N., Dimas, E., Mwilambwe-Tshilobo, L., Dagher, A., Koellinger, P., Nave, G., . . . & Bzdok, D. (2020). The default network of the human brain is associated with perceived social isolation. *Nature Communications, 11*(1), 1–11. https://doi.org/10.1038/s41 467-020-20039-w

Springham, N., Thorne, D., & Brooker, J. (2014). Softer: Looking for oxytocin in art therapy. *International Journal of Art Therapy, 19*(1), 31–42. https://doi.org/10.1080/17454 832.2014.882366

Sproston, N. R., & Ashworth, J. J. (2018). Role of C-reactive protein at sites of inflammation and infection. *Frontiers in Immunology, 9*, 754. https://doi.org/10.3389/fimmu.2018.00754

Stahn, A. C., Gunga, H. C., Kohlberg, E., Gallinat, J., Dinges, D. F., & Kühn, S. (2019). Brain changes in response to long Antarctic expeditions. *New England Journal of Medicine, 381*(23), 2273–2275. https://doi.org/10.1056/NEJMc1904905

Startev, V., Jordanova, M., & Petev, J. (2011). Oxidative stress, obesity and chronic inflammation in smokers according to smoking duration and heaviness. *European Respiratory Journal, 38*, 1099.

Steenkamp, M. M., Litz, B. T., & Marmar, C. R. (2020). First-line psychotherapies for military-related PTSD. *Journal of the American Medical Association, 323*(7), 656–657. https://doi.org/ 10.1001/jama.2019.20825

Stinley, N. E., Norris, D. O., & Hinds, P. S. (2015). Creating mandalas for the management of acute pain symptoms in pediatric patients. *Art Therapy, 32*(2), 46–53. https://doi.org/ 10.1080/07421656.2015.1028871

Suffren, S., La Buissonnière-Ariza, V., Tucholka, A., Nassim, M., Séguin, J. R., Boivin, M., . . . & Maheu, F. S. (2021). Prefrontal cortex and amygdala anatomy in youth with persistent levels of harsh parenting practices and subclinical anxiety symptoms over time during childhood. *Development and Psychopathology: First View*, 1–12. https://doi.org/10.1017/S095457942 0001716

Sweeney, T. (2013). *Eco-art therapy: Creative activities that let earth teach*. Author.

Taber, K. H., Black, D. N., Porrino, L. J., & Hurley, R. A. (2012). Neuroanatomy of dopamine: Reward and addiction. *Journal of Neuropsychiatry and Clinical Neuroscience, 24*(1), 1–4.

Taleb, N. N. (2014). *Antifragile: Things that gain from disorder* (Incerto). Random House Incorporated.

Talwar, S. (2010). An intersectional framework for race, class, gender, and sexuality in art therapy. *Art Therapy, 27*(1), 11–17. https://doi.org/10.1080/07421656.2010.10129567

Tanaka, S., Komagome, A., Iguchi-Sherry, A., Nagasaka, A., Yuhi, T., Higashida, H., . . . & Tsuji, C. (2020). Participatory art activities increase salivary oxytocin secretion of ASD children. *Brain Sciences, 10*(10), 680. https://doi.org/10.3390/brainsci10100680

Tang, M., Hofreiter, S., Reiter-Palmon, R., Bai, X., & Murugavel, V. (2021). Creativity as a means to well-being in times of COVID-19 pandemic: Results of a cross-cultural study. *Frontiers in Psychology, 12*, 265. https://doi.org/10.3389/fpsyg.2021.601389

Tedeschi, R. G., & Calhoun, L. G. (1996). The Posttraumatic Growth Inventory: Measuring the positive legacy of trauma. *Journal of Traumatic Stress, 9*(3), 455–471. https://doi.org/ 10.1007/BF02103658

Thich Nhat Hanh. (2014). *No mud no lotus*. Parallax Press.

Thorpe, S., Fize, D., & Marlot, C. (1996). Speed of processing in the human visual system. *Nature, 381*, 520–522. https://doi.org/10.1038/381520a0

Tinio, P. P. (2013). From artistic creation to aesthetic reception: The mirror model of art. *Psychology of Aesthetics, Creativity, and the Arts, 7*(3), 265. https://doi.org/10.1037/a0030872

Tomova, L., Wang, K. L., Thompson, T., Matthews, G. A., Takahashi, A., Tye, K. M., & Saxe, R. (2020). Acute social isolation evokes midbrain craving responses similar to hunger. *Nature Neuroscience, 23*(12), 1597–1605. https://doi.org/10.1038/s41593-020-00742-z

Trumpff, C., Marsland, A. L., Basualto-Alarcón, C., Martin, J. L., Carroll, J. E., Sturm, G., . . . & Picard, M. (2019). Acute psychological stress increases serum circulating cell-free mitochondrial DNA. *Psychoneuroendocrinology, 106*, 268–276. https://doi.org/10.1016/j.psyneuen.2019.03.026

Twain, M. (1869). *The innocents abroad, or the new Pilgrim's Progress.* Seawolf Press.

Ulrich, M., Keller, J., & Grön, G. (2016). Neural signatures of experimentally induced flow experiences identified in a typical fMRI block design with BOLD imaging. *Social Cognitive and Affective Neuroscience, 11*(3), 496–507. https://doi.org/10.1093/scan/nsv133

Umeda, T., Isa, T., & Nishimura, Y. (2019). The somatosensory cortex receives information about motor output. *Science Advances, 5*(7), eaaw5388. https://doi.org/10.1126/sciadv.aaw5388

Unwalla, K., Cadieux, M. L., & Shore, D. I. (2021). Haptic awareness changes when lying down. *Scientific Reports, 11*(1), 1–7. https://doi.org/10.1038/s41598-021-92192-1

U.S. Department of Health and Human Services, Office of Disease Prevention and Health Promotion. (2021). Social determinants of health. *Healthy People 2030.* https://health.gov/healthypeople/objectives-and-data/social-determinants-health

Vaisvaser, S. (2021). The embodied-enactive-interactive brain: Bridging neuroscience and creative arts therapies. *Frontiers in Psychology, 12*, 1495. https://doi.org/10.3389/fpsyg.2021.634079

Van den Bosch, M., & Odesang, A. (2017). Urban natural environments as nature-based solutions for improved public health: A systematic review of reviews. *Environmental Research, 158*, 373–384. https://doi.org/10.1016/j.envres.2017.05.040

van der Kolk, B. A., van der Hart, O., & Marmar, C. R. (1996). *Dissociation and information processing in posttraumatic stress disorder.* In B. A. van der Kolk, A. C. McFarlane, & L. Weisaeth (Eds.), *Traumatic stress: The effects of overwhelming experience on mind, body, and society* (pp. 303–327). Guilford Press.

Vander Weele, C. M., Siciliano, C. A., Matthews, G. A., Namburi, P., Izadmehr, E. M., Espinel, I. C., . . . & Tye, K. M. (2018). Dopamine enhances signal-to-noise ratio in cortical-brainstem encoding of aversive stimuli. *Nature, 563*(7731), 397–401. https://doi.org/10.1037/aca0000286

Van Lith, T., & Spooner, H. (2018). Art therapy and arts in health: Identifying shared values but different goals using a framework analysis. *Art Therapy, 35*(2), 88–93. https://doi.org/10.1080/07421656.2018.1483161

Van Rullen, R., & Thorpe, S. J. (2001). The time course of visual processing: From early perception to decision-making. *Journal of Cognitive Neuroscience, 13*(4), 454–461. https://doi.org/10.1162/08989290152001880

Venturino, A., Schulz, R., De Jesús-Cortés, H., Maes, M. E., Nagy, B., Reilly-Andújar, F., . . . & Siegert, S. (2021). Microglia enable mature perineuronal nets disassembly upon anesthetic ketamine exposure or 60-Hz light entrainment in the healthy brain. *Cell Reports, 36*(1), 109313. https://doi.org/10.1016/j.celrep.2021.109313

Verhallen, A. M., Renken, R. J., Marsman, J. B. C., & Ter Horst, G. J. (2021). Working memory alterations after a romantic relationship breakup. *Frontiers in Behavioral Neuroscience, 15*, 60. https://doi.org/10.3389/fnbeh.2021.657264

Vygotsky, L. S. (1978). *Mind in society: The development of higher psychological processes.* Harvard University Press.

Walker, M., Kaimal, G. Koffman, R., & DeGraba, T. J. (2016). Art therapy for PTSD and TBI: A senior active-duty military service member's therapeutic journey. *The Arts in Psychotherapy, 49*(2), 10–16. https://doi.org/10.1016/j.aip.2016.05.015

Walker, M., Kaimal, G. Myers-Coffman, K., Gonzaga, A. M. L., & DeGraba, T. J. (2017). Active-duty military service members' visual representations of PTSD and TBI in masks.

International Journal of Qualitative Studies on Health and Well-Being, 12(1), 1267317. https://doi.org/10.1080/17482631.2016.1267317

Walker, M. S., Stamper, A. M., Nathan, D. E., & Riedy, G. (2018). Art therapy and underlying fMRI brain patterns in military TBI: A case series. *International Journal of Art Therapy, 23*(4), 180–187. https://doi.org/10.1080/17454832.2018.1473453

Wallace, K. (2021, May 18). You are a network. *Aeon.* https://aeon.co/essays/the-self-is-not-singular-but-a-fluid-network-of-identities

Wamsley, E. (2021). 034 Dreaming as constructive episodic future simulation. *Sleep, 44*(Suppl. 2), A15. https://doi.org/10.1093/sleep/zsab072.033

Wang, S., Segev, I., Borst, A., & Palmer, S. (2021). Maximally efficient prediction in the early fly visual system may support evasive flight maneuvers. *PLOS Computational Biology, 17*(5), e1008965. https://doi.org/10.1371/journal.pcbi.1008965

Weil, S. (1970). *First and last notebooks* (translated by R. Rees).

Weinberg, T. (2018). Gaining cultural competence through alliances in art therapy with Indigenous clients. *Canadian Art Therapy Association Journal, 31*(1), 14–22. https://doi.org/10.1080/08322473.2018.1453214

Welke, D., Purton, I., & Vessel, E. A. (2021). Inspired by art: Higher aesthetic appeal elicits increased felt inspiration in a creative writing task. *Psychology of Aesthetics, Creativity, and the Arts.* Advance online publication. https://doi.org/10.1037/aca0000393

Whitaker, R. (2002). *Mad in America.* Basic Books.

Whiting, J. (2018). Resonance between indigenous art and images captured by microscope. http://theconversation.com/the-resonances-between-indigenous-art-and-images-captured-by-microscopes-105120

Whiting, K. (2020, October 21). These are the top 10 job skills of tomorrow—and how long it takes to learn them. World Economic Forum. https://www.weforum.org/agenda/2020/10/top-10-work-skills-of-tomorrow-how-long-it-takes-to-learn-them/

Willander, J., & Larsson, M. (2006). Smell your way back to childhood: Autobiographical odor memory. *Psychonomic Bulletin & Review, 13*(2), 240–244. https://doi.org/10.3758/BF03193837

Wilson, D. A., & Stevenson, R. J. (2003). The fundamental role of memory in olfactory perception. *Trends in Neuroscience, 26*, 243–247. https://doi.org/10.1016/S0166-2236(03)00076-6

Wilson, E. O. (1984). *Biophilia.* Harvard University Press.

Winch, G. (2014). *Emotional first aid: Healing rejection, guilt, failure, and other everyday hurts.* Penguin.

Winner, E. (2018). *How art works: A psychological exploration.* Oxford University Press.

Winner, E. (2021, April 22). *Changed by art.* Aeon. https://aeon.co/essays/works-of-art-compel-our-attention-but-can-they-change-us

Wohlleben, P. (2016). *The hidden life of trees: What they feel, how they communicate—Discoveries from a secret world* (Vol. 1). Greystone Books.

Wordsworth, D. (2017, April 27). *What if Maslow was wrong?* Medium: Becoming Alight. https://medium.com/becoming-alight/the-refugee-rethink-part-4-what-if-maslow-was-wrong-27eb49707548

World Health Organization. (2014). *Mental health: Strengthening our response.* https://www.who.int/features/factfiles/mental_health/en/

World Health Organization. (2021). *Social determinants of health.* https://www.who.int/health-topics/social-determinants-of-health#tab=tab_1.

Wu, W. L., Adame, M. D., Liou, C. W., Barlow, J. T., Lai, T. T., Sharon, G., . . . & Mazmanian, S. K. (2021). Microbiota regulate social behaviour via stress response neurons in the brain. *Nature, 595*, 409–414. https://doi.org/10.1038/s41586-021-03669-y

Xiang, W., Chen, S., Sun, L., Cheng, S., & Bove Jr, V. M. (2016). Odor emoticon: An olfactory application that conveys emotions. *International Journal of Human-Computer Studies, 91*, 52–61. https://doi.org/10.1016/j.ijhcs.2016.04.001

Xue, H., Lu, K., & Hao, N. (2018). Cooperation makes two less-creative individuals turn into a highly-creative pair. *NeuroImage, 172*, 527–537. https://doi.org/10.1016/j.neuroimage.2018.02.007

Yan, W., Zhang, M., & Liu, Y. (2021). Regulatory effect of drawing on negative emotion: A functional near-infrared spectroscopy study. *The Arts in Psychotherapy, 74*, 101780. https://doi.org/10.1016/j.aip.2021.101780

Zak, P. J. (2015, January). Why inspiring stories make us react: The neuroscience of narrative. In *Cerebrum: The Dana forum on brain science* (Vol. 2015). Dana Foundation.

Zeman, A. (2021). Blind mind's eye. *American Scientist, 109*(2), 110–117. https://doi.org/10.1511/2021.109.2.110

Zhu, R., & Mehta, R. (2017). Sensory experiences and consumer creativity. *Journal of the Association for Consumer Research*, 2(4), 472–484.

Zwir, I., Del-Val, C., Hintsanen, M., Cloninger, K. M., Romero-Zaliz, R., Mesa, A., Arnedo, J., Salas, R., Poblete, G. F., Raioharju, E., Raitakari, O., Keltikangas-Jarvinen, L., de Erausquin, G. A., Tattersall, I., Lehtimaki, T., & Cloninger, C. R. (2021). Evolution of genetic networks for human creativity. *Molecular Psychiatry, 27*, 354–376. https://doi.org/10.1038/s41380-021-01097-y

Index